MW00417178

PROUD SOUTH

curated by
Lidewij Edelkoort
with Lili Tedde &
Mariola Lopez Mariño

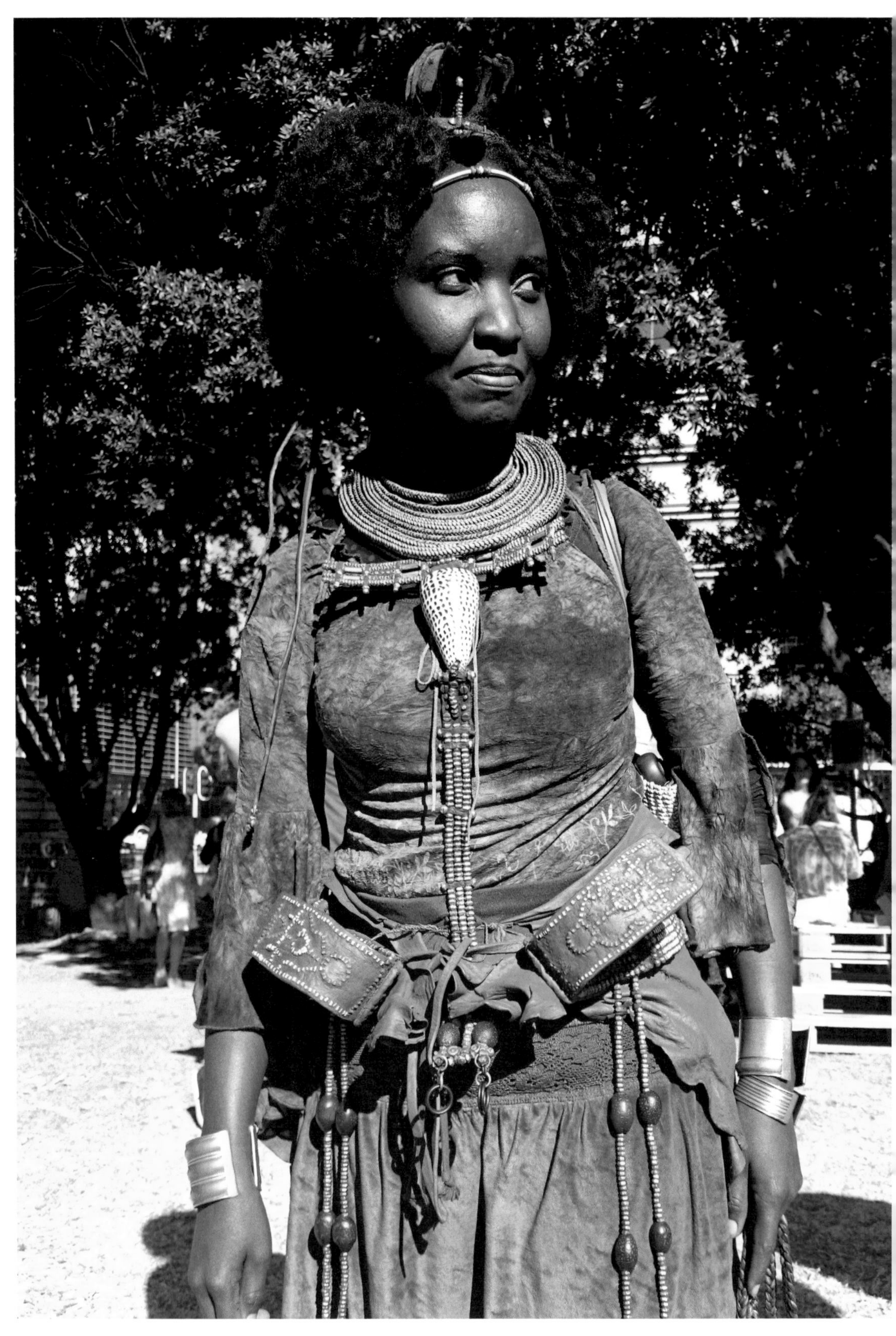

photo Daniel Costa – image taken in South Africa

FOREWORD

It was upon meeting the amazing Muthoni Kimani (a graphic designer with a great love for textiles and baskets) at the Design Indaba conference that I finally realised the time had come. Emancipation was accomplished, self-esteem rekindled, and roots recognised and adopted. Her distinctly South African allure made my heart beat faster and my mind expand. What I had been anticipating was now a reality, and needed to be nurtured to flourish. The south is waking up and grasping global opportunities that are being explored. It took a long incubation period for its immense talents to gain confidence but now we can feel the planet tremble with excitement, the globe is exploding with expectation. *L.E.*

PROUD & SOUTH

by Lidewij Edelkoort

Gradually, a southern generation of creatives is standing up, expressing local craft, embracing regional materials, recognising ancestral practices and cherishing indigenous values. A new idiom is born from the ruins of post-colonial influences and a strong emancipation movement, a sense of excitement that is discernible and feels like being in a pressure cooker, creating local flavours with a sense of urgency. It was just a matter of time for the whistle to start singing and hissing, tossing and turning, announcing that the time had come to serve these local recipes to the world.

That time has come. And creativity is shaking up the lethargic northern patterns of making and remaking, serving up the same old things repeatedly and in concordance. The fashions and photography from the south are original, as in *from origin*, and creative, as in *from creation*, as pure as a newborn and as sage as an elder, a strange combination of the naïve with the knowledgeable, a heady mixture of youthful energy with ancient wisdom. Each garment has a soul, and each photo knows how to capture one, elevating fashion to an altogether other domain of totemic and emphatic strength. Ordinary items are lifted from their everyday functions, acquiring outsider status and insider knowledge, being both unique and universal. These strange powers gravitate around each other like atoms of a creative aesthetic bomb, waiting to explode on the centre stage of fashion, captured by gifted designers and intelligent brands. They are then eternalised by exceptional photographers who have made it a point to open the floodgates of southern creativity, cascading new ideas into an otherwise morose and repetitive landscape of fashion design, meandering with a sense of wonder, unfolding the power of expression for what southern design can become.

Styling is an integral part of southern photography, often initiated by those who make the

photo Rogério Cavalcanti – Brazil

pictures, integrating found materials, diverting commercial packaging and citing ethnic origins with obvious tongue-in-cheek delight. Sorting out the good memories from traumatic recollections, the past is cuddled and pummelled at the same time, extracting inner struggles and building self-esteem in the process. And last but not least, we need to mention the power of people in contemporary casting who choose archetypes to figure out the content of fashion. Fathers and sisters and neighbours are instrumental when modelling with a naïve posture that gives clothes real emotional value, while otherworldly models elevate garments to become iconic and unforgettable. A handful of happiness distributed with true human presence. The models smile!

The amazing strength of southern articulation comes together, celebrating the different regions and their very own interpretations of what it is to be southern and proud to be so. From the delicate colours and elaborate textiles defining South Asia to the exotic and botanical materials governing Latin America to the fringed and brighter textures found across Africa, fashion goes from elegant to outlandish to exuberant, yet certain traits cross borders and oceans and develop what can be considered as southern design.

An obsession with materials, crafted finishes and details is dominant everywhere and often sourced at artisanal workshops or villages, where it is possible to sustain ancient making practices, with belief in cooperation as a model. Colours and patterns that play games with volumes and modes of wrapping and layering, are at once covering and exposing body language. Delivering grace to the clothes in movement. An innate sense of wild styling uses accumulation to reach excellence and uniqueness, bringing recycling within the realm of reincarnation. Faith in humanity finds its foundations in a cocktail of religious belief systems that are rooted in Animistic practices. The future is spirited or will not be.

Indigenous knowledge from the south will become the guiding light for a world at the edge of destruction, gently steering us to a better understanding of the earth and its principles as well as how to bring us back to analogous and archaic building, farming, fishing and fashion making. Slowing down production and sharing governance.

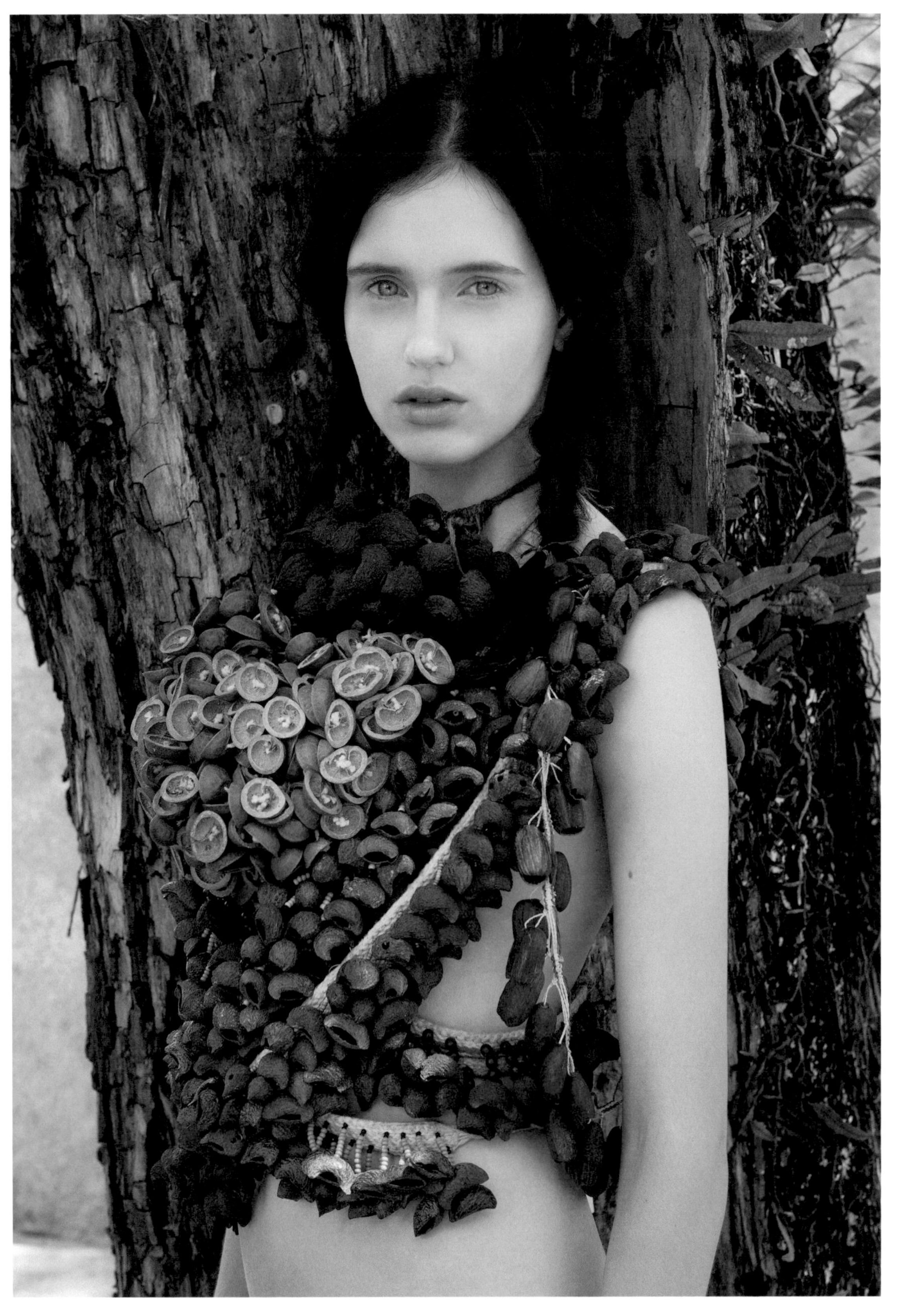

photo Rogério Cavalcanti *design* Monica Carvalho – Brazil

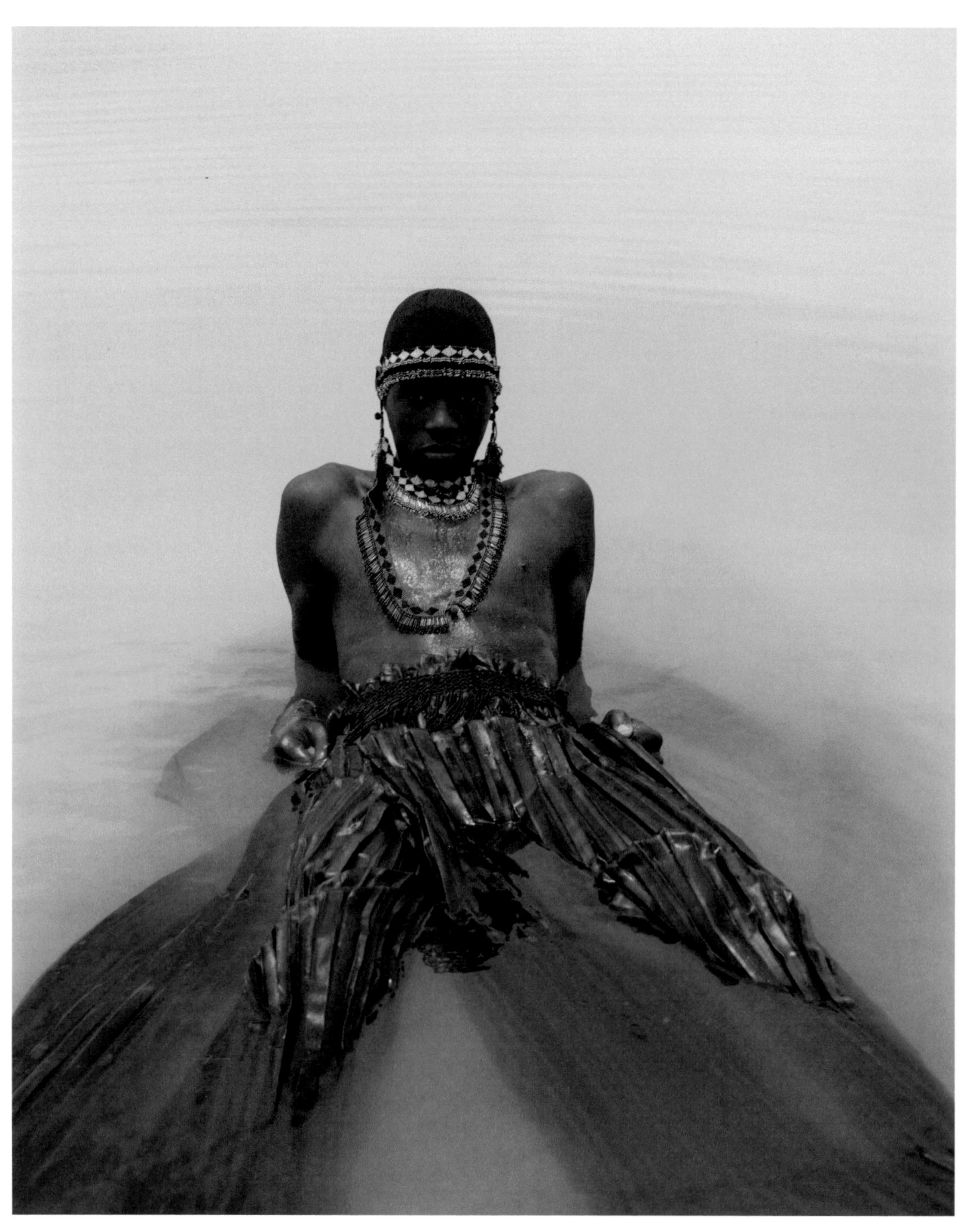

photo Kyle Weeks *design* Lukhanyo Mdingi – South Africa

PROUD & TOUCHED

As long as I have been working, which means almost half a century, I have been engaged with southern countries, designing collections, curating events, giving lectures, stimulating local expression. From developing clothes for Indian companies when I was a young woman to indigo crafts in West Africa, and from publishing magazines on booming Brazil to curating an exhilarating exhibition on South African design, my experience has often been similar in all these diverse regions. The most important recurring comment from the southern audiences was that they were running behind one season and therefore felt condemned and compelled to imitate and follow the western expressions of design and fashion. My answer would invariably be that it depends on how one looks at this calendar and that we could just as easily argue that the south is running one season ahead all others and therefore should consider itself a front-runner…

Designing western clothes in eastern mills has made me keenly aware of the restricted rules of western fashion, where local colour and fantasy were not allowed to bloom. As a young woman, I encountered amazing southern people that introduced me to their cultures, which has given me early insight into the discrepancies between the hemispheres, with public opinion favouring the reasonable north above the thriving south for no cultural reason.

Feeling adopted by craftswomen creating indigo tie and dye patterns in Benin has put me in touch with their ancestors, drinking a Fanta together to celebrate the deceased. Attracted to the earth of Africa, the gardens of India and the forests of Brazil, it was nature that instructed me that something was terribly wrong with this continually repressive colonial system and I have never ceased to see excellence in the exuberance of the south. Editing the words of the women of the Yawanawá tribe, narrating their lifestyle and emancipated profession of gathering berries in the Amazon rainforest, taught me that our ideas of well-being are nowhere near their outspoken optimism and feminism, and that the world has a lot to learn by harvesting their wisdom.

In this book, I pay homage to the southern regions that have educated me and elevated my actions to become inclusive of all earthlings, celebrating the earth, animals, people and materials. Paying respect to all sentient beings.

L.E.

PROUD & GROUNDED

◇◇◇◇◇◇◇◇◇◇◇◇◇

Discovering the origin of southern aesthetics is important for understanding design decisions and photographic perspectives that are often intuitive yet compose the austral expression of materials, shapes and pictures. Learning from the traditions of indigenous cultures that include body painting, textile design and ritual decoration, while witnessing how this history is expanded by contemporary creatives with dignity and respect, one can map out some of the different influences that constitute southern design and photography. A sense of earth and sky, a quest for body and soul, the starkness of dots and wax, the vibrance of the spiritual and the embrace of all that blooms are each chapters from the same book on the future creativity from the south. Hovering between abstract minimalism and absolute maximalism, these currents will cultivate new fashions in the decades to come. This final liberation from the residue of post-colonial references will set the stage for an emancipated domain in design. *L.E.*

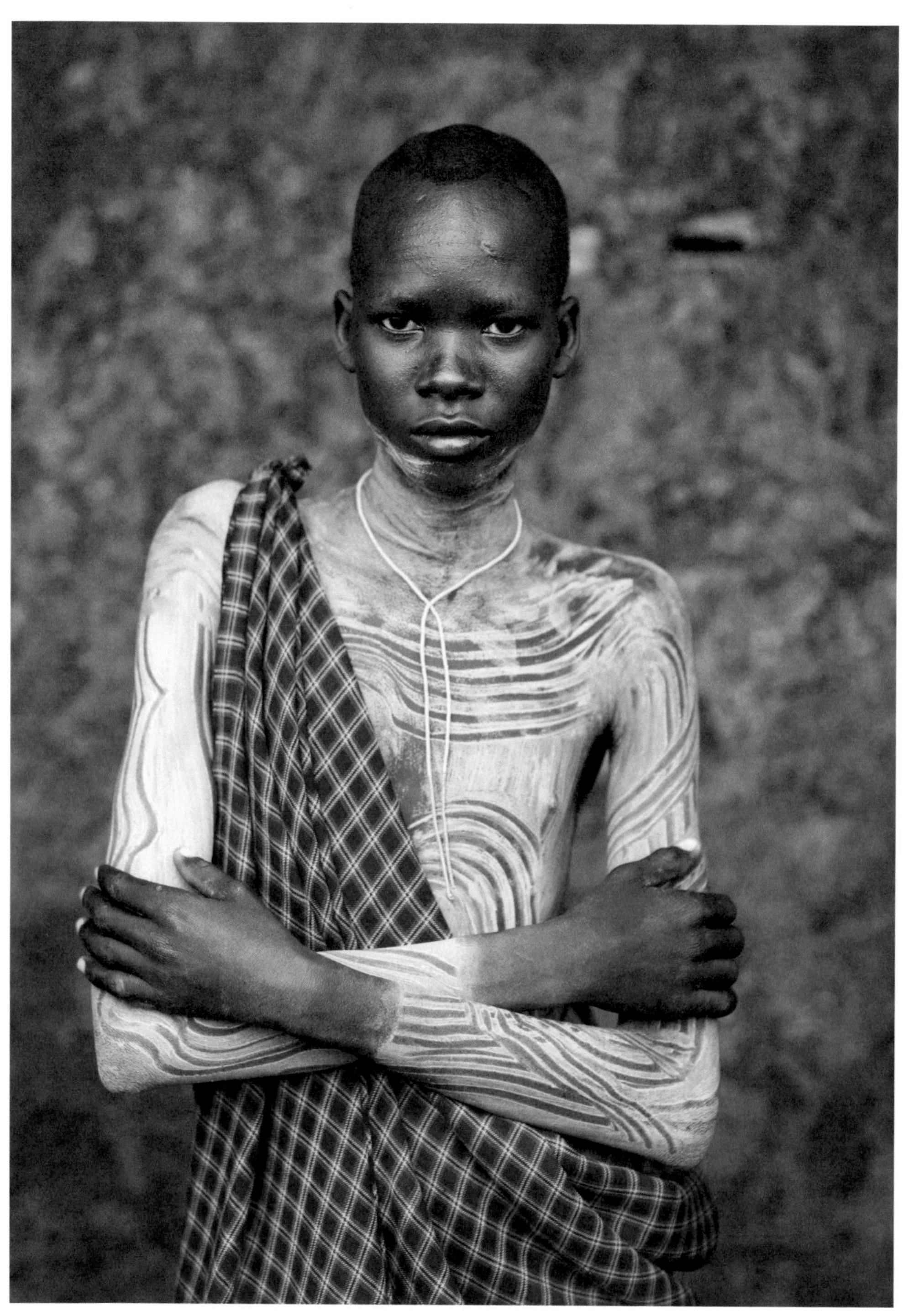

photo Eric Lafforgue – image taken in Ethiopia

opposite page, clockwise

photo Gleeson Paulino / GQ – Brazil
photo Trevor Stuurman – South Africa
photo Erdi Doğan *design* Hatice Gökçe – Turkey
photo John-Paul Pietrus – Philippines *design* Kenneth Ize – Nigeria

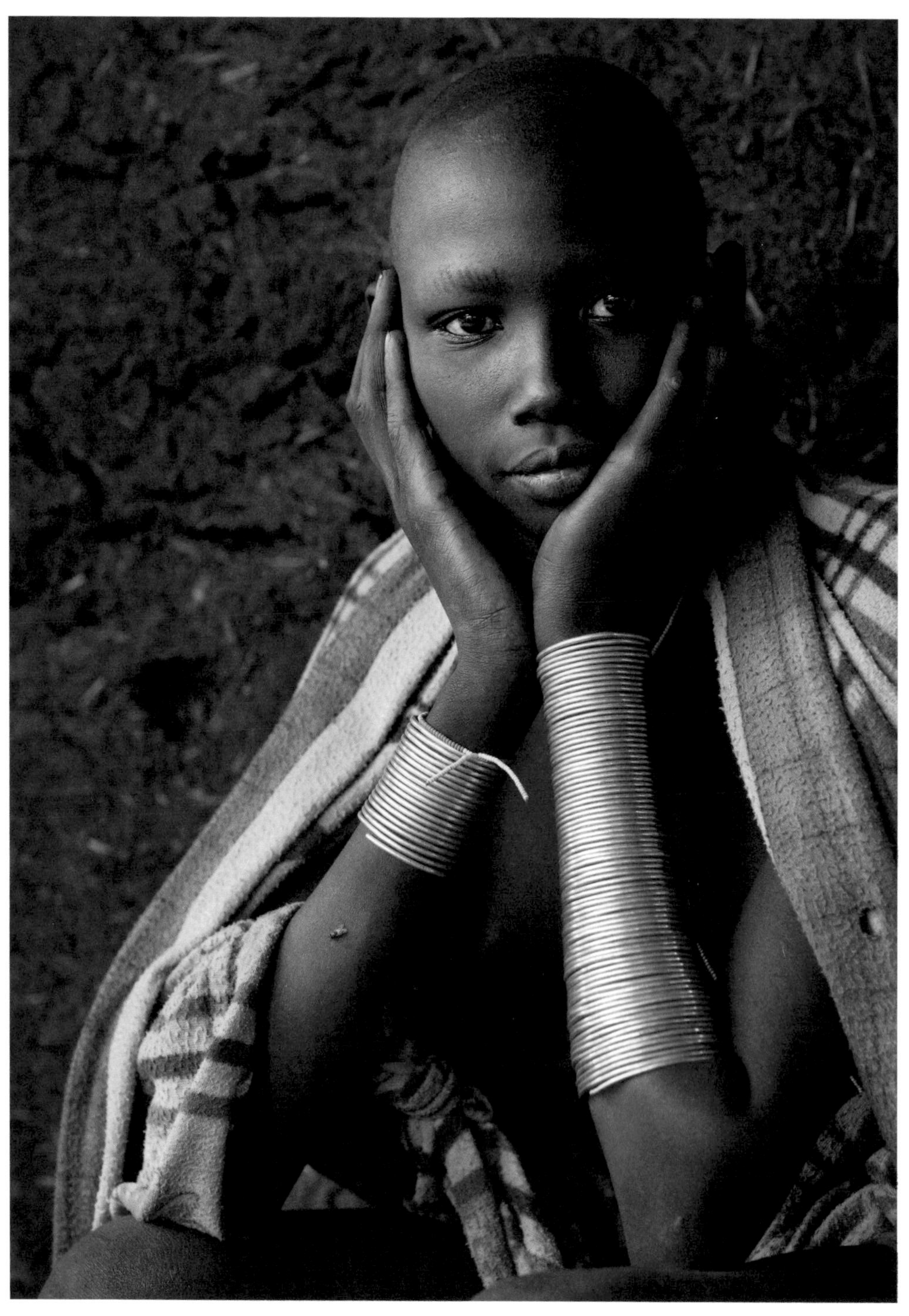

photo Eric Lafforgue – image taken in Ethiopia

opposite page, clockwise

photo Kenji Nakamura *design* Samuray Martins – Brazil
photo Eric Lafforgue – image taken in Tanzania
photo Eric Lafforgue – image taken in Ethiopia
photo Gabrielle Kannemeyer – South Africa

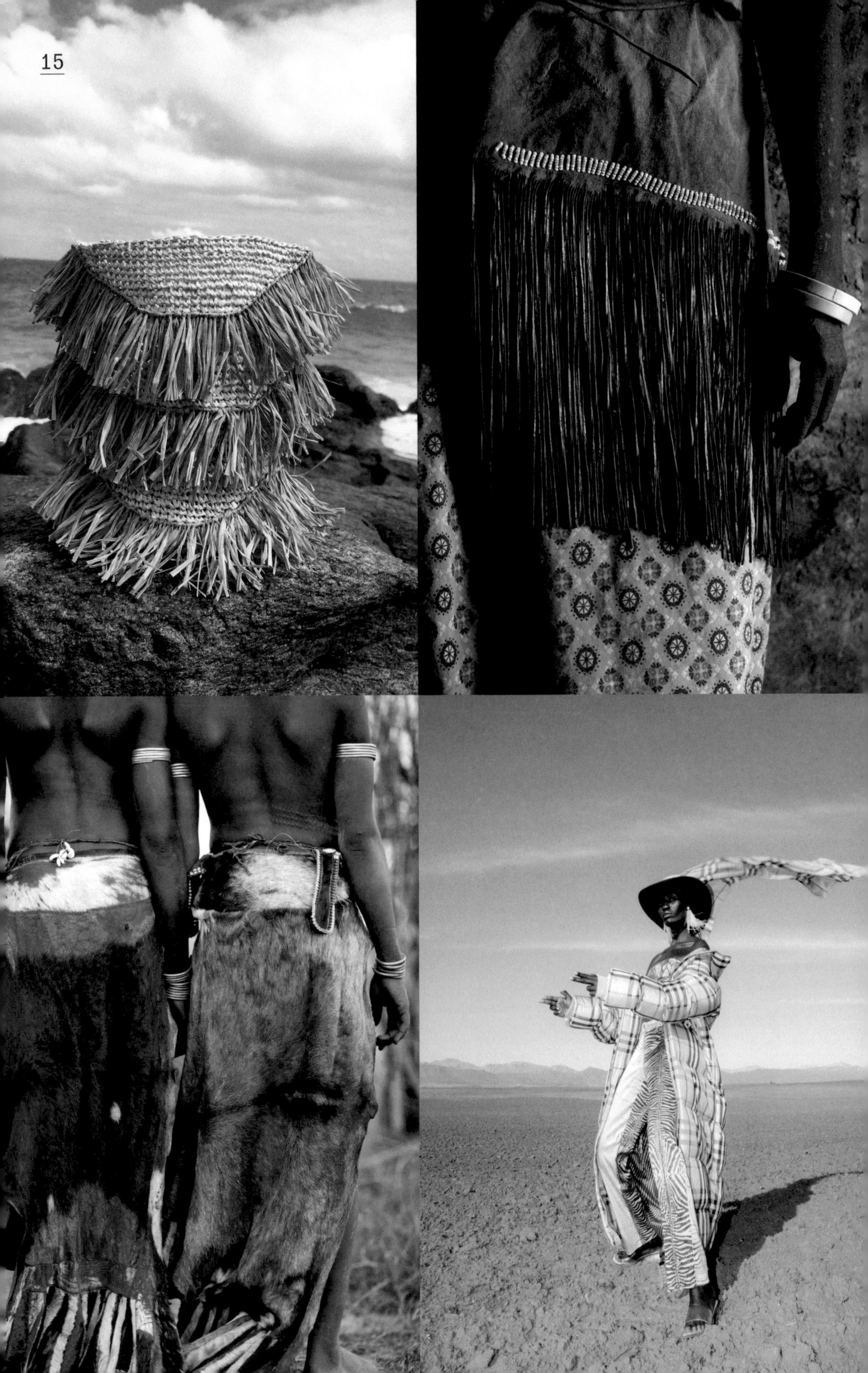

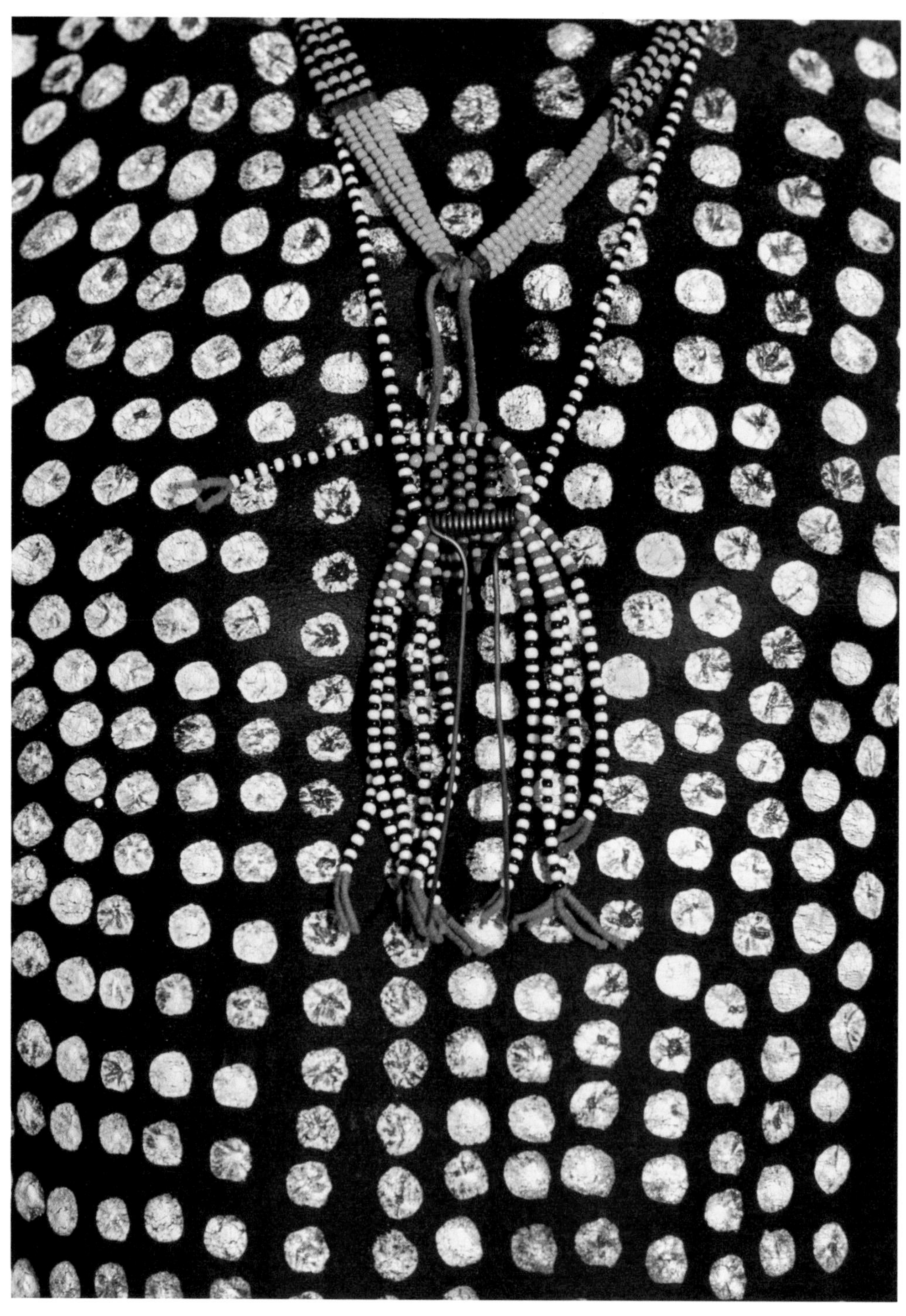

photo Art Wolf – image taken in Ethiopia

opposite page, clockwise

photo Leonor von Salisch *design* Buki Akomolafe – Nigeria
design Marimekko – Finland
photo Heather Moore *design* Skinny laMinx – South Africa
photo & styling Adele Dejak – Kenya

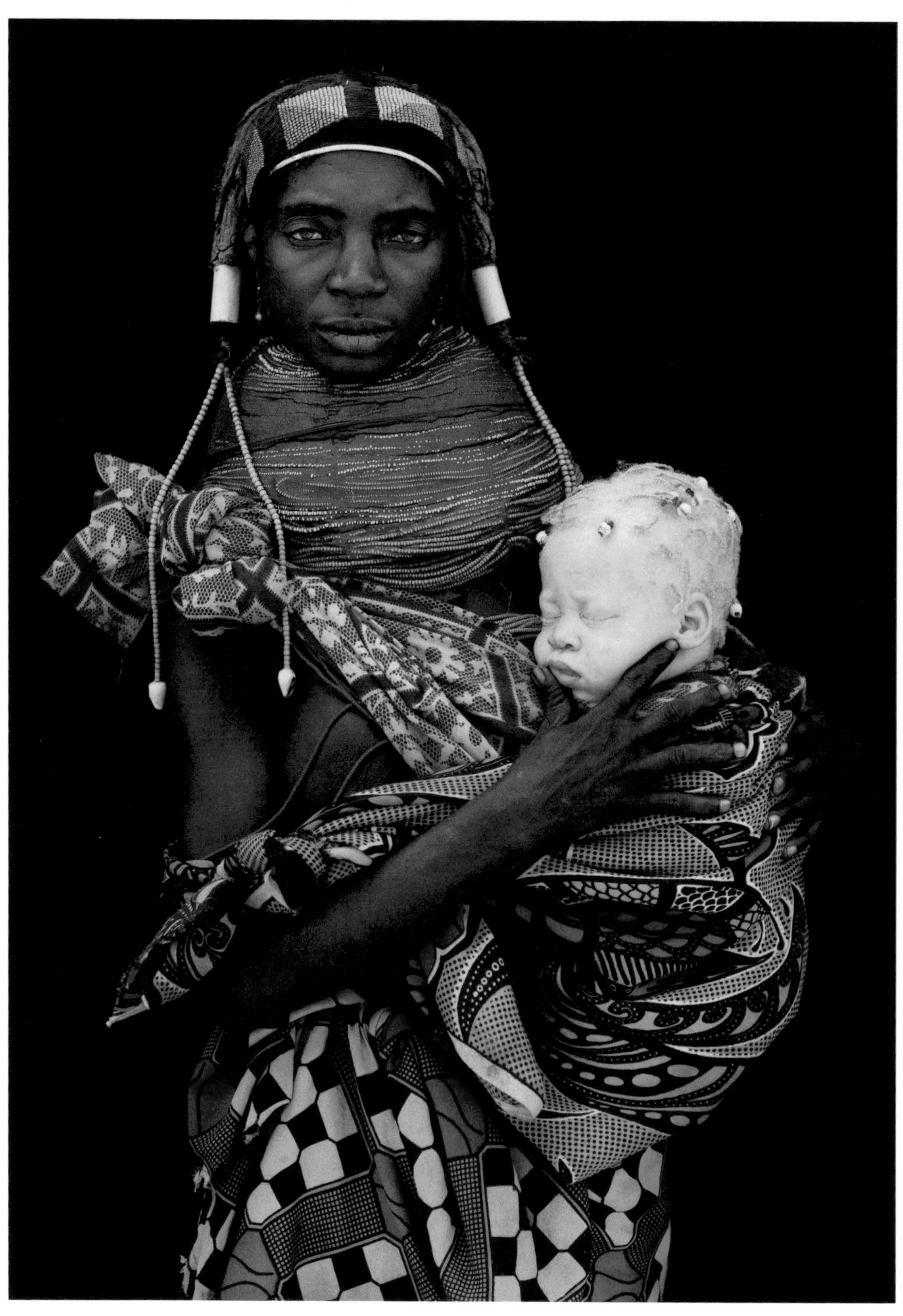

photo Eric Lafforgue – image taken in Angola

opposite page, clockwise

photo Trevor Stuurman – South Africa
photo Gleeson Paulino / Elle – Brazil
photo Bruno Gomes *design* Meninos Rei – Brazil
photo Ed Suter *design* Tsidi Ramofolo – South Africa

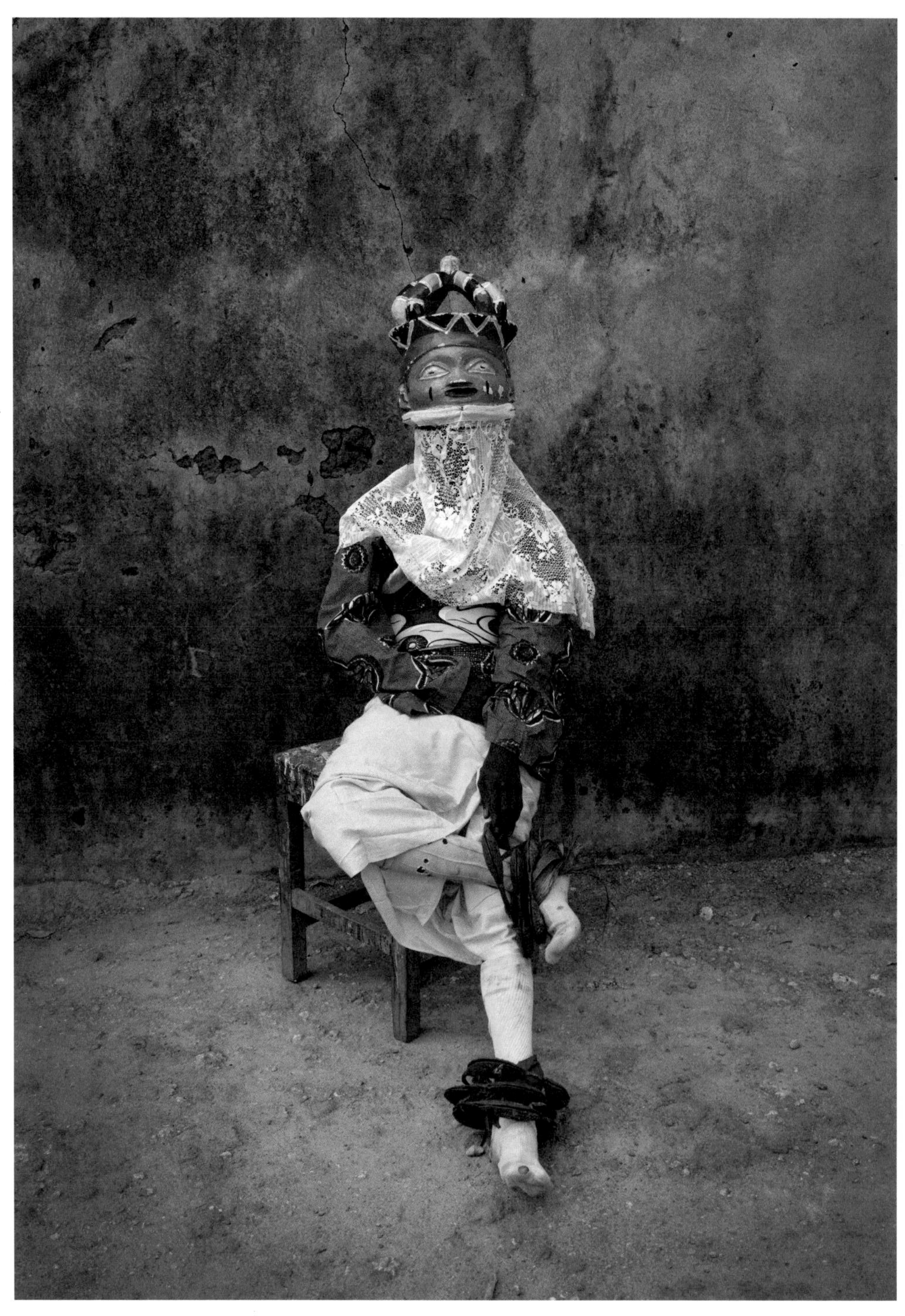

art Leonce Raphael Agbodjelou / Jack Bell Gallery – Benin

opposite page, clockwise

photo Naveli Choyal *design* Tigra Tigra – India
photo Leslie Payró *design* Carla Fernández – Mexico
photo Mous Lambarat – Morocco
photo Pedro Santos *design* Laura Laurens – Colombia

photo Eric Lafforgue – image taken in Saudi Arabia

opposite page, clockwise

photo Chris Saunders *design* Sheila-Madge – South Africa
photo Pretika Menon *design* Shirin Salwan – India
photo Ivory Campbell *design* Joy Julius – Nigeria / Switzerland
photo Justin Polkey / Vogue India – South Africa

photo Tom McShane – image taken in South Sudan

opposite page, clockwise

photo Pedro Loreto *design* Uxuá – Brazil
photo Bikramjit Bose *design* Eka Design Studio – India
photo Bikramjit Bose *design* Eka Design Studio – India
photo Menty Jamir *design* Eka Design Studio – India

art Leonce Raphael Agbodjelou / Jack Bell Gallery – Benin

opposite page, clockwise

photo Rogério Cavalcanti *design* João Pimenta – Brazil
photo photographer unknown – image taken in India
art Leonce Raphael Agbodjelou / Jack Bell Gallery – Benin
photo Rogério Cavalcanti *design* João Pimenta – Brazil

AYEGBAJEJE

PROUD & DEVOUT

◇◇◇◇◇◇◇◇◇◇◇◇◇

A committed culture that embraces several belief systems at once connects the southern continents, layering original spirituality with what is left from colonial Catholicism, missionary Protestantism and historical Islamic fragments. Blended with strands of Hinduism, Taoism and Buddhism, these faiths can unite in a universal celebration. Especially in multicultural countries such as Brazil and South Africa, some people are collecting and worshipping African twins, Christian crosses, Buddha sculptures and the Virgin Mary, for sentimental reasons. With a return to Animism, the religion of all religions, the idea that all beings are alive and worthy of respect takes hold of a new generation of disciples to venerate nature as a central energy, respecting the rock and river and the twig and feather. As the sum of devotion accumulates into a creative, holistic faith, fashion and photography register the interconnected systems with an ardent sense of styling that uses enveloping shapes and zealous patterns, with celestial accessories on models that play their inter-religious roles, embodying gods with gusto. *L.E.*

photo & art direction Marianne Marplondon – UK

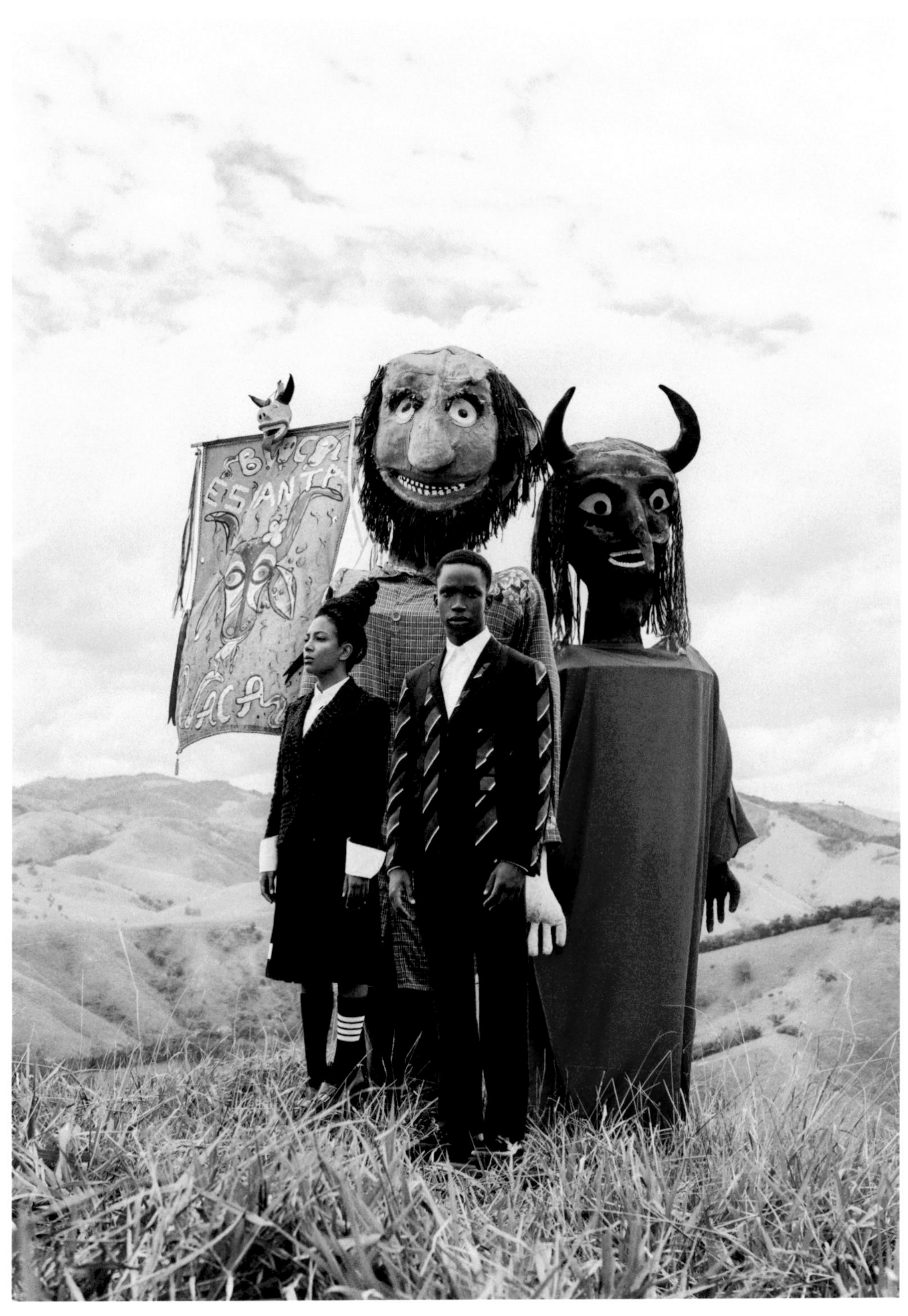

photo Gleeson Paulino *design* Nataal x Thom Browne x Farfetch – Brazil

photo Stephen Tayo – Nigeria

photo & art direction Marianne Marplondon – UK

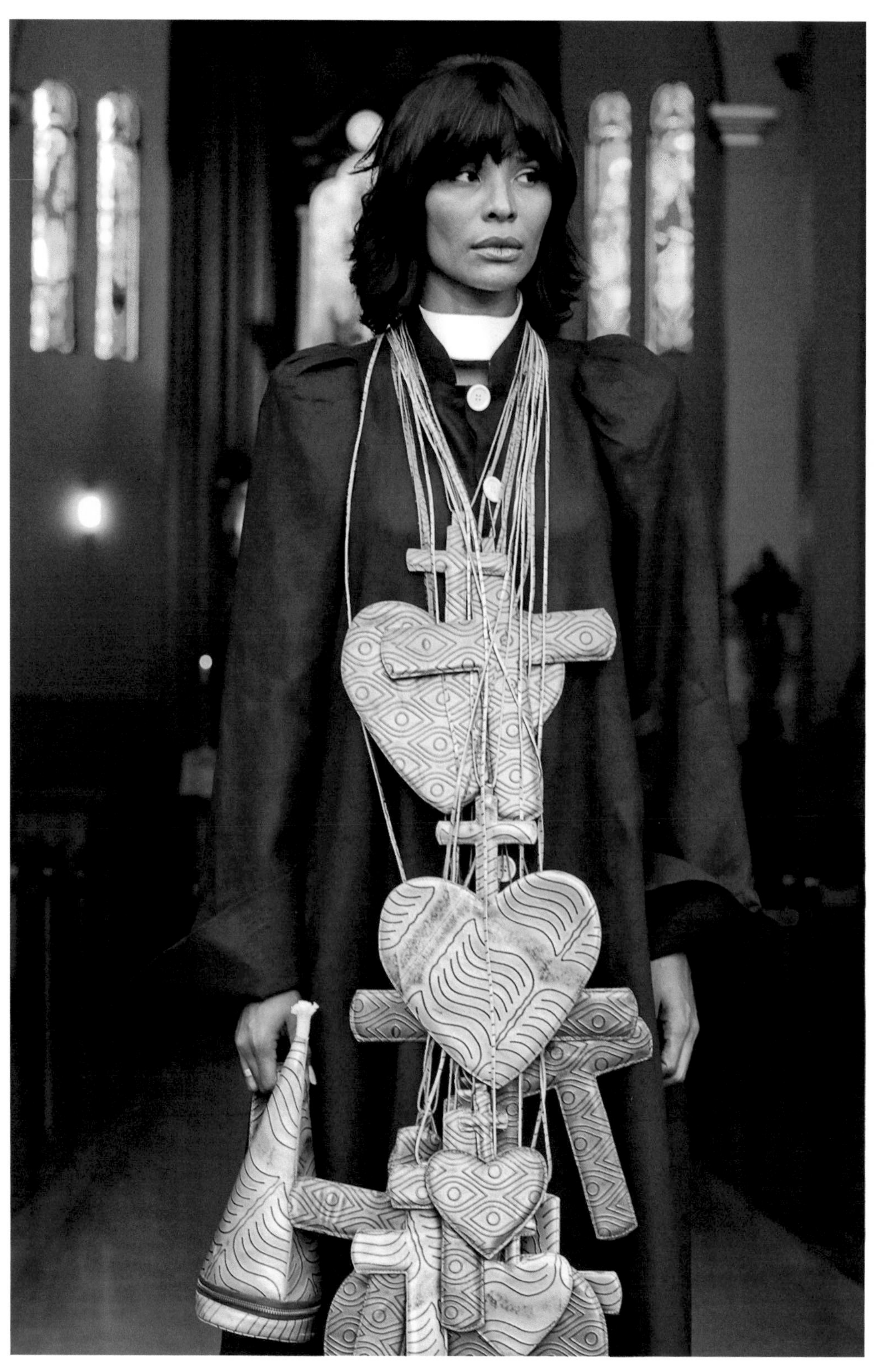

photo Augusto Pena *design* Ronalgo Fraga – Brazil

photo Mous Lamrabat – Morocco

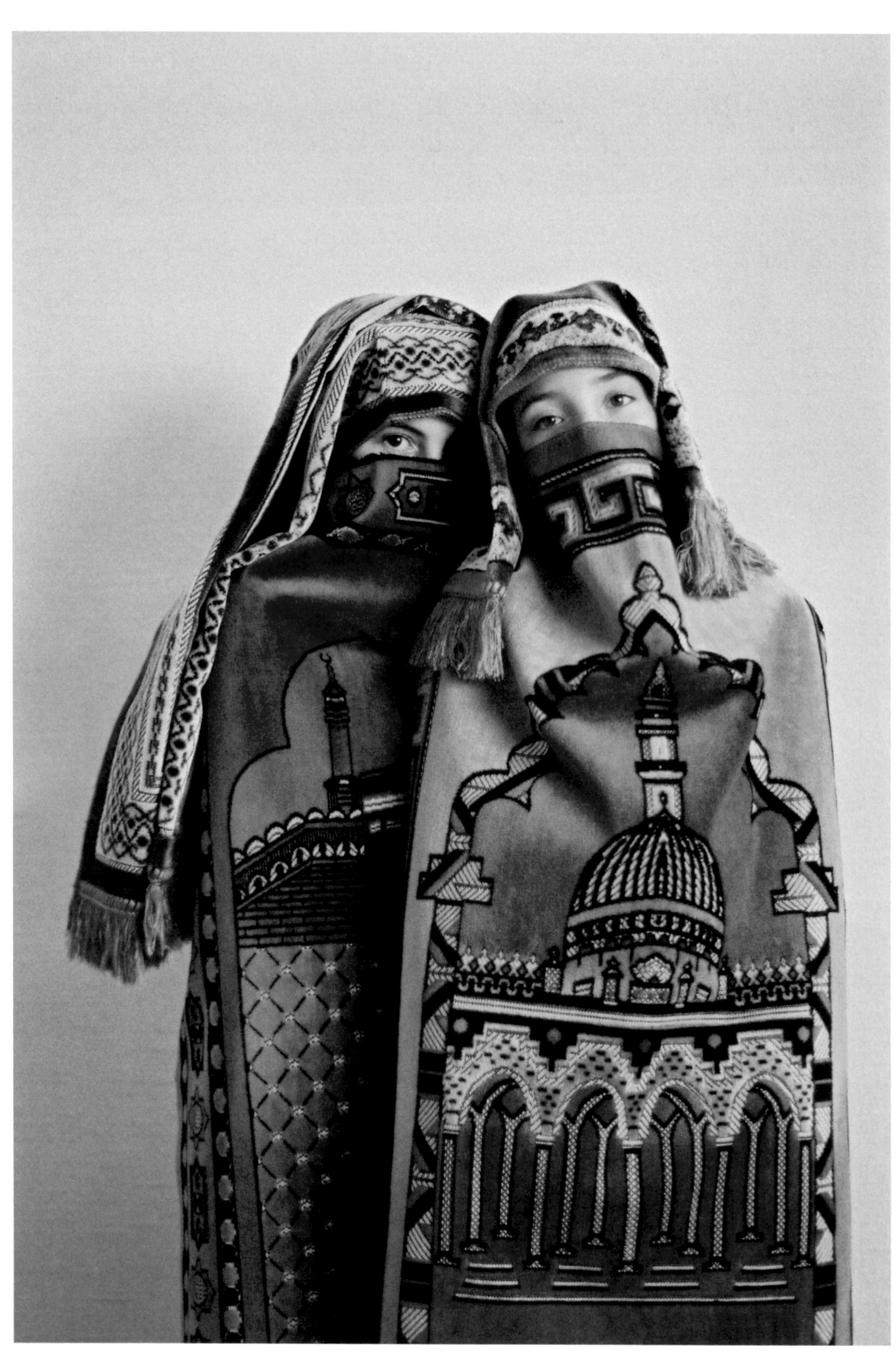

photo Mous Lamrabat – Morocco

art Leonce Raphael Agbodjelou / Jack Bell Gallery – Benin

photo Mous Lamrabat – Morocco

photo Gleeson Paulino – Brazil

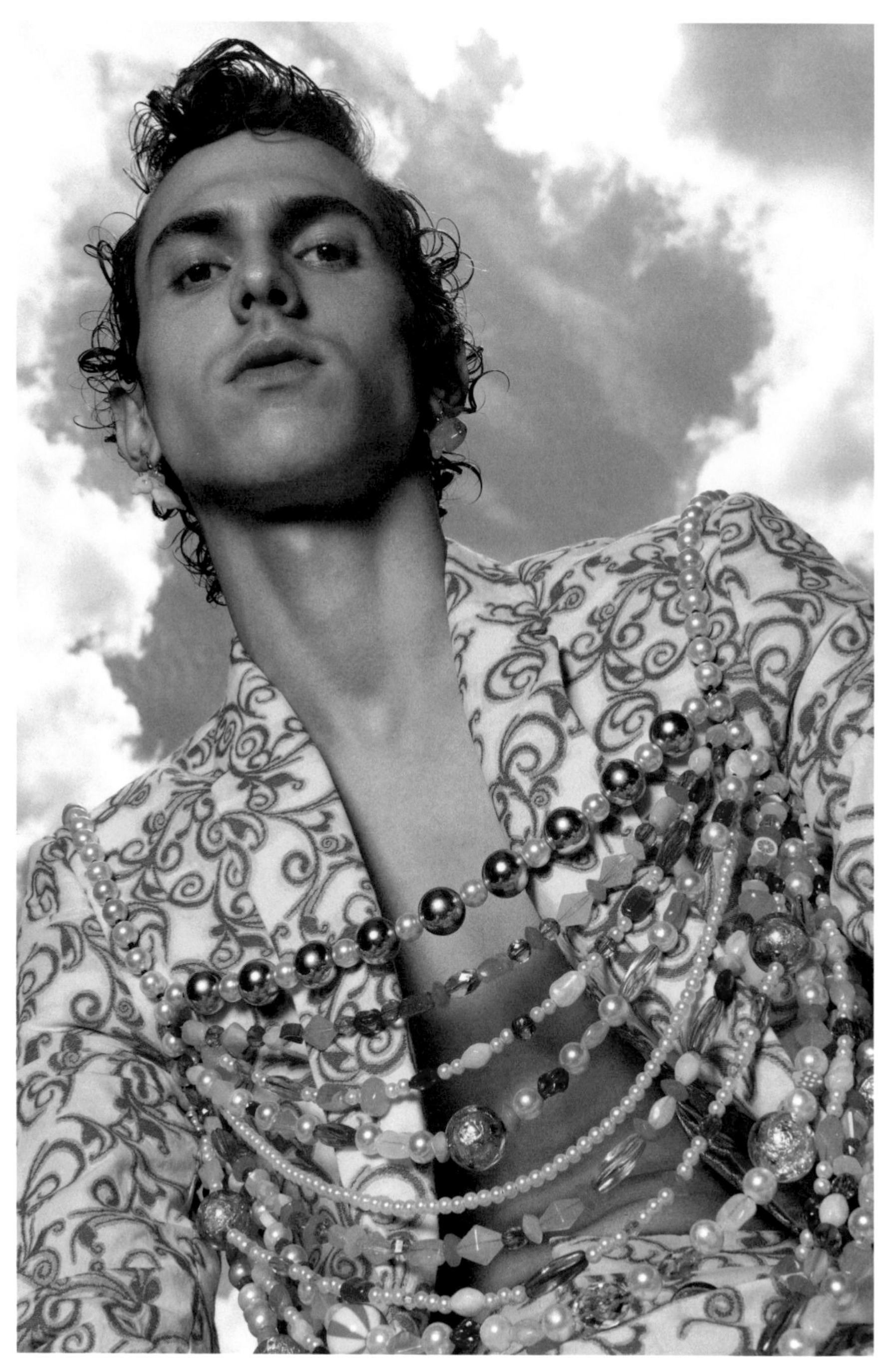

photo Rogério Cavalcanti *design* Ronaldo Fraga / Renauxview – Brazil

photo Ruy Teixeira – Brazil

photo Phyllis Galembo – USA

photo Ruy Teixeira – Brazil

PROUD & HUMOUR

photography by Mous Lamrabat
– Morocco –

In these photos, the proud and naïve way to wear counterfeit logos on clothes is rendered with down-to-earth humour and humanity. Having been raised in Belgium yet born in Morocco explains the body of work of Mous, as he is known. A self-made photographer, the trained designer exchanged the confined measures of interior architecture for the vast landscapes of his motherland that anchor his majestic subjects, exploring the religions of capitalism and consumerism through the scarf, veil and burka of tradition. A weird and fascinating way of messaging which is at once abstract and narrative. Combatting racism and sectarism with an absolute approach, one can detect the designer behind the photographer in the way he constructs his images, playing with proportion and perspective. Channelling outsider art from within his culture. His use of intense colour set against neutral backgrounds, featuring one iconic detail, makes each photo a manifesto, simply telling the truth with graphic sharpness. Acting as posters fighting for equality, integration and acceptance of the other. The knowledge of the inner stirrings of his people makes the work anthropological, peeling away the proud and doubting stirrings of the soul that are defining contemporary Moroccan culture, cutting to the core of its humanity. Happiness and resilience are essential qualities of Moroccans' intense identity. Unveiling xenophobia and dismantling prejudice have become the heroic hallmarks of Mous Lambarat's work that, due to its stark symbolic simplicity, is able to change the way we explore southern complexity. *L.E.*

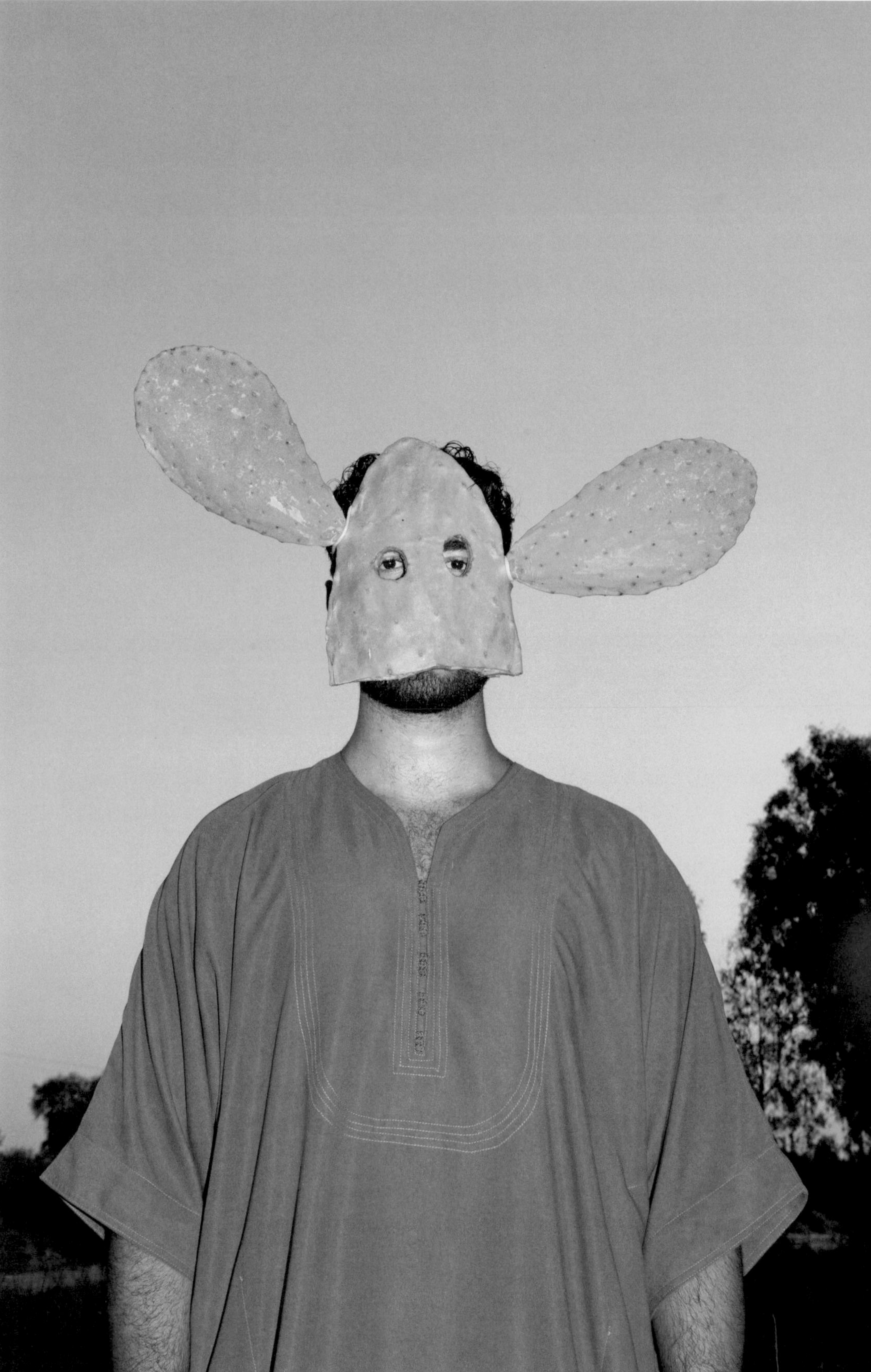

CDG
29
SIMAR
A
300

PROUD & LABOUR

◇◇◇◇◇◇◇◇◇◇◇◇

A universal revival of work clothes resonates in the south, bringing back ample shapes and precise stitching in sturdy fabric constructions. Young people turn to workwear to dress stylishly and economically, indulging in uniform fashions. These sober clothes echo a past of working the land, building houses and creating craft. Labour has been cherished for centuries, providing for extended families and bringing the possibility of climbing the handmade social ladder, ascending with organic energy, organising guilds, building schools, discerning excellence, giving out national treasure titles. Labour has elevated living standards and still does, but also severely punishes people working in desert climates, in polluted city centres and in mountainous arid regions, earning their incomes in faraway countries to escape poverty. As labour is also at the root of slavery, where massive amounts of people were singled out and forced to do the master's work, contemporary work clothes can be seen as silent homages to the ancestors, carrying their pain and pride in plain sight, as clothes that never forget. *L.E.*

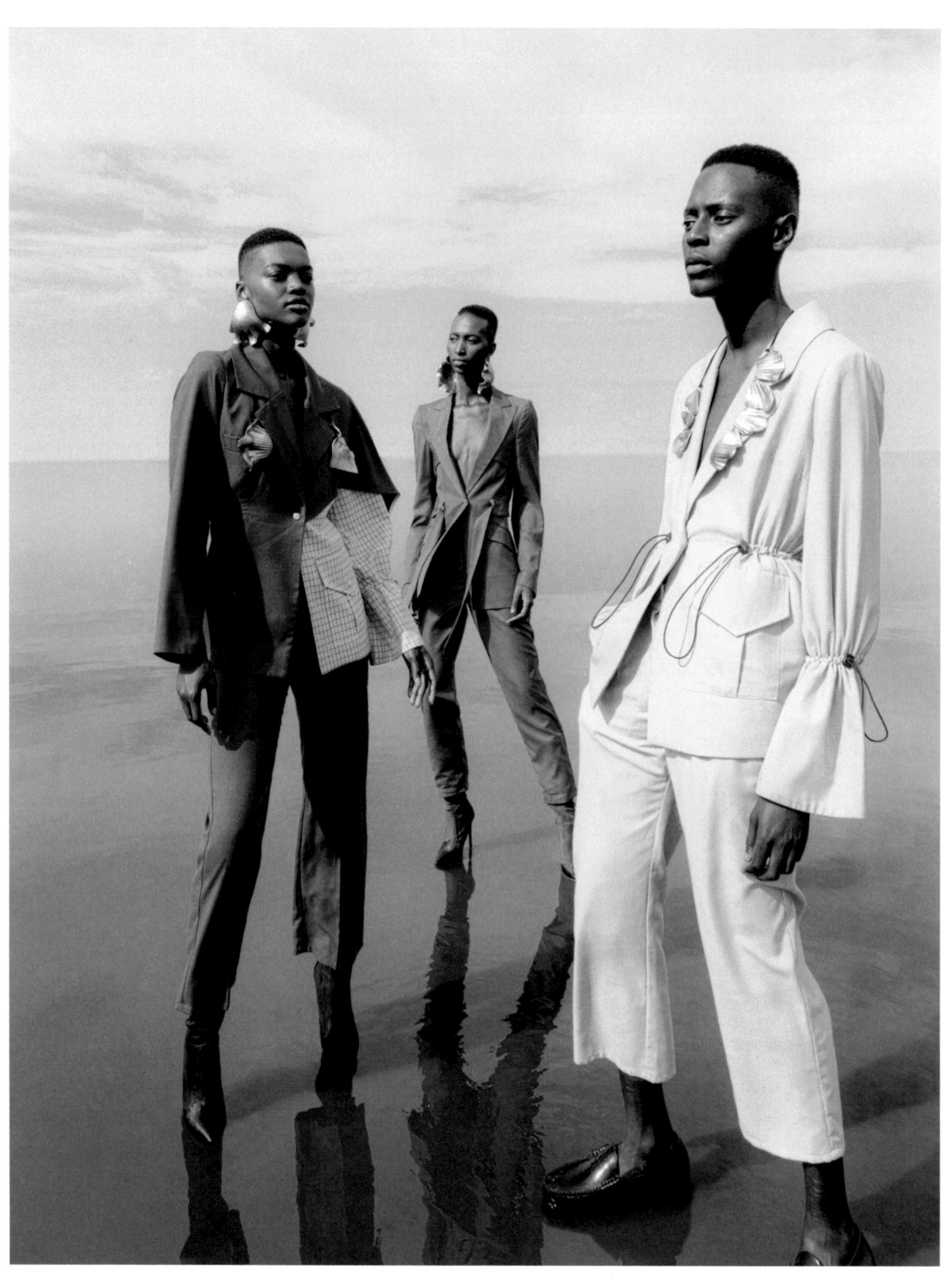

photo Kristin Lee Moolman *design* Thebe Magugu – South Africa

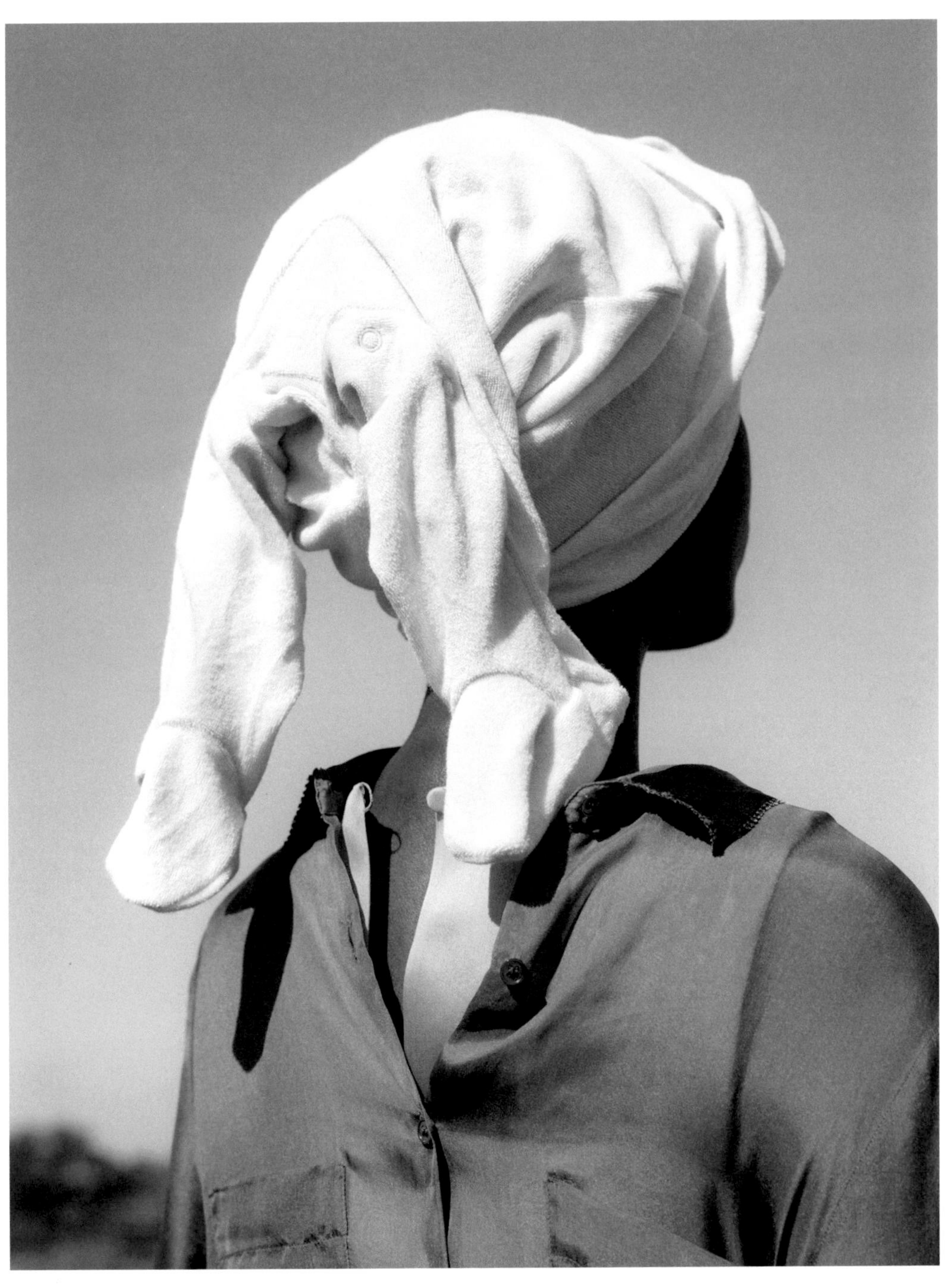

photo Jackie Nickerson – USA / UK

photo Menty Jamir *design* Eka Design Studio – India

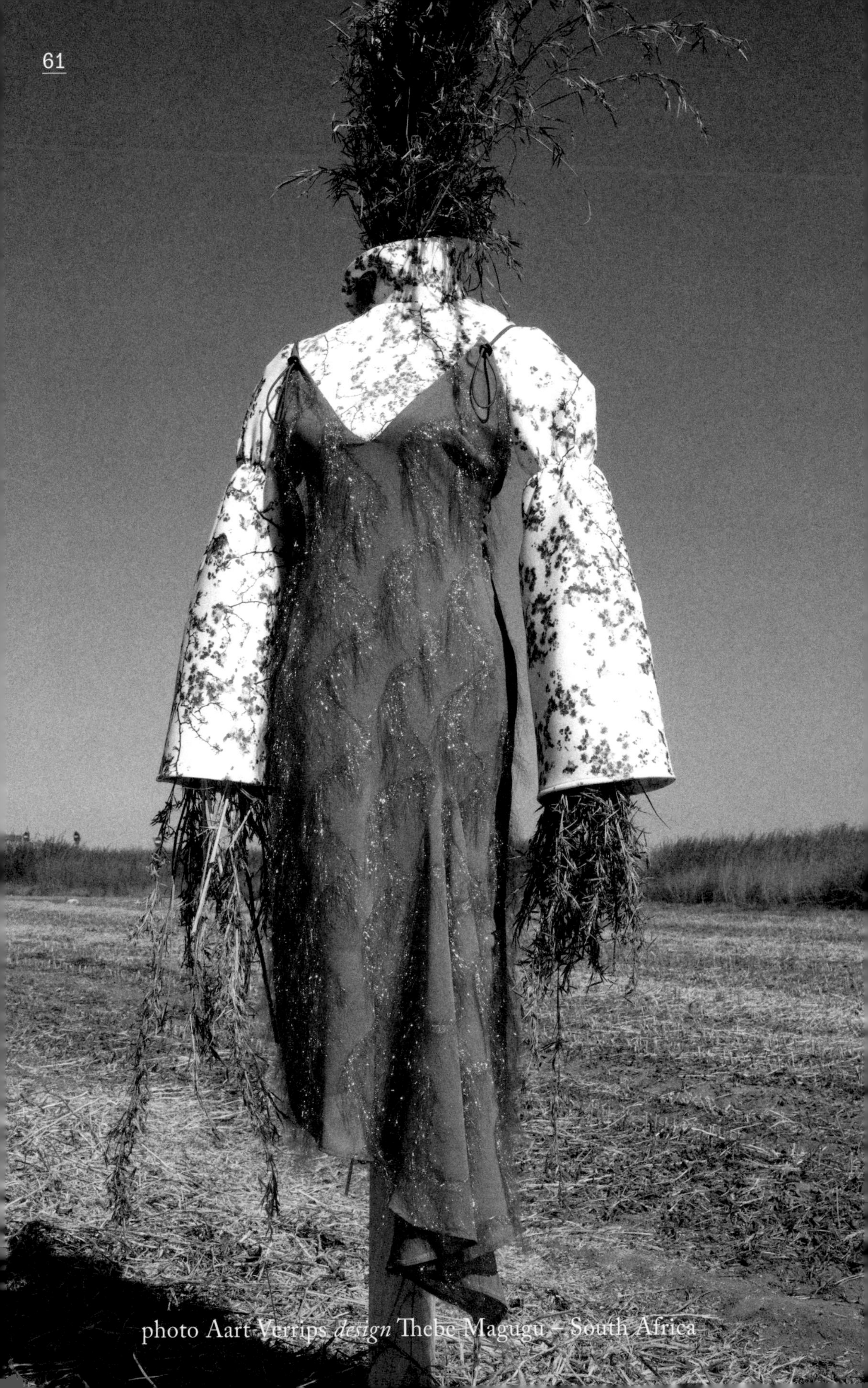

photo Aart Verrips *design* Thebe Magugu – South Africa

photo & art direction Francesco Visone – Tenerife

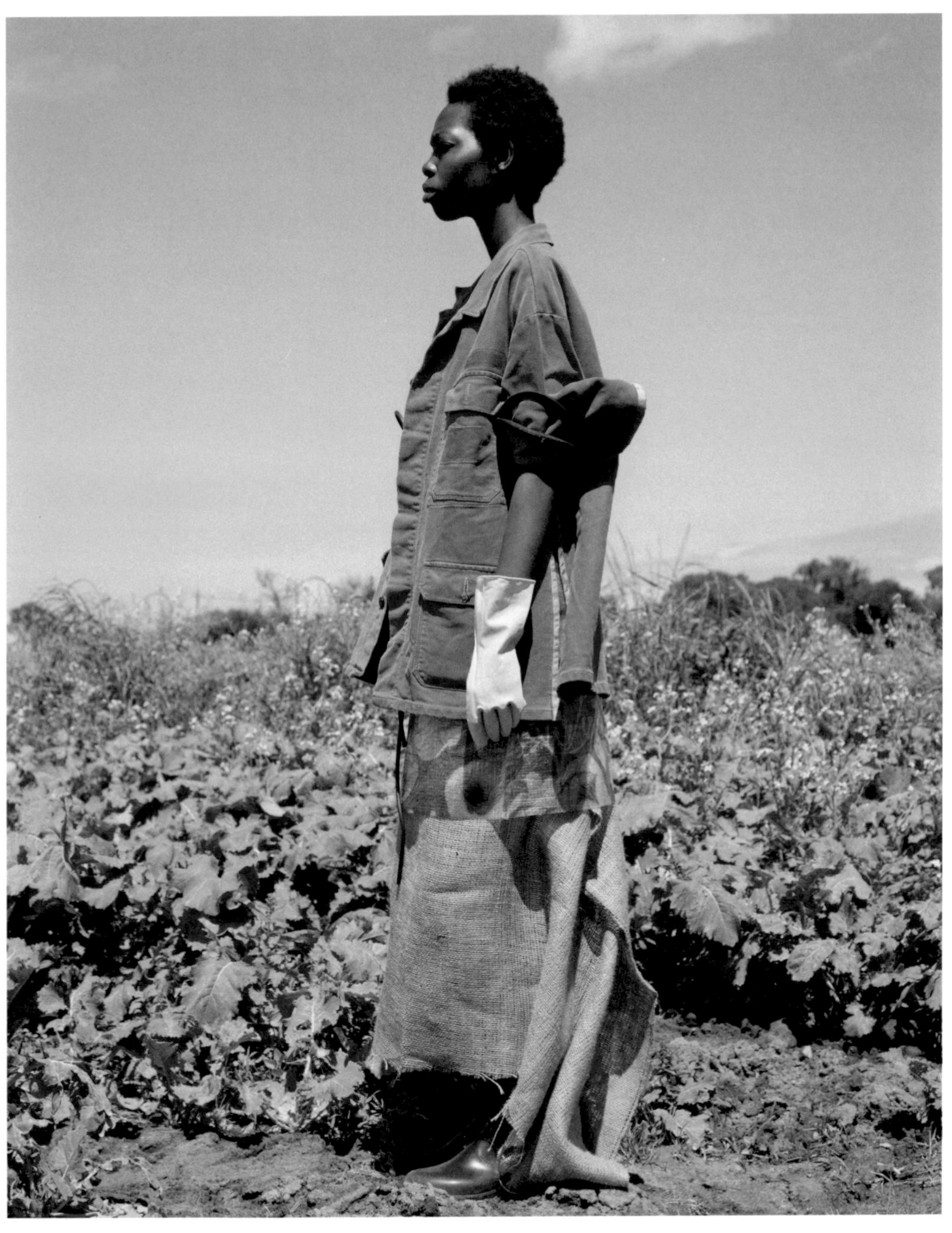

photo Jackie Nickerson – USA / UK

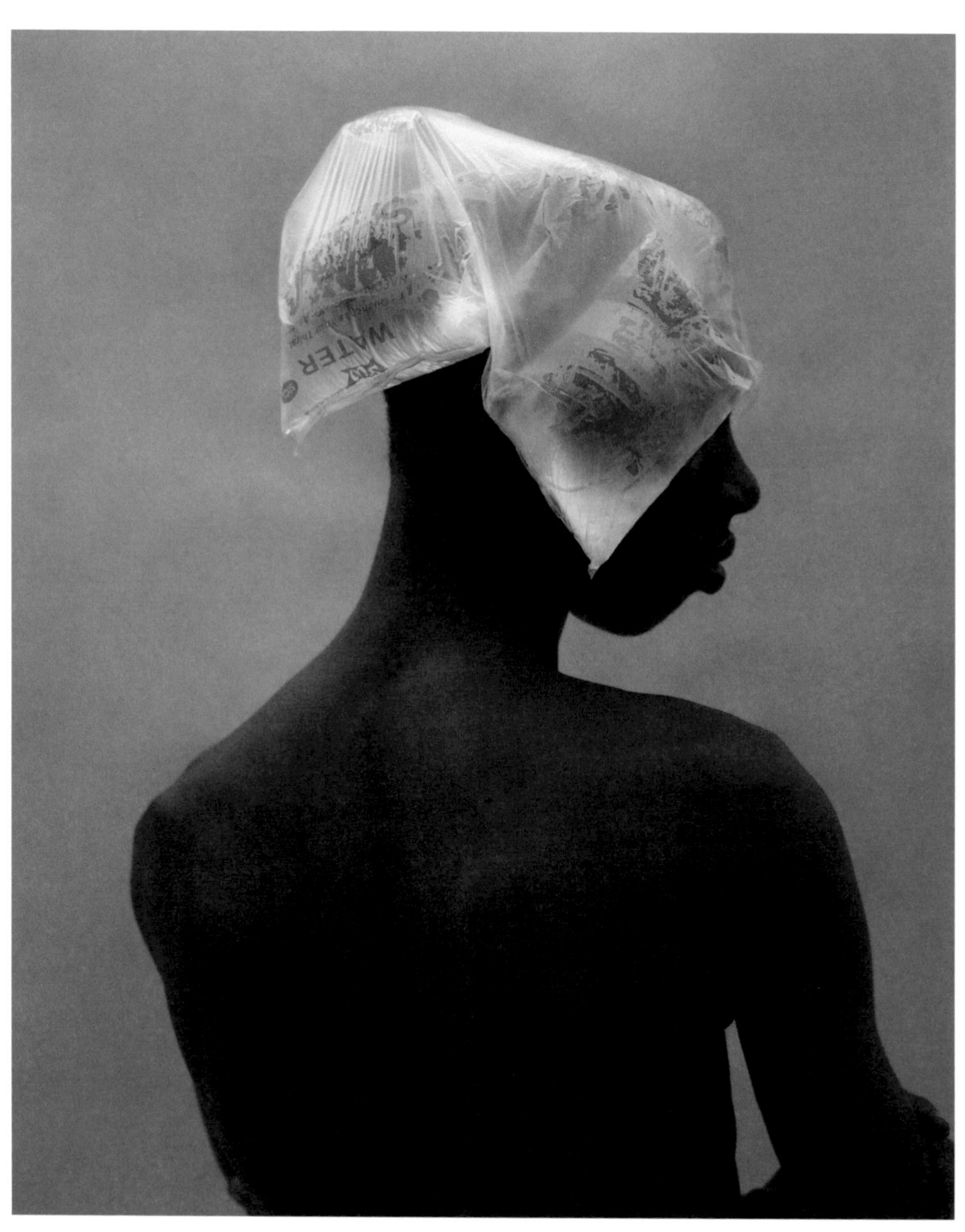

photo Lakin Ogunbanwo – Nigeria

photo Travys Owen *design* Lukhanyo Mdingi – South Africa

photo & styling Ismail Zaidy – Morocco

photo Menty Jamir *design* Eka Design Studio – India

photo Jaime Rubiano *design* Esteban Cortazar – Colombia

photo J'dee Allin *design* Hamaji – Kenya

photo Omar Victor Diop – Senegal

PROUD & SOURCE

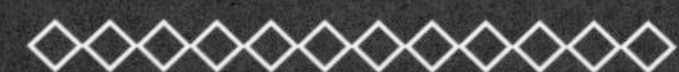

If one colour is to symbolise the south, it must be indigo, the magical green plant that turns textiles blue. The oldest known indigo fragment was found in Peru some six thousand years ago. Mysteriously, its use was discovered in the Americas and Asia, as well as Africa, at approximately the same time, long before boats would sail to connect these places, simultaneously inspiring people to use the same miracle plant. The indigo leaves first must ferment into a green drab, getting ready to deliver the beautiful blue hue which has coloured textiles for centuries. People learned to play with tie and dye patterns, inventing intricate ikat weaving, obtaining resist printing, experimenting with dip-dyeing and doing endless studies in blue, from celestial to midnight, almost black-blue. Indigo is known to appease the mind, open the spirit, comfort the skin and provide good sleep; a well-being recipe that helps explain the growing appetite for dyeing processes all over the world. Those that craft indigo are believed to have eternal life, giving the hue a spiritual dimension. *L.E.*

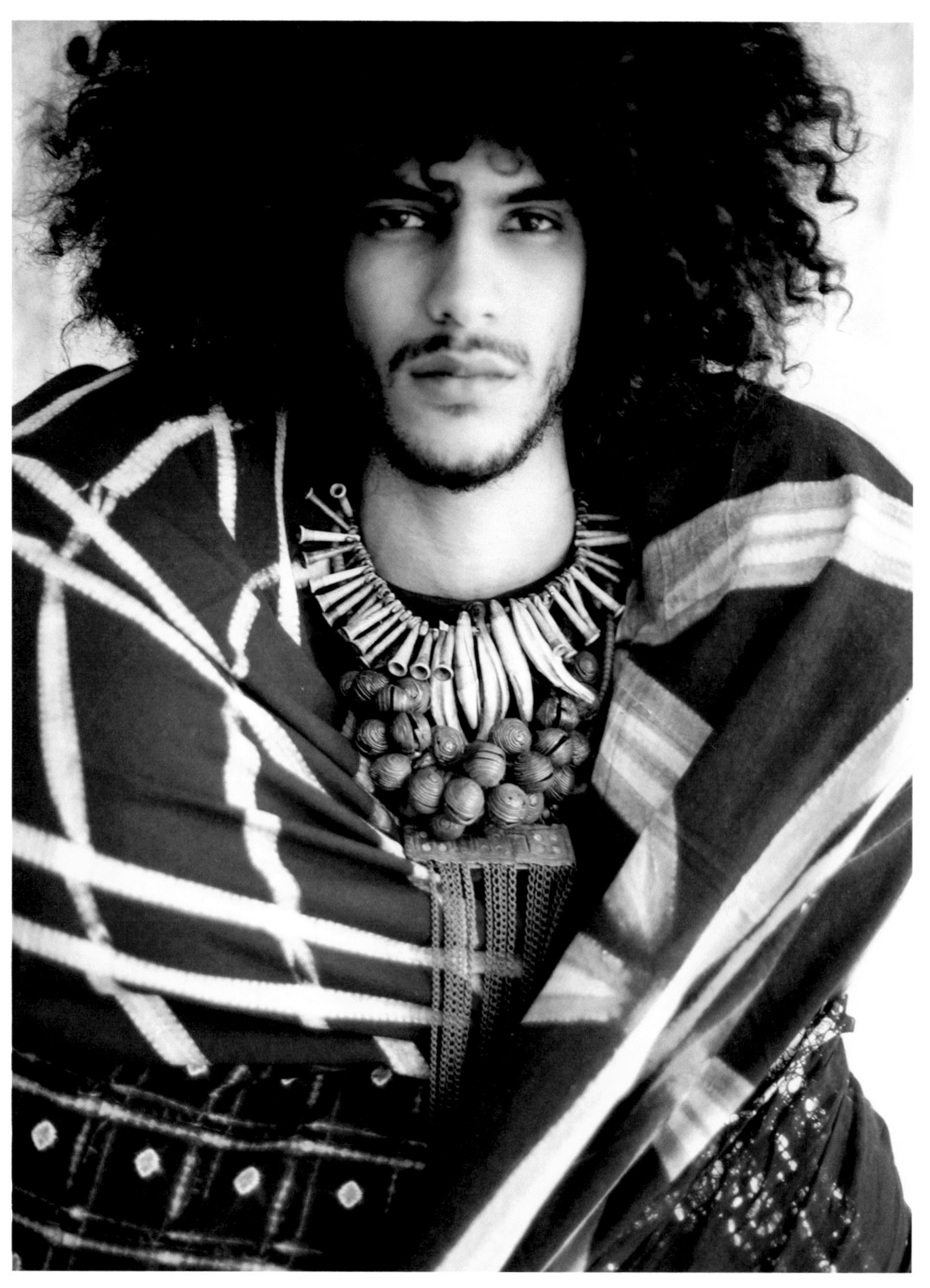

photo Marie Taillefer *design* Heartwear – Benin
photo Trevor Stuurman – South Africa

photo Cynthia Anderson *design* Nur Zahra – Indonesia
photo Gabrielle Kannemeyer *design* Daily Paper – South Africa

photo Marie Taillefer *design* Heartwear – Benin
photo Wilbert Das *design* Uxuá – Brazil

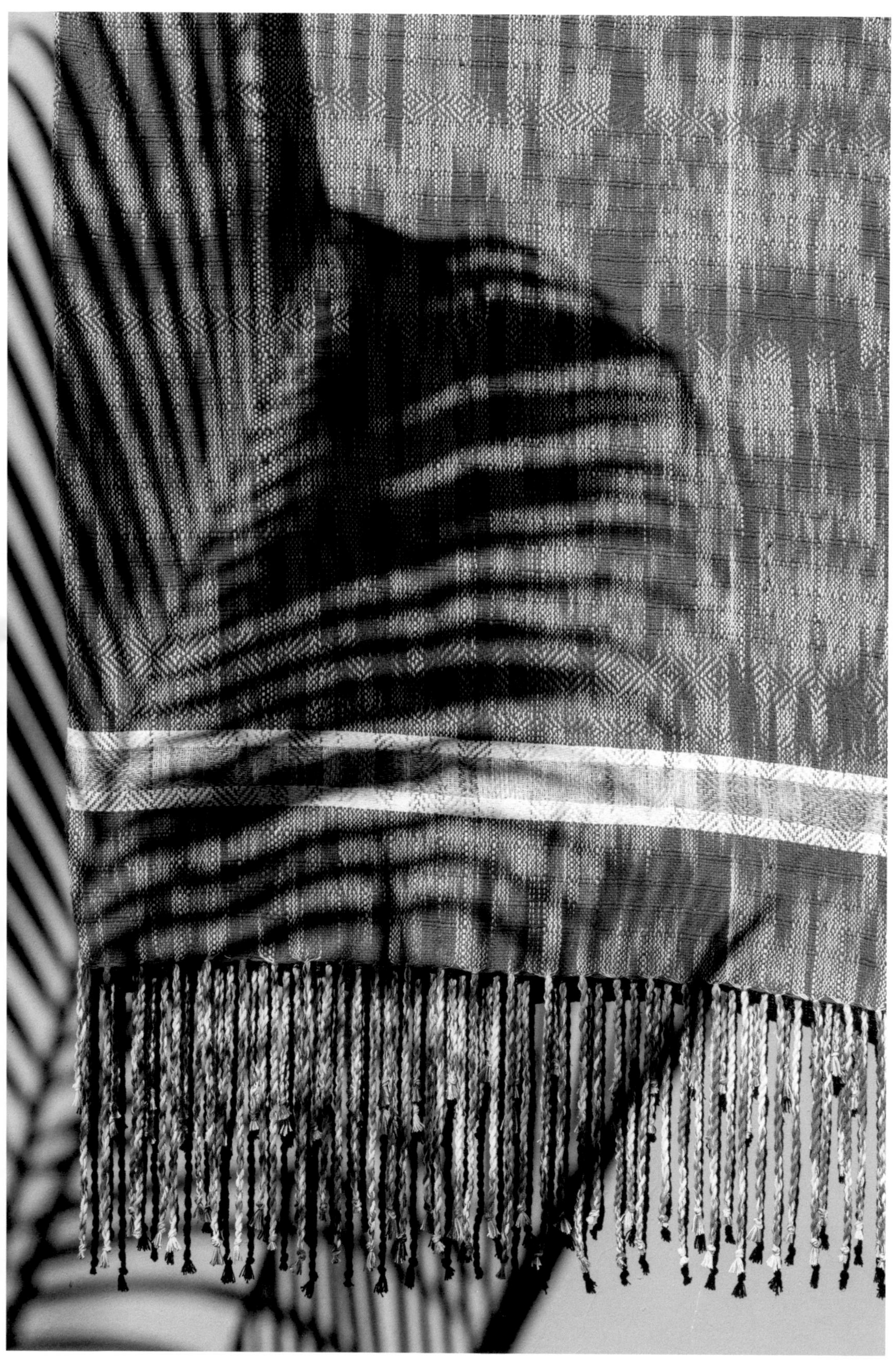

photos Marie Taillefer *design* Heartwear – Benin

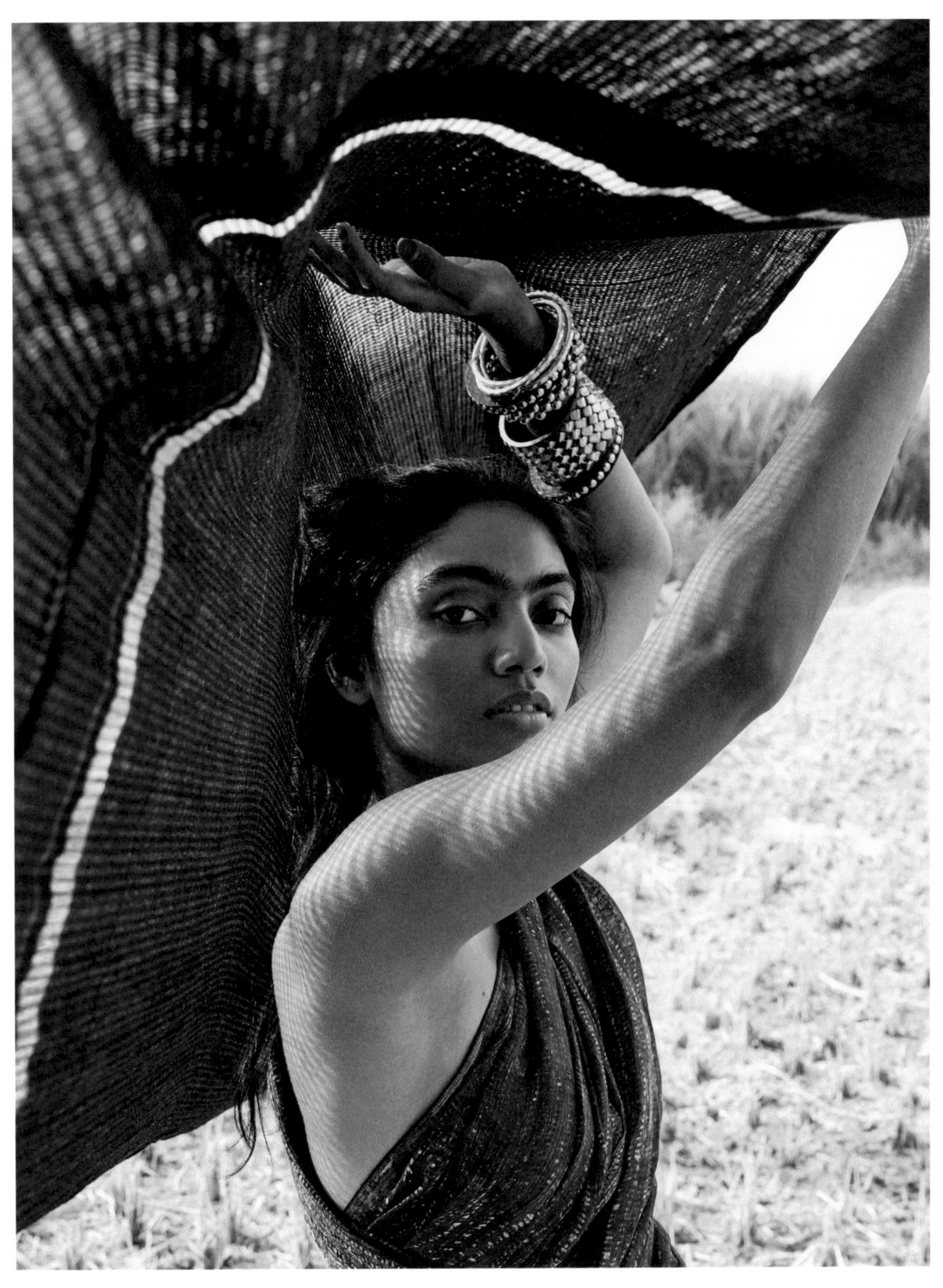

photo Justin Polkey *design* Anavila – India
photo Bharath Ramamrutham *design* Sabyasachi Mukherjee / CITTA – India

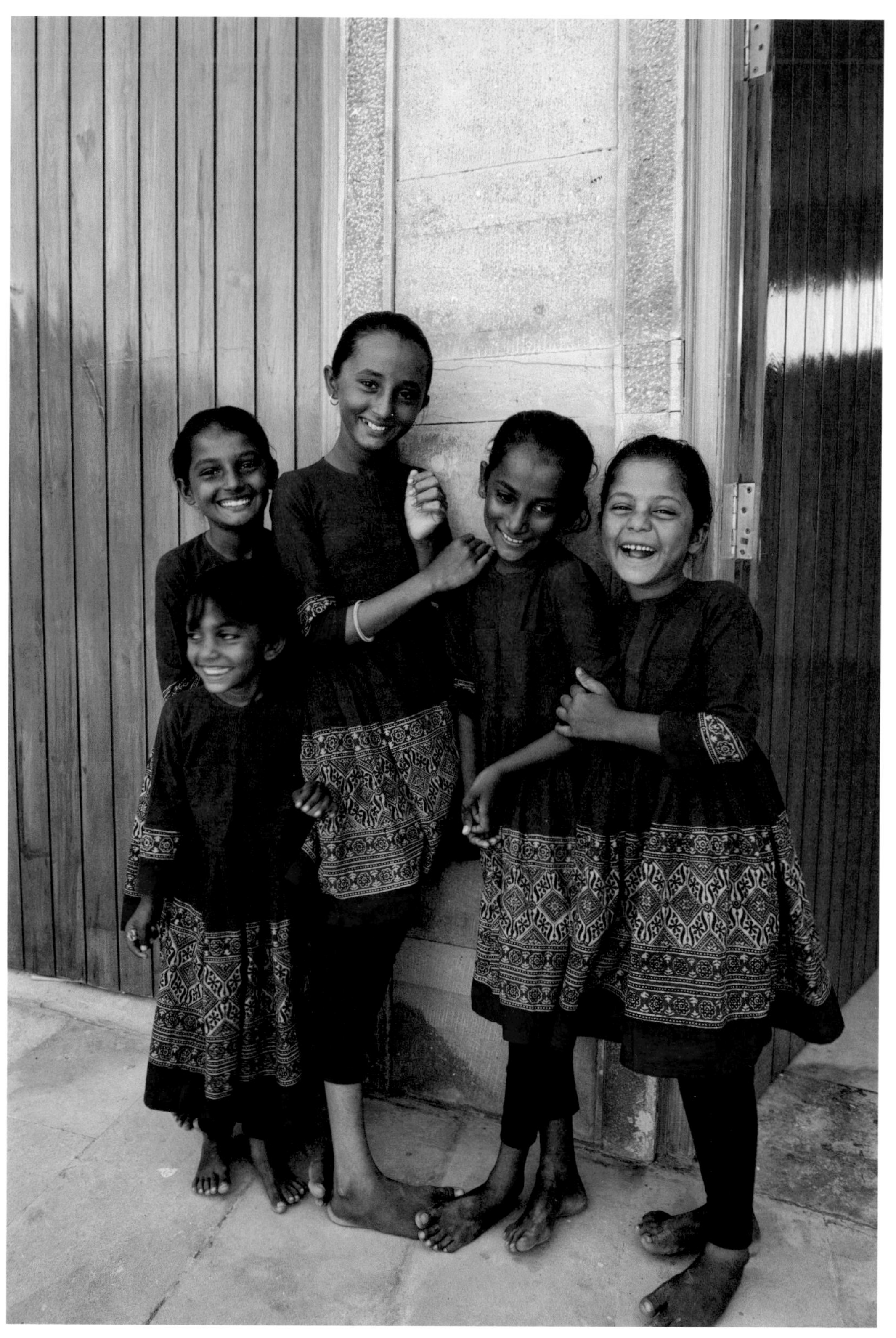

PROUD SOUND, THE RISE OF THE PROUD SOUTHERNER

by Kavita Parmar

"May you live in interesting times."

Whether a Chinese curse or an ironic English expression, the disputed origins of this phrase make it seem like a perfect fit to define the current zeitgeist. Everything around us is up for questioning: institutions, systems, governments and gender roles.

There seems to be a general sense of mistrust of just about everything we assumed as baseline. How we find ourselves in such chaos might have to do with the abundance of information. The magnitude of the new information landscape which can only be defined as an explosion, an overload, or without exaggeration, a tsunami when measured in data bits, is mind-blowing indeed (information generated from 2001 to 2002 was more than all information generated by humanity until then). As the amount of information available to the public increased, the authoritativeness of any one source decreased. Uncertainty is an asset corrosive to authority.

Although people with nostalgia feel that as authority is questioned it seems unsettling and even dangerous, to those of us with faith in our humanity these are truly exciting times which allow for a rewrite, giving us a chance to construct a brand new narrative. We can take this moment to examine our biases and question what we have taken for granted, what we lost and what we gained. This is fundamental to course correction, which without doubt is the urgent need of the hour, before we hurl ourselves into unknown forms of forewarned dystopia.

As humanity we have gone through this a few times before. Out of these moments of confusion and chaos, new ideas will arise to hopefully give a positive shape to our future. One of the ideas that is close to my heart is the recalibration of the balance between the north and south. To just give some perspective, according to the UN, by 2100 the population of the global north will have grown by only 0.3 billion to 1.28 billion (11.8% of the global population), while that of the global south will have grown by 3.7 billion to 9.6 billion (88.2% of the global population). Until this past century the power was tipped very much in favour of the north as it was mostly in control of the capital, assets and flow of information.

For some context, I was born in an India that was claiming its place on the world map and wanted to prove that it was modern. Hence, we made the classic error of mirroring those we were told were winners, the ones to emulate, the developed nations, the first world and the so-called civilised ones. Of course these voices represented authority as they controlled the information, it was their story.

The old colonialist powers from the north, when left with no option but to go home, seeded self-doubt with such arrogance that we, who were tired of fighting for the most basic human rights in our own land, fell for the script, hook, line and sinker. We spent decades trying to deny the authenticity of our aesthetic and to abandon our innate wisdom, to behave just like the northerners, in the name of progress. We unlearned our facts to repeat their truths. We dressed to fit in, feigned our accents to please, even straightened our hair and whitened our skins and denied our inner anger. We aimed at top universities, cool clubs, the right companies, even if it was just to fill the diversity quotas to continue the charade.

And then it all started changing more quickly than ever; in less than two decades not only has there been an explosion in the generation of information but the southern economies have grown exponentially. This has allowed for a questioning of the established storyline.

A great example is the story of an extinct textile called Dhaka Muslin. Nearly two hundred years ago this sublime fabric was the epitome of luxury. In the great exposition of treasures organised by Prince Albert in 1851, amongst over a hundred thousand objects on show from the remotest corners of the empire, the item that was voted most precious was this almost invisible muslin. It is said that a metre of the very fine muslin would be worth the equivalent of 45,000 pounds today. This gossamer-like fabric was hand spun and handwoven by expert weavers in a country associated with the opposite of luxury.

The knowledge to make this muslin no longer exists because in the name of progress the faster and cheaper model was adopted, resulting in the total annihilation of this craft and heritage know-how. A very special indigenous cotton plant was replaced by a higher-yielding variety which did increase output but also consumed much more water, damaging the planet. We replaced quality with quantity, as the narrative of success was defined by the leaders of the Industrial Revolution. Dhaka has gone from making the most luxurious fabric worn by the elite to the centre of throwaway fast fashion, making its artisans slaves to a western need for cheap goods, produced in inhumane conditions.

The good news is that there is a powerful quiet revolution taking place and most of it is playing out in the global south. Through my work I have had the fortune to be up close with indigenous communities, small designers, artists, creatives and activists working on real solutions around the globe in the most remote parts of the planet.

The new generation of Indians and other southerners do not have the self-doubt I grew up with. They are rediscovering their roots, reclaiming their aesthetic and rewriting another narrative. As I travel around the south it is exciting to see creatives in all fields develop their own unapologetic singular vision. They fearlessly borrow from the old and patch it with the current to construct the future. It blurs the lines so often that it causes discomfort to an audience trained to think in boxes, for them it feels confusing as it cannot be defined by old maxims. They allow themselves to inhabit different realities at the same time; the very ancient that seems to be nearly primal, inherited from their ancestors, and the futuristic that they have adopted as their own in this hyper-connected world. It is the opposite of binary, as it is full of fluid contradictions. They seek no consensus as the movements are quite new, raw and honest. They don't pretend to know all the answers but are exploring the scenarios of the past and willing to ask the hard questions, working without fear.

And gosh, it is exciting, as it is messy and authentic and real. The good news is that if we allow it to flourish and nurture it a little, a truly global alternative narrative is taking shape and we will all be richer for it. Rich in experiences and interactions. The timing couldn't be better as the crumbling of the old edifices in just about every industry is allowing for behavioural diversity to bubble up and jostle for space as former authorities are being replaced. We must have radical faith in our capacity to adapt to change, our ability to create newness and our irreplaceable need for human connections.

As we reignite the engines may we be brave enough to consider another way forward. We have the unique opportunity to allow for ancient wisdom, hidden for so long, to speak up and share its experience and vision. Southerners who have long been told to keep their mouths shut and watch from the sidelines have new ideas fuelled with ancestral wisdom that they have been intuitive enough not to abandon.

I do believe the time has come for the proud south and may we all be wise enough to listen, observe and encourage.

PROUD & HOUSE

◇◇◇◇◇◇◇◇◇◇◇◇◇◇

design by Péro
photography by Dolly Devi
– India –

Discovering the House of Péro felt like a gift: a breath of fresh air, defined by a new personal idiom, with over-the-top romantic dresses, flowing skirts and floating tops. An adventure sparked from a knowledge of textiles and a love of clothes, in the hands of the Indian designer Aneeth Arora who studied both aspects, which is rare in today's fashion world. When she uses lace, she uses an avalanche of antique laces, patching patterns together from found bits and pieces. When she uses flowers, she generously scatters them all over, underlined with lace trims. When she uses embroidery, it is done by hand and stands out, engineered on colourwoven grounds. She crafts her creations with excessive detailing that makes the clothes unique and valuable; they feel like gems and become even more endearing when they are wrapped in muslin bags fastened with textile gris-gris. At times, the dresses look like Laura Ashley on steroids. Even the shoes are loaded with frills and tassels so as to vibrate positive energy when they walk. The whimsical aspect of the clothes makes them potent and transforms the romantic into the contemporary. The secret of Arora's quirky dainty edge rests in her textile processes, where materials pass from the hands of one craftsperson to another and another, an Indian tradition of creating one-of-a-kind pieces that are cherished and preserved. To be continued… *L.E.*

PROUD & TOUCH

◇◇◇◇◇◇◇◇◇◇◇◇◇◇

Southern comfort is brought by southern creativity, mastering the art of crafts that touch hands as much as hearts. Seducing with gathered textiles that are designing tactility and fantasy, such as fringes, frills and pompoms to rattle while dancing. Standing out from the surface, these elaborate embellishments give dimension to festive garments that dabble in applications. Quilting uses leftover materials, recycling the waste of the west into elaborate austral beauty. Haberdashery has the knack to lift a vintage dress out of oblivion, embroideries retrace history and ancestry, and patchworks tell stories of magical days gone by when stitching becomes magic while telling stories. Crochet turns knits into gardens, tassels turn volume into fur coats, rags make outfits shudder with movement and laughter. Creative communities unite to deal with the problems of over-production, designing one-off pieces to gain creative traction, without burdening the planet with more of the same old stuff. Making the south the centre of reincarnation. *L.E.*

photo Mous Lambarat – Morocco
photo Trevor Stuurman – South Africa

photo Vaishnav Praveen *design* Ka-Sha – India
photo Pedro Loreto *art direction* Flora Velloso – Brazil

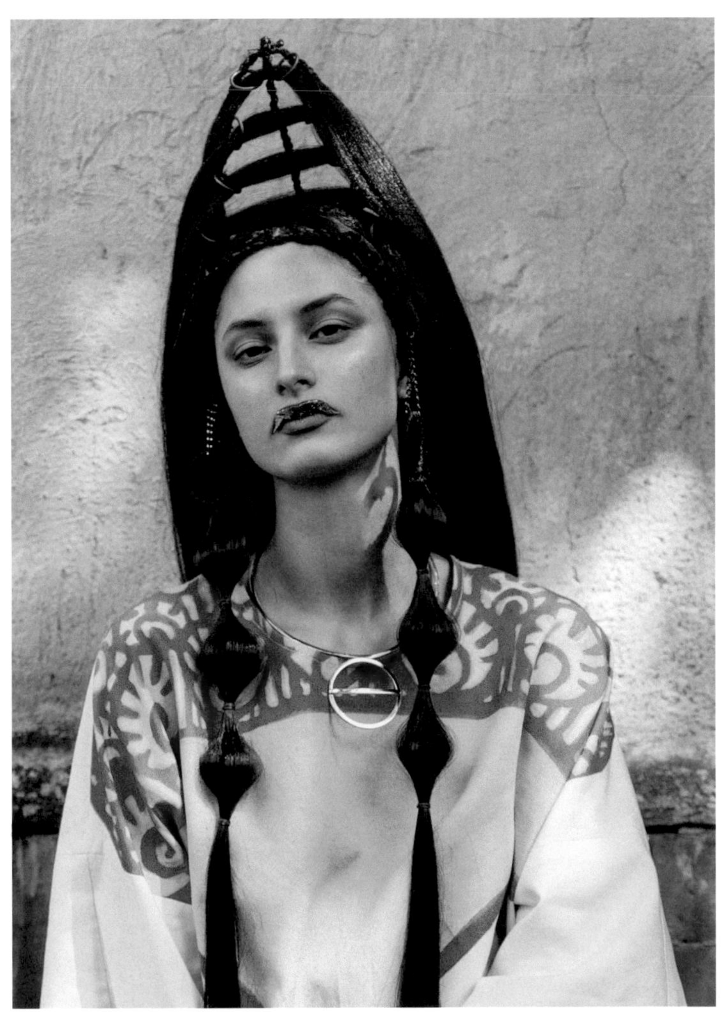

photo Ramiro Chaves & Dorian Ulises López
design Carla Fernández – Mexico
photo Sandra Blow *design* Carla Fernández – Mexico

next spread *photos* Tom Barreto *design* Ana Clara Watanabe – Brazil

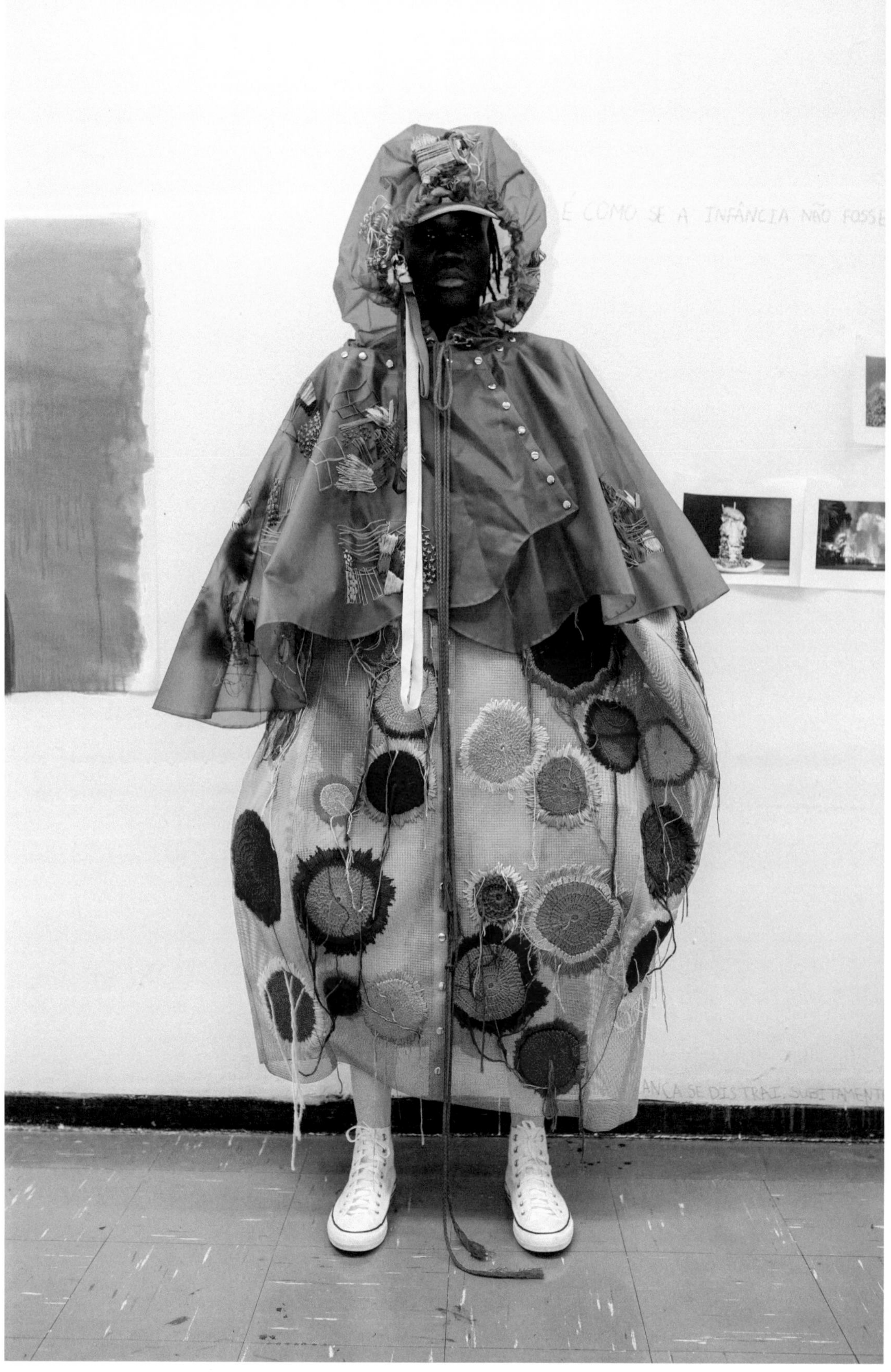
É COMO SE A INFÂNCIA NÃO FOSSE
ANÇA SE DISTRAI, SUBITAMENT

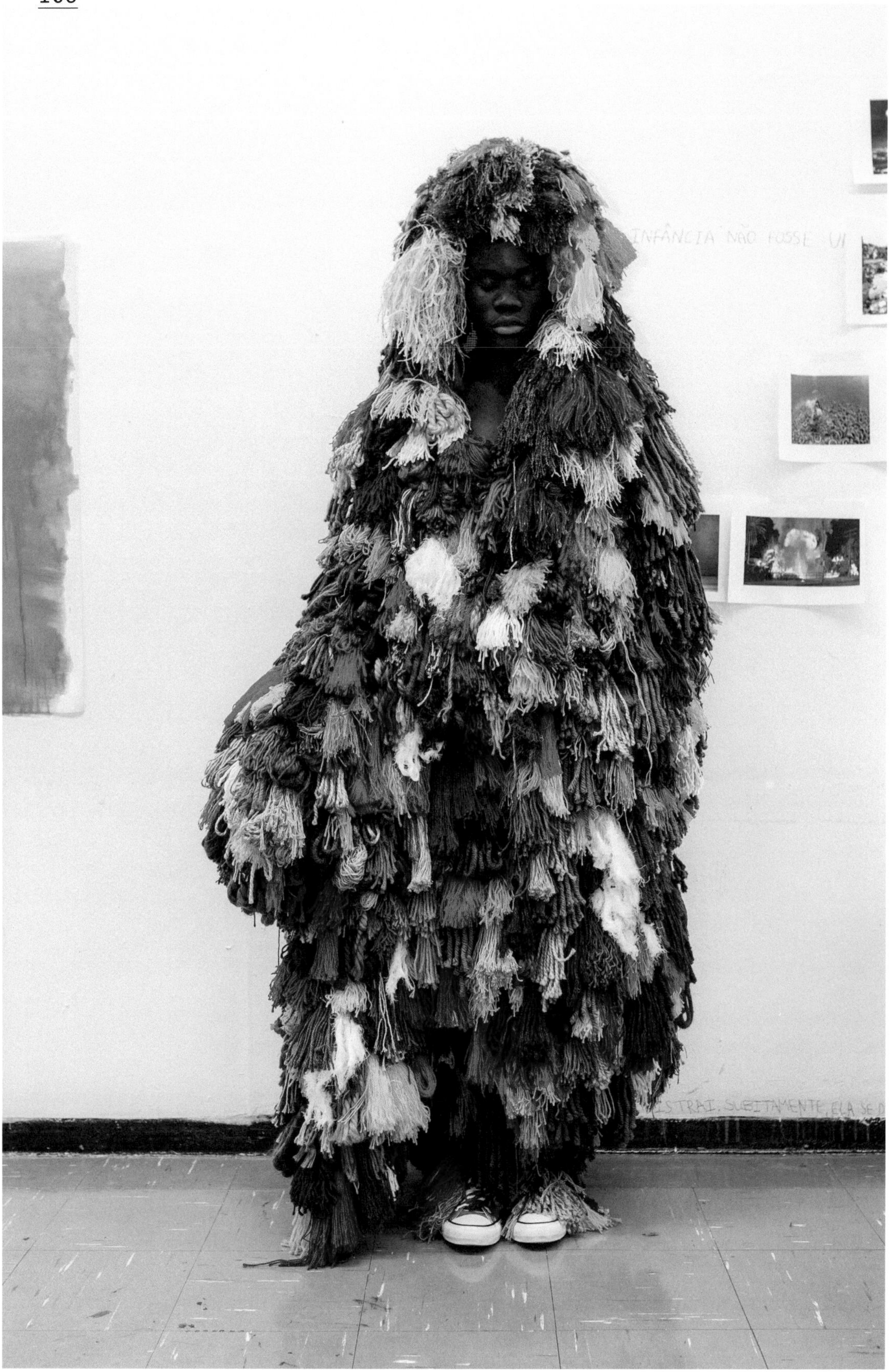
INFÂNCIA NÃO FOSSE
SUBITAMENTE, ELA SE

photo Alan Sosa Latournerie *design* Thais Pérez Jaén – Mexico
photo Pedro Santos *design* Laura Laurens – Colombia

photo Raphael Lucena *design* Farm – Brazil
photo Hick Duarte *design* Fernanda Yamamoto / Vogue – Brazil

photo Gleeson Paulino *design* João Pimenta – Brazil
photo Luke Houba *design* Lukhanyo Mdingi – South Africa

photo Rafael Arroyo *design* Thais Pérez Jaén – Mexico
photo Pedro Loreto *design* Uxuá – Brazil

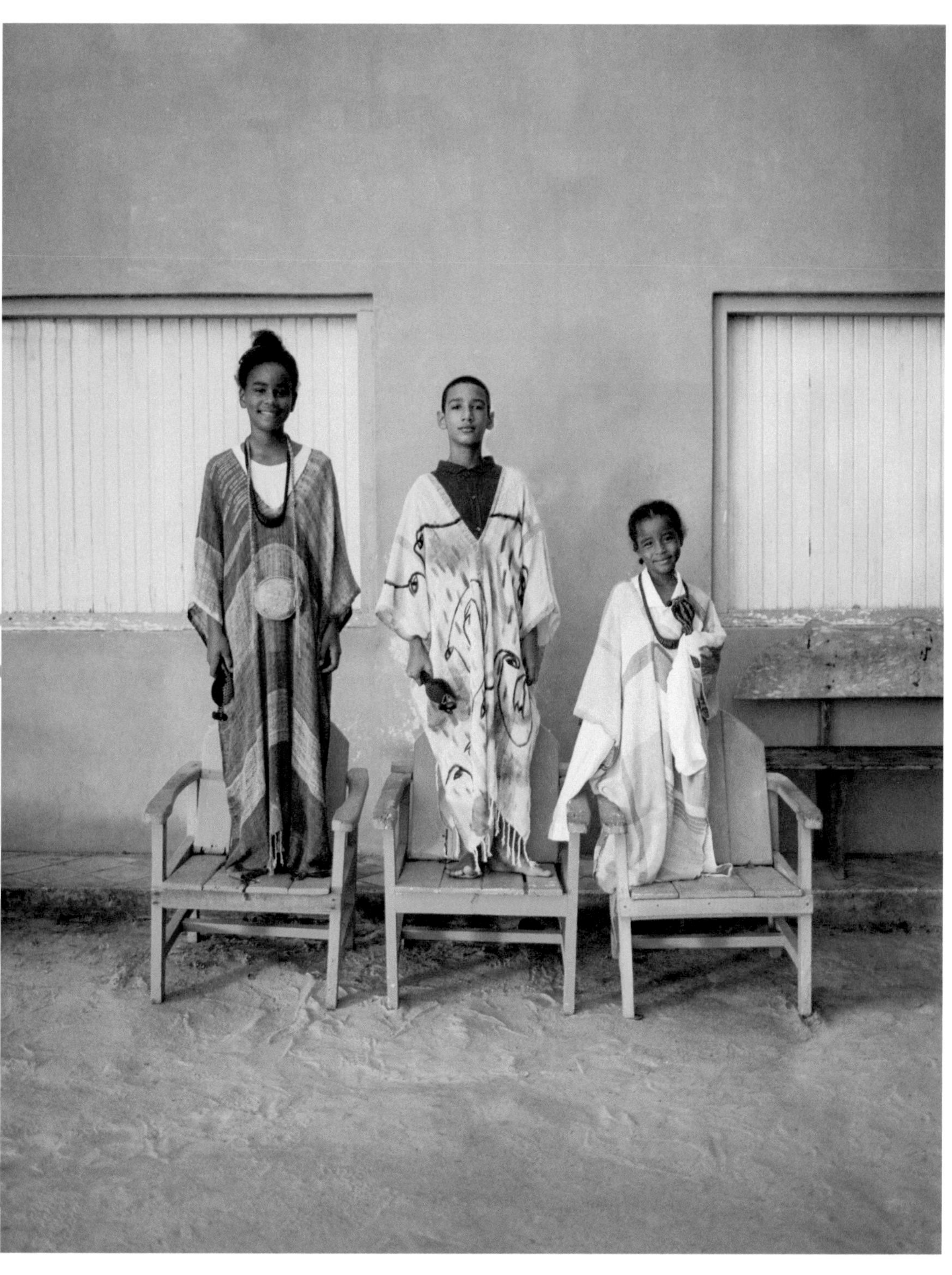

PROUD & YOUNG

◇◇◇◇◇◇◇◇◇◇◇◇◇◇◇

The nomadic history of wax prints is astounding. The patterns are derived from Javan batiks which were traded by Dutch merchants, taking the resist dye textiles from Southeast Asia to Africa where they became popular, inspiring interpretations that are brighter and more graphic. Although there are local trends and great differences in colour and subject matter, something in the making of wax patterns must make people happy since the textiles exude such fresh and dynamic energy. Mostly used for wrapped outfits, they seem to have a life of their own and even get names that express their intentions, such as a motif with mobile phones that might be called *'allo, 'allo?* or a fabric with knives and forks named *bon appétit!* This appetising sense of selling a mood more than a print might explain why the bold materials are now used for young interiors in great pattern mixes, making rooms smile and chairs jump for joy. *L.E.*

photo & design Sandrine Alouf – France

photo Jacobus Snyman *design* Chu Suwannapha – South Africa

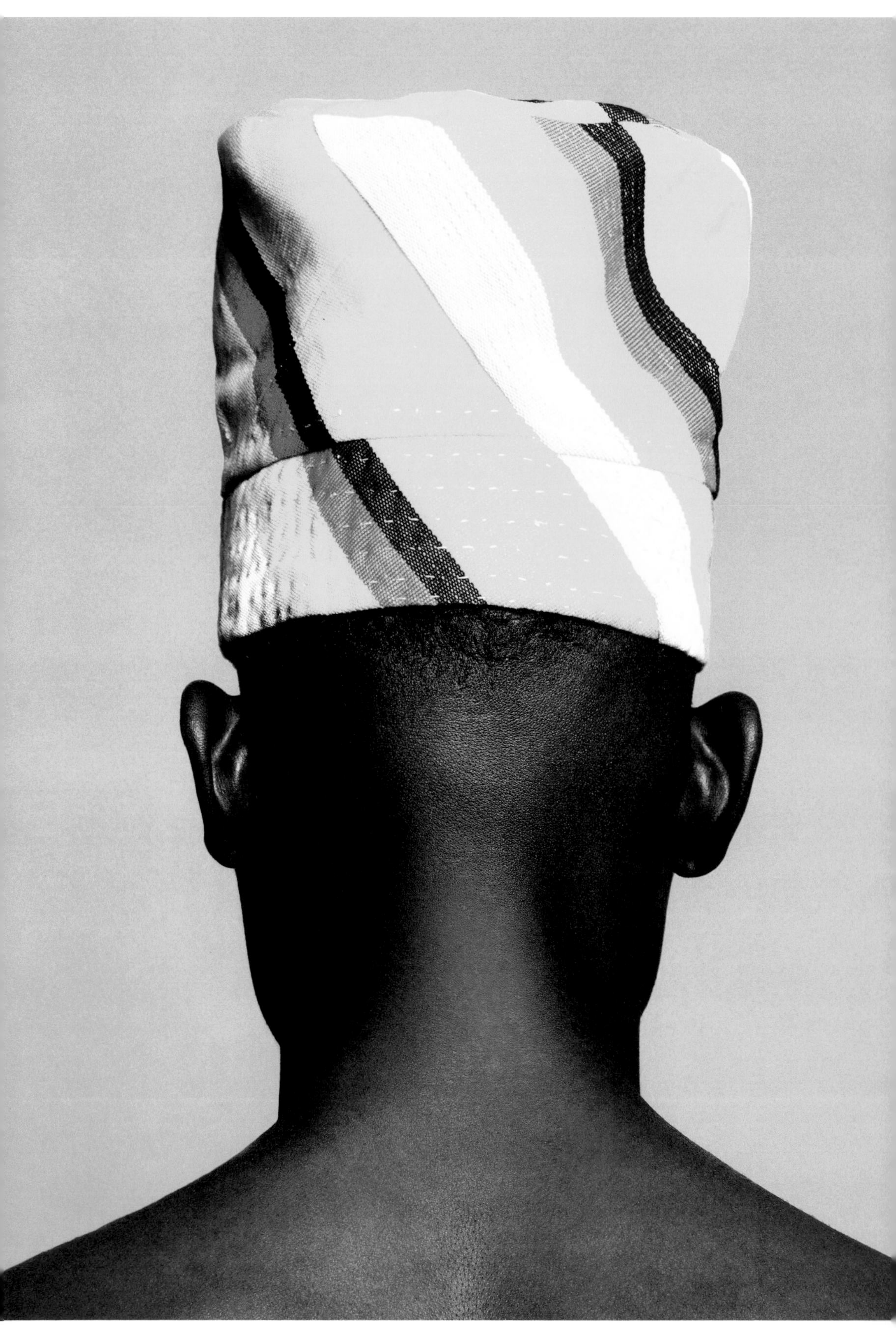

photo Lakin Ogunbanwo – Nigeria

design Flavia del Pra – Brazil

design CSAO – Nigeria

photo Jackie Nickerson – USA / UK

photo & design Sandrine Alouf – France

photo Jacobus Snyman *design* Chu Suwannapha – South Africa

PROUD & ARDOUR

photography by Ramiro Chaves
and Ana Hop *for* Carla Fernández
– Mexico –

She has gained international acclaim for documenting the rich textile history of her beloved Mexico. The passion of designer Carla Fernandez – a striking Mexican with a handsome husband, like a modern-day Frida and Diego – has fuelled her ethical fashion venture since the turn of the century, and has made her a famous cultural figure in the world of art. Her consistency and bravery led her to share her knowledge of indigenous clothes, becoming contemporary fashion that is rare and a great example if we want the world to change. From the traditional shapes of Mexican dress that incorporates the square and the rectangle, she lays down the rules of modern tradition and how to make it contemporary by abstracting its essence. Using weaving, embroidery and collage, she brings together collections that have an international following but are proudly from the south. With her mobile laboratory she investigates artisan communities all over the country to collect and preserve their knowhow, including their crafts, in fellow designer collections. Her clothes that are made by hand are essential to the work, since each piece has its own soul and character, and she recognises their immense value in the manifesto *Fashion as Resistance* that describes her commitment to decolonialisation, social justice and the future of fashion. A future where a fashion house explores new meaning in luxury, positioning it as an agent of ethical change. *L.E.*

Rosa Vázquez Pérez

Araceli Hernández Ruiz

Cristina Hernández

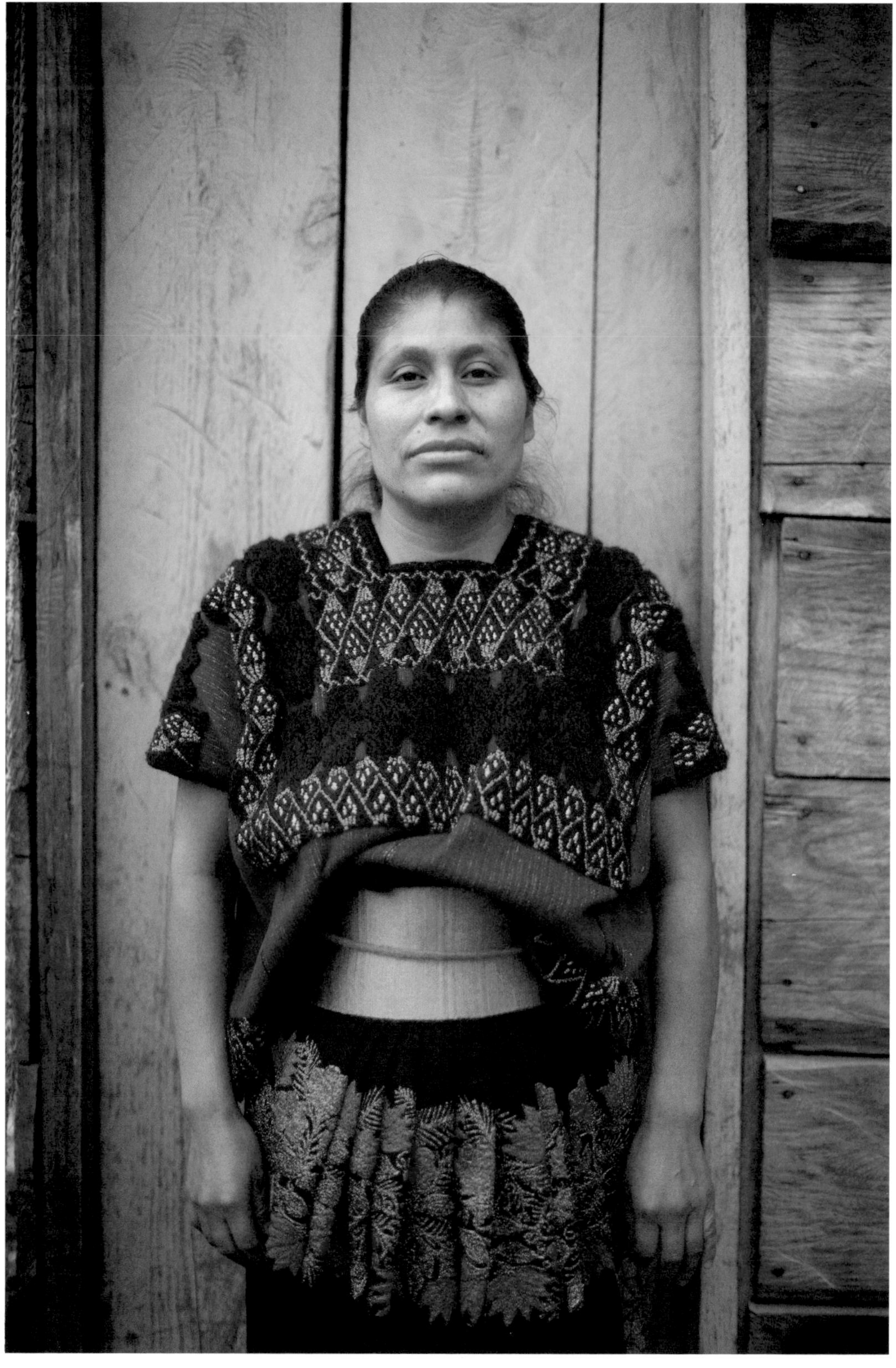

Carmela Pérez

Juana López

Manuela Patishtán Pérez

MANIFESTO OF FASHION AS RESISTANCE

by Carla Fernández

One day we woke up and realised we could not care less about what happens in Paris.

We do what they told us not to do. Our way of doing things seems suicidal to business schools: We work in a country in which 68 different languages are spoken. Textiles are our lingua franca. Among ourselves we speak in fingers, palms and cubits. Our garments smell of smoke. They are woven and embroidered next to the stove. We create few of them, and we do it slowly. We are like grasshoppers in the field: small but rambunctious. We use fabrics that were woven to be treasured. A huipil is an open book. Its brocade tells the story of how a caterpillar morphs into a butterfly. The same rectangle that is a skirt in the morning becomes a mat in the afternoon and a blanket at night.

It is up to us to put an end to fashion as trash. We do not design garments to end up rotting in a dump. We say no to bloodsucking transnational corporations and to the mass production that is so detrimental to our planet. Anonymous assembly is for the plunderers of souls. No to the false neoliberal urgency that, season after season, prioritises volume over care. No to uniformity. No to the vile automated consumerism that favours all things foreign. Let us not fool ourselves, we all participate in fashion. Yes to insubordinate creativity. Yes to work free of distress.

1 to be original is to go back to the origin

In Mexico high fashion is made in the mountains, the deserts and the jungles. We make fashion alongside people whose roots are in the earth from which they sustain themselves.

In the mountains, an artisan harvests cotton, collects seven branches with which to make a backstrap loom and, seated on a woven palm mat, she makes a panel of fabric. If tomorrow the petroleum supply is depleted, if there is no electricity or internet and the industry is paralysed, she will still do what she does. She will continue making her own clothing, growing her own food and building her own home. She will do tomorrow just as she does today, and just as her ancestors have done for centuries. The capacity to transform materials into sustenance is a key element in a way of life commensurate with nature, in which rituals, world views and sciences are intertwined. We pose this question: Who should be learning from whom?

2 fashion is not ephemeral

Death to planned obsolescence! Which renders expendable all it draws into its abyss of waste. The best design is not that which disintegrates, but that which remains. We want our clothes to last so that their whisper will be heard by other generations. Fashion is not ephemeral; neither is our planet, nor our relationships. Our relationships with the communities with whom we collaborate are abiding and fond.

3 tradition is not static

For more than three thousand years those who weave and embroider have transmitted their fundamental knowledge from mother to daughter. If their techniques have survived, it is precisely because they are a form of expression. In them the subjective and the collective are simultaneously manifested.

Still, tradition is not suspended in time: in small towns and artisan communities styles change and evolve; creativity is awake, not dormant, and it gives way to new and unexpected designs.

4 square root

In the western tailoring system, encoded in cuts and curves, what predominates is the silhouette of the person wearing the clothes, rather than their fabric or history. But Mexican indigenous clothing results from joining together square and rectangular panels. It is a unique textile origami that uses these two figures as the base from which to construct any other form using folds, pleats and stitching. This system of patterning interests us for both its vernacular significance, which we consider the path to the future, and for its constructive and architectural quality.

The geometric clothes worn by indigenous women can be read like open books that tell the life stories of the weavers who made them. If a page were cut out or divided with seams, it would be impossible to read the entire narrative. We gave this system the name *la raíz cuadrada*, the square root, because we work with the roots of Mexico and this way of square patterning as tools of design.

5 the origin of the textile is the earth

There sprout the seeds of the plants from which fibres are created. Cotton, with its brown and white mound, brims with the events of the Americas, which flow from its roots to its leaves, transmitting vitality. Work done by hand turns the fibres into textiles. Designs are conceived with the body and the mind in an organic procedure. The earth manifests its generosity in our clothes.

Their colours and textures narrate stories: the wool of San Juan Chamula is submerged in mud for days so that it never loses its intense and brilliant black. The tricolour skirts of southern Oaxaca feature blue obtained from indigo, representing the sky; stripes of red made by macerating the cochineal insect, representing fertility; and purple drawn from the caracol púrpura, a coastal sea snail, symbolizing power and death. The material is transformed by subtly awakening the natural elements under the influence of the hands, the mind and the heart.

6 in true luxury there is no oppression

How could we take pride in the luxury of our work if our production chain depended on the oppression of our workers or the overexploitation of our planet's resources?

True luxury is when the enjoyment and pleasure of some do not come at the cost of the suffering of others. True luxury is organizing a generous and gratifying system of work. Our notion of luxury is based on admiration of the fine, delicate artistic richness that comes from artisans' hands.

No to anonymous manufacturing. No to the theft of imagination for the exclusive benefit of commerce. No to the notion that the work of some is worth more than the work of others. No to the supremacy of the idea over the manufacture.

We understand that artisan processes require time to think, time to learn, time to transform and transcend. Upon this notion of what it means to make, we build long-term relationships with a commitment to fair compensation as a symmetrical reflection of effort.

7 everybody is beautiful and emanates vitality

These two principles must be honoured with a way of dressing that celebrates the diversity of all silhouettes. In this variety of forms we visualise sculptures in movement, in transit, occupying the street. The majority of our clothes are not sized, as we reject an arbitrary ideal of beauty. This is why our styles must be flexible, adaptable and modular while staying in harmony with the person who wears them.

8 the client as a collector

We hope that those who wear our designs will be more than clients, that they will be participants in and sentinels of a legacy at risk of extinction, that they will know the origin of each piece, understand its symbolic and material worth and the values and techniques of the people who made it. By collecting fragments of the textile history of Mexico, our clients become its custodians. Our greatest satisfaction is when our creations are not stored in a drawer but constantly worn and used to revitalize the idea of Mexican fashion and its art of ancestral origin.

9 we are one and we are many

To be a company means we learn every day from each other and from ourselves; we discover the limits of who we are as individuals and what we are as a team. We dream of growing and work to achieve it. We weave a web of collaborations that connects us, sustains us and makes us stronger to face the enormous challenge of maintaining a creative, independent and economically unconstrained fashion line.

Our network is full of indispensable people who daily reinvent their own work methods, far from the structures of fashion imposed by external variables. Despite our rebellious system, within which we produce at a measured pace with complicated logistics and sustainable growth, we never forget that we are a business. We have firm goals that are only attainable if a group of people is committed to its core, as determined and passionate as the peak of the popocatépetl is tall, and willing to come together to work for a common goal.

10 the processes are a legacy

When we travel Mexico with our mobile design lab, more than anything we see the opportunity to learn and the emergence of work done together. Our clothes tell the hidden stories of Mexico. To understand their complexity and beauty we must make visible the artisan techniques that bring them to life. When conceiving the designs, the artisan involves her material and emotional being. She does not mechanically repeat; she varies, combining new figures and silhouettes. We denounce those who copy Mexican embroidery to fabricate it outside of its context. We raise our voices and join the song that makes the serpent's tail flick back and forth as it moves between past and present. The future is handmade!

PROUD & LOUD

◇◇◇◇◇◇◇◇◇◇◇◇◇◇

design by Maxhosa
– South Africa –

He was one of the first designers to graduate with a collection of knitwear dedicated to his origins. Laduma Ngxokolo intrinsically knew that his cultural heritage was of essential value to the world. After he staged his fashion show during the renowned Design Indaba conference in Cape Town, in front of a vast and critical audience of international designers, his peers jumped to their feet in a standing ovation, some with tears in their eyes. Everybody felt that this was a seminal moment, turning values upside down as an emancipation of southern design. The eponymous Xhosa-inspired Maxhosa brand was born. He had returned to the villages of his childhood to take stock of the coloured bead patterns made by local women for centuries. Patterns that already translated to blankets and beaded artefacts, but that never had been repositioned on contemporary clothes. The power of colour and craft designed a collection that seemed to become a Missoni of the south, manipulating yarns, stitches and motifs to create intricate total looks of knitwear. Straight as an arrow, shouldered like a warrior, solid as a rock, and as stubborn as a kid, he listened to this primal call and expanded Maxhosa into a thriving fashion label. His shows are events, his collaborations are famous, and his personal aura has made his roots even more recognisable. He is a relentless ambassador of his southern tribe. *L.E.*

photo Trevor Stuurman
photo Andile Buka

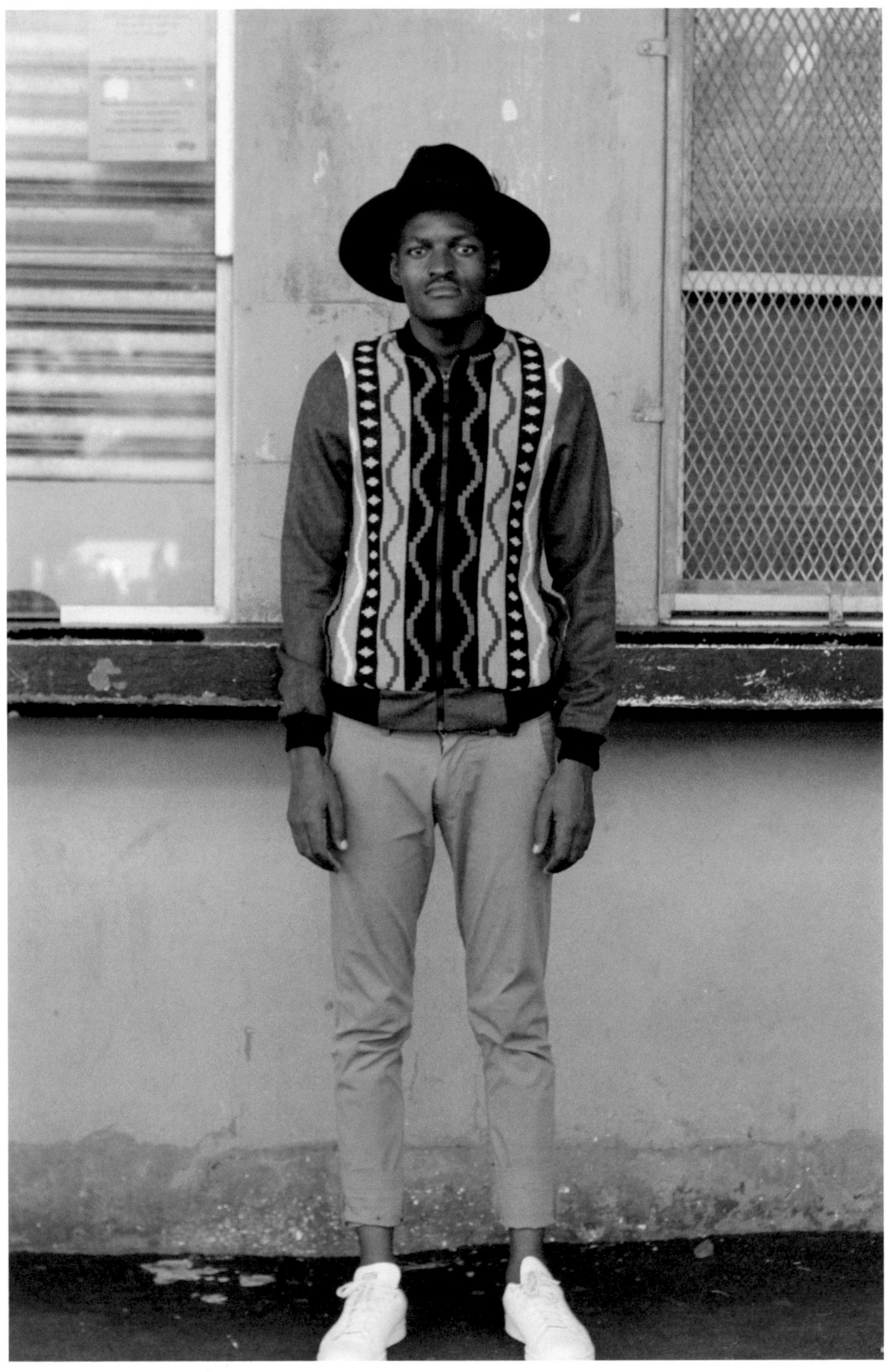

photo Gareth Cattermole
photo Trevor Stuurman

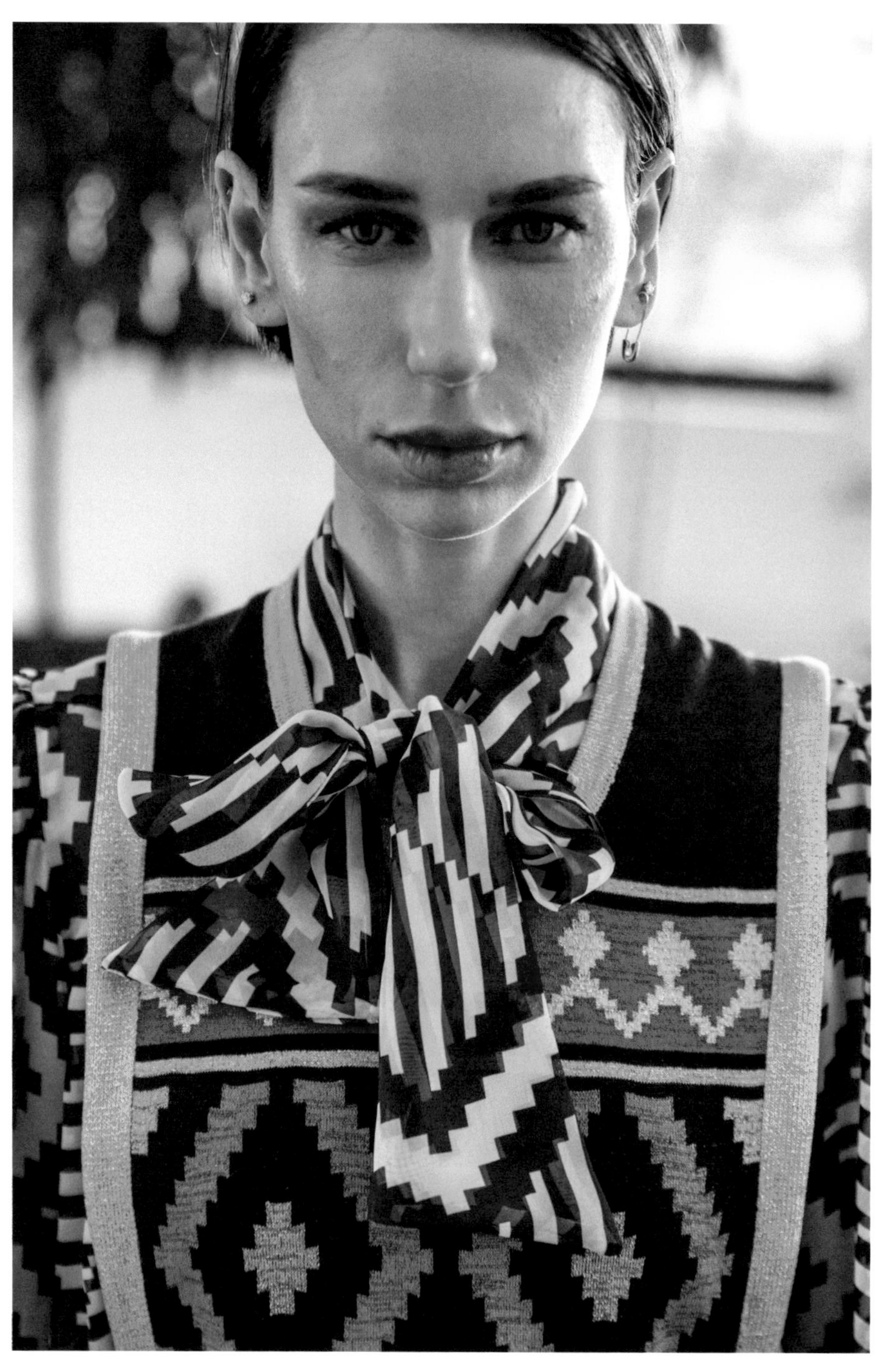

photo Arthur Dlamini
photo Andile Buka

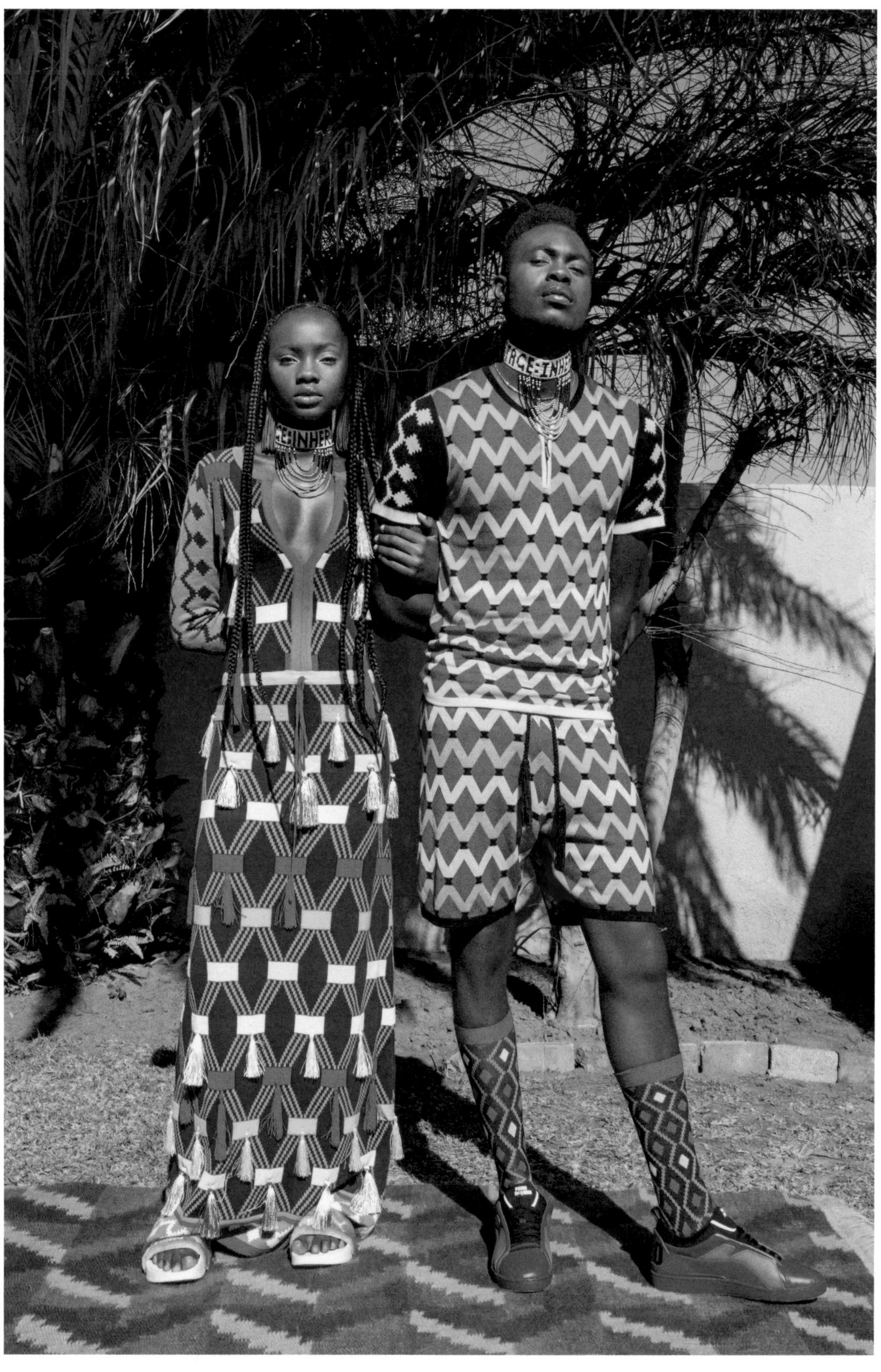

PROUD & SOUK

Accumulation is the southern way to express exuberance and it is in accumulation that we find the way designers want to affirm their signature, photographers want to portray their singularity and stylists want to show their magical skills in evoking the dream. They construct the dream of the naïve young princess, the spiritual male model or naughty kids playing model, that all display their infatuation with add-on design pieces such as bags and hats and caps, as well as scarfs and scarfs and more scarfs, worn as identity makers, as religious tokens or as luxury items. Finding their luck in the souk of seduction, they hunt for new things such as hair pins, using the head as another field of experimentation. The way the accumulated south has embraced accessories was born centuries ago when the adornments came to the first humans from shells and grasses and gris-gris, making the individual stand out. This innate need for personalised decoration is creating a new world, turning it upside down.

L.E.

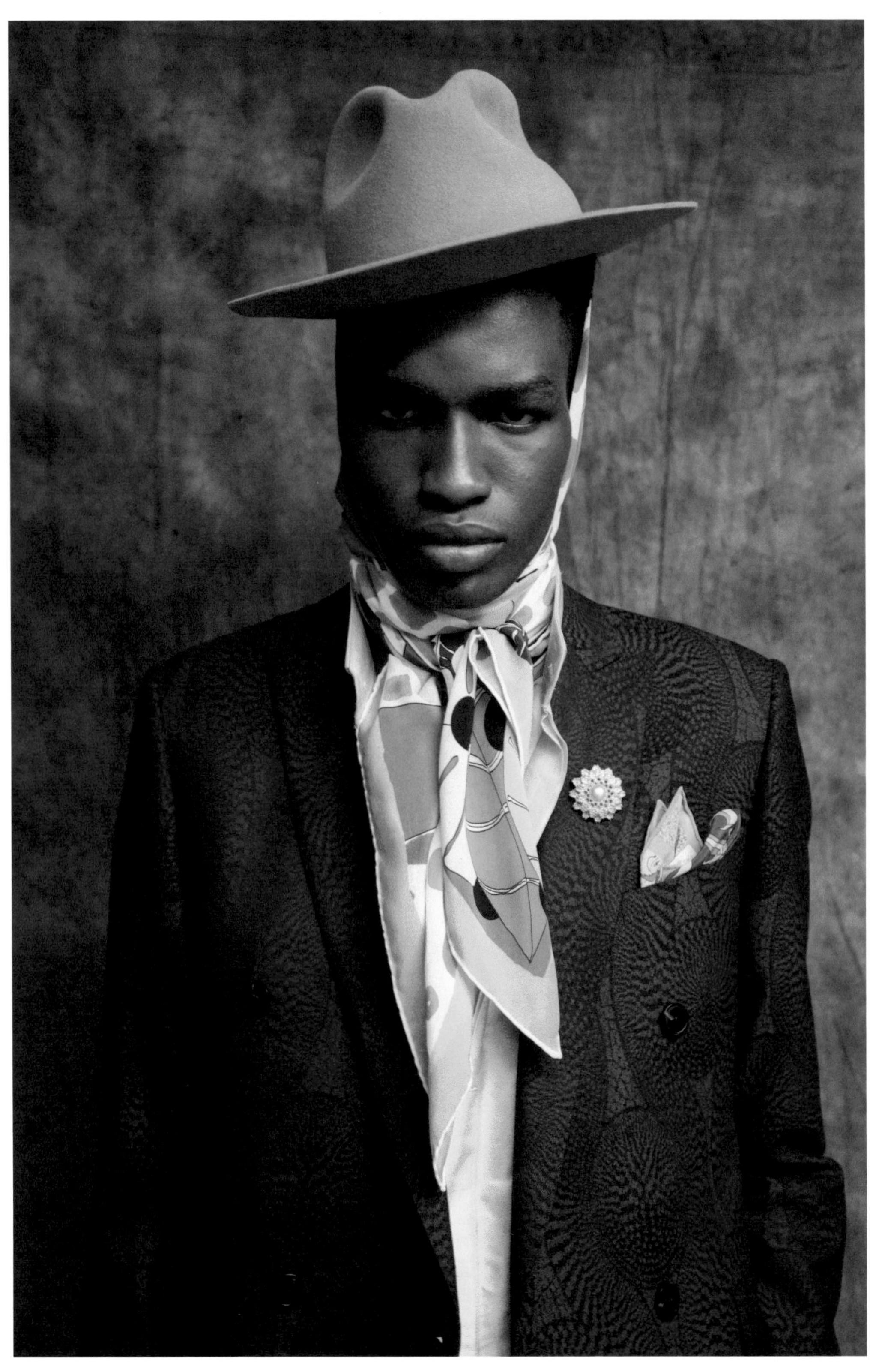

photo Trevor Stuurman – South Africa

photo Mous Lambarat – Morocco

photo Carol Wehrs *design* Farm – Brazil

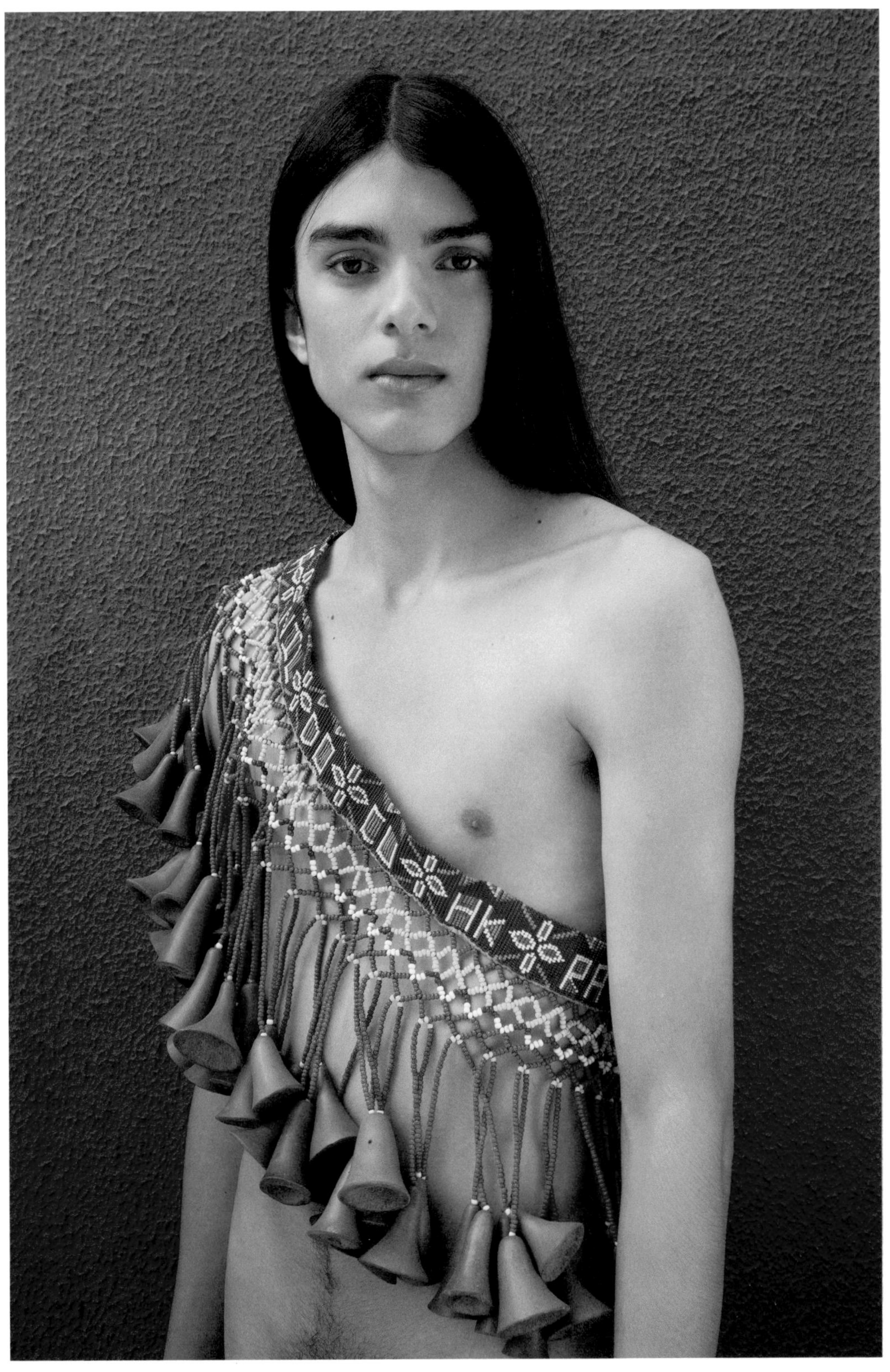

photo Rogério Cavalcanti – Brazil

photo Travys Owen *design* Orange Culture – Nigeria

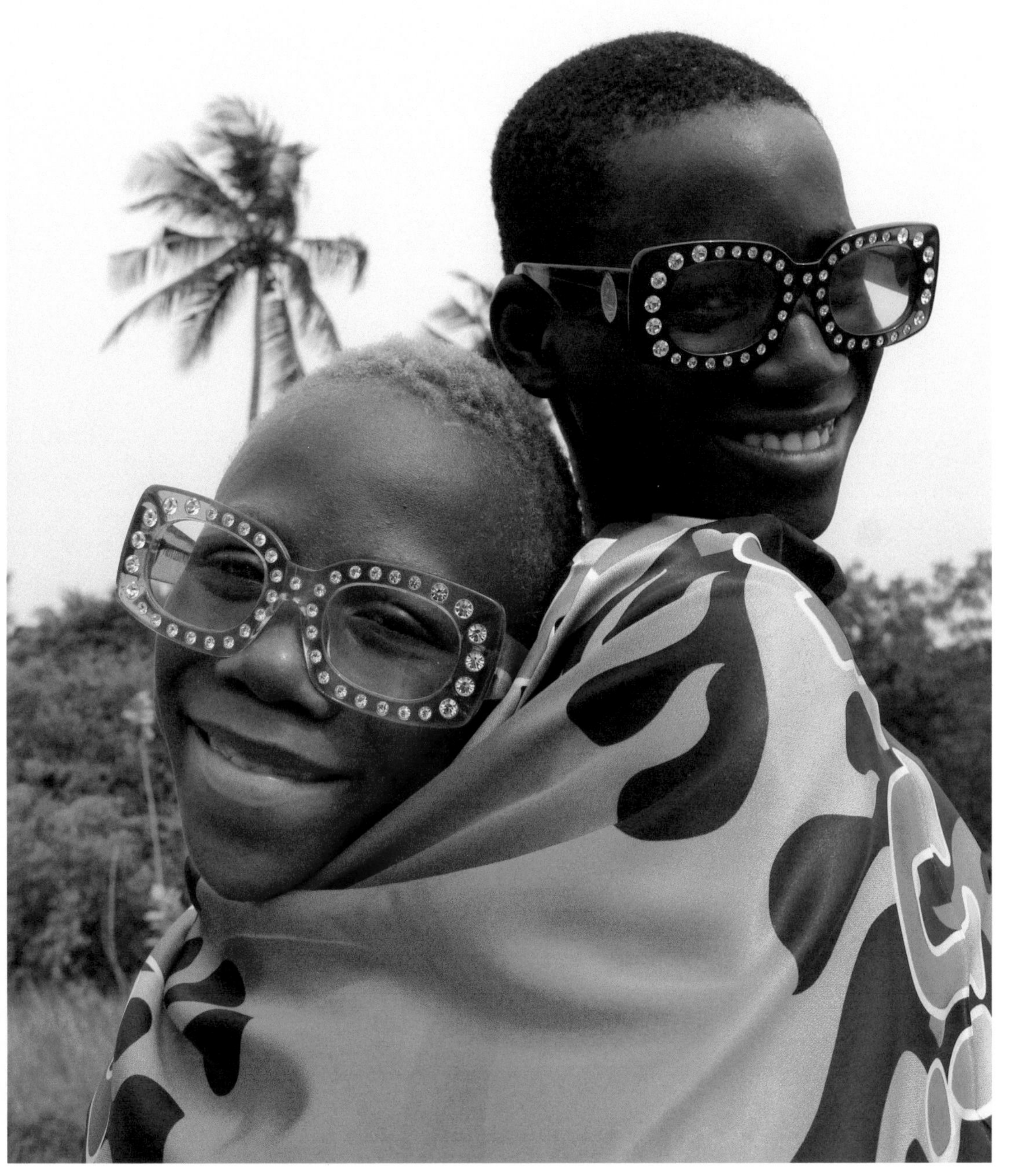

photo Stephen Tayo – Nigeria

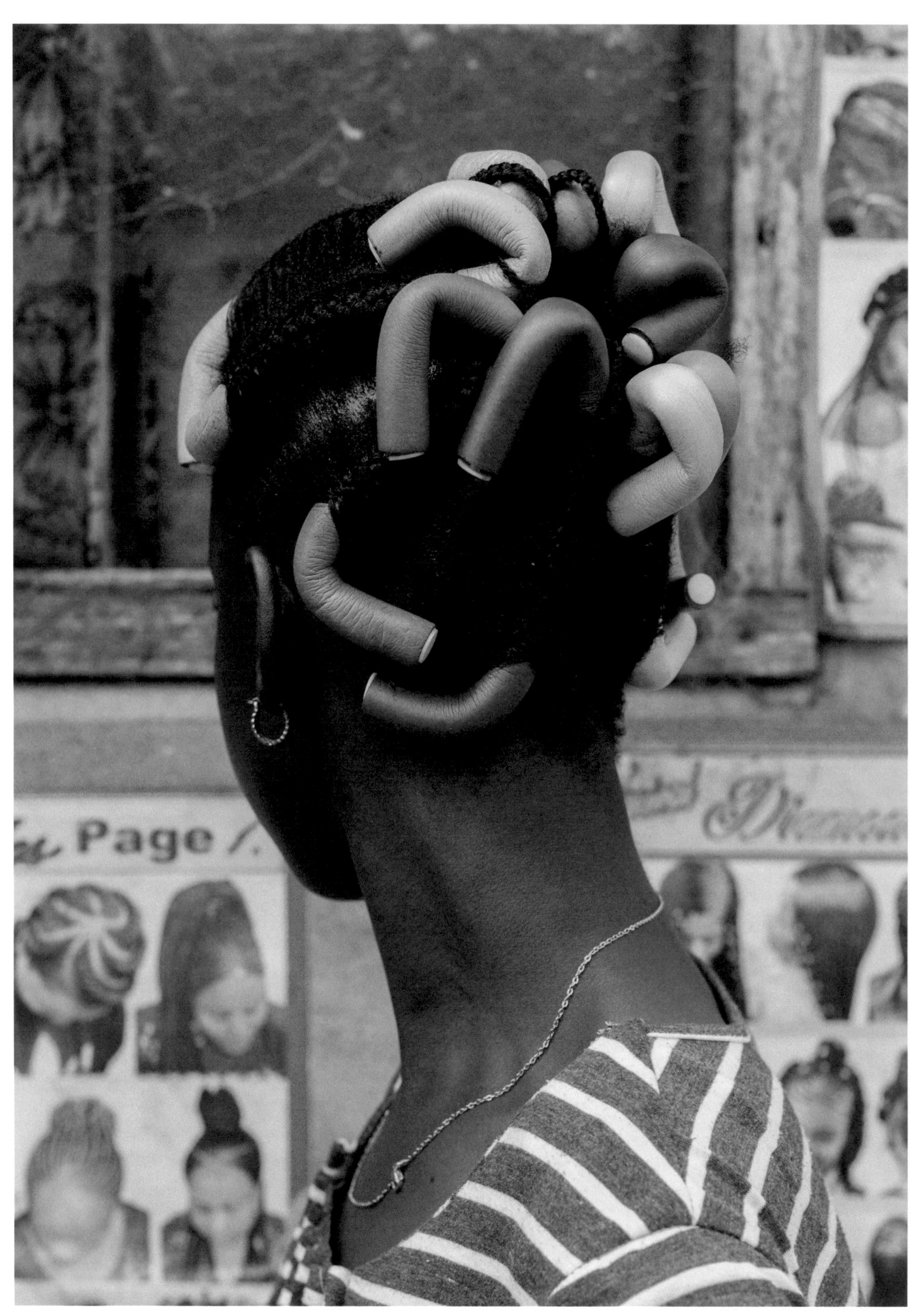

photo Stephen Tayo – Nigeria

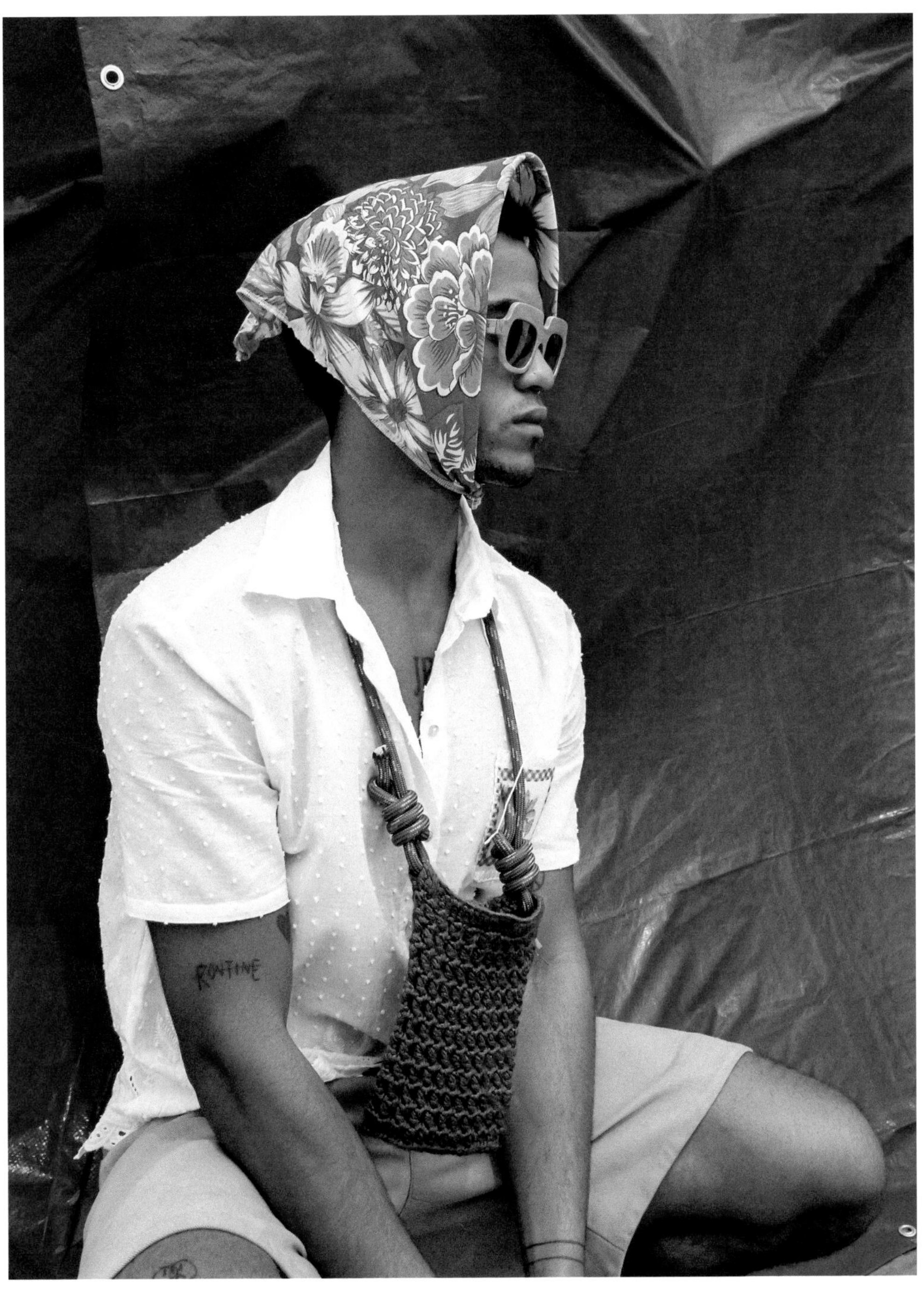

photo Matilde Cunha *design* Savio Drew / Casa Obi – Brazil

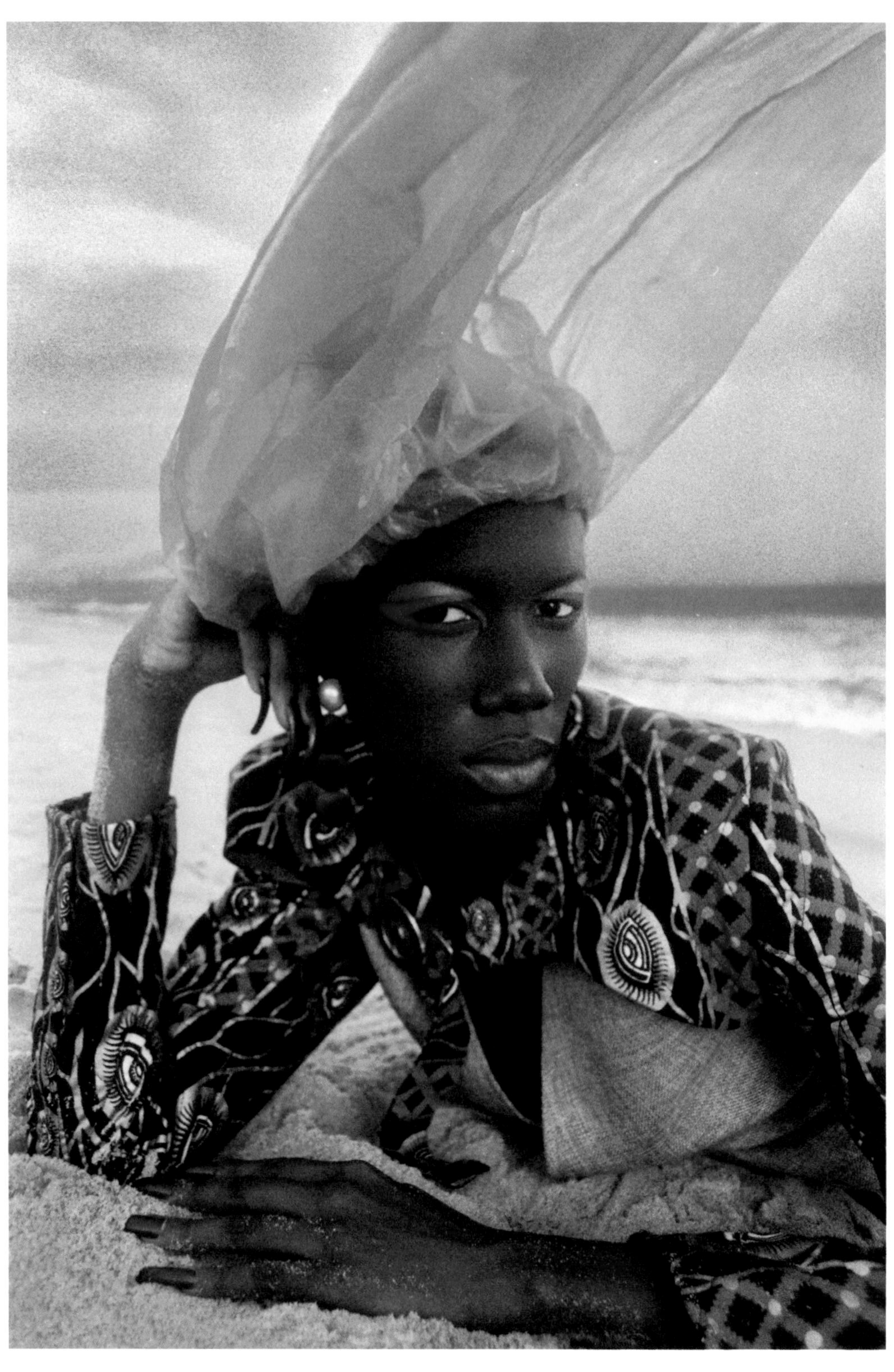

photo Louis Philippe de Gagoue *design* Ngadi Smart / Vlisco&co – Nigeria

photo Javier Falcon *design* Meche Correa – Peru

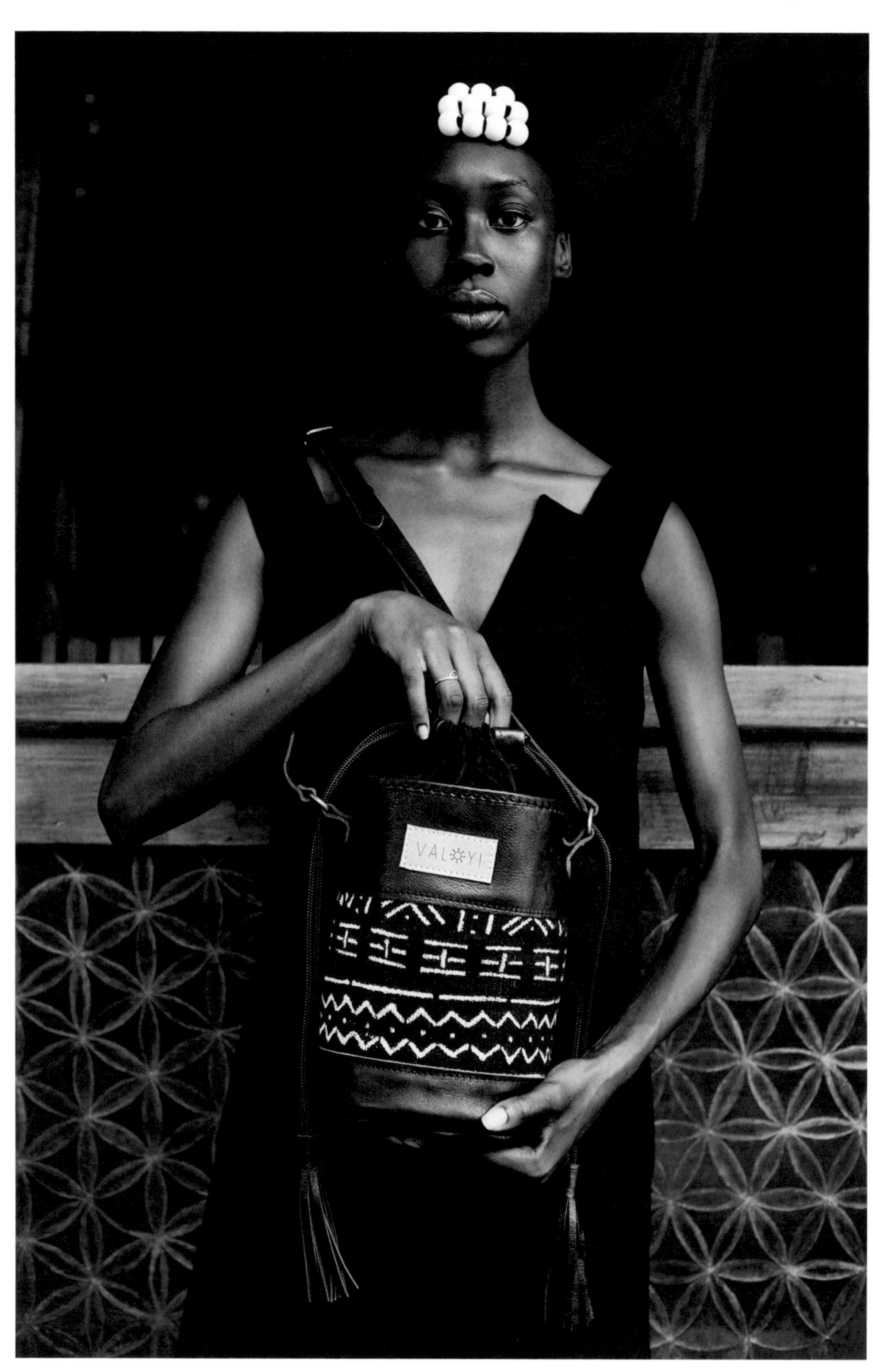

photo Saskia Wegner *design* Valoyi – South Africa

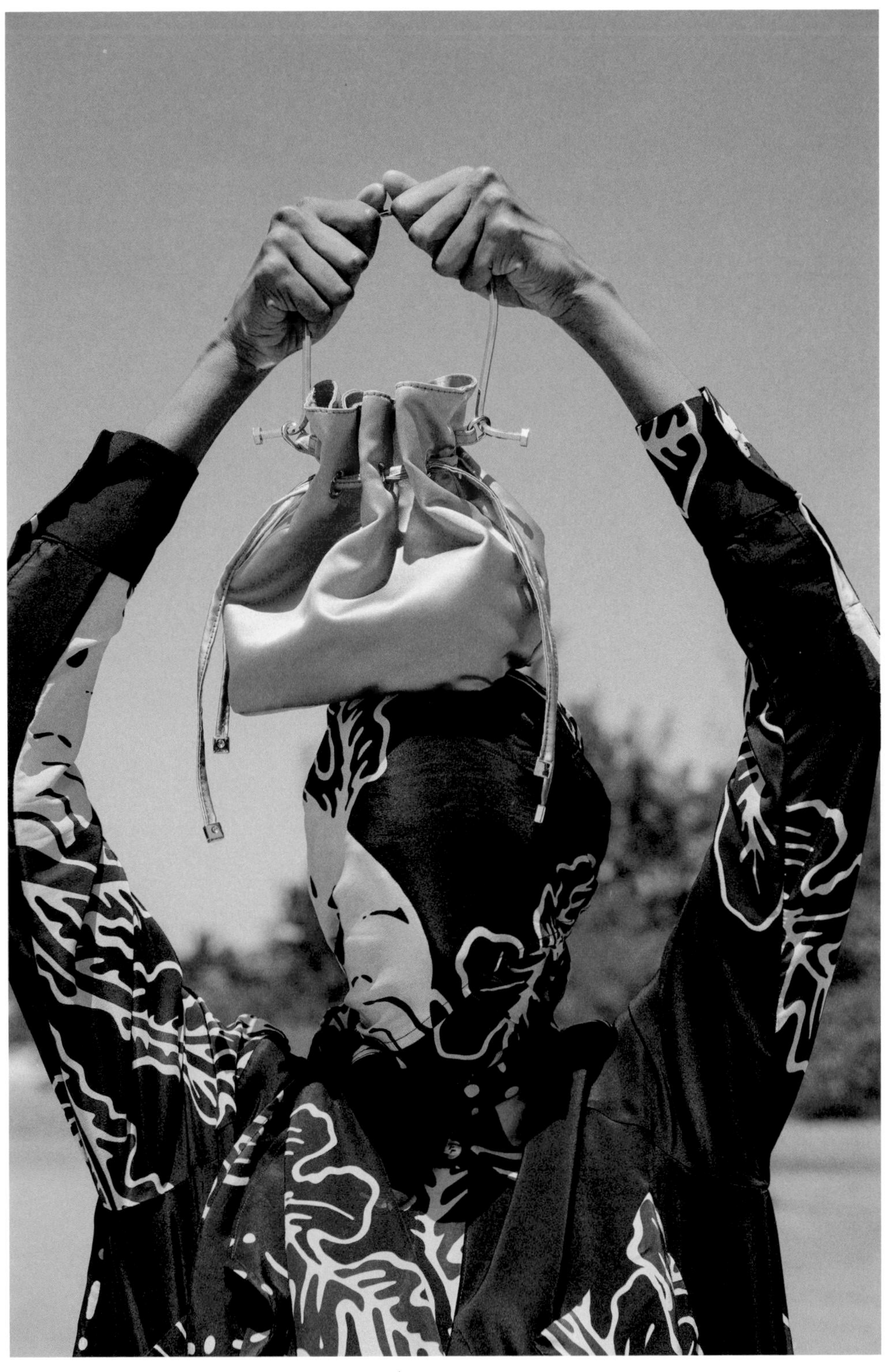

photo Bruna Sussekind *design* Betina De Luca + Waiwai – Brazil

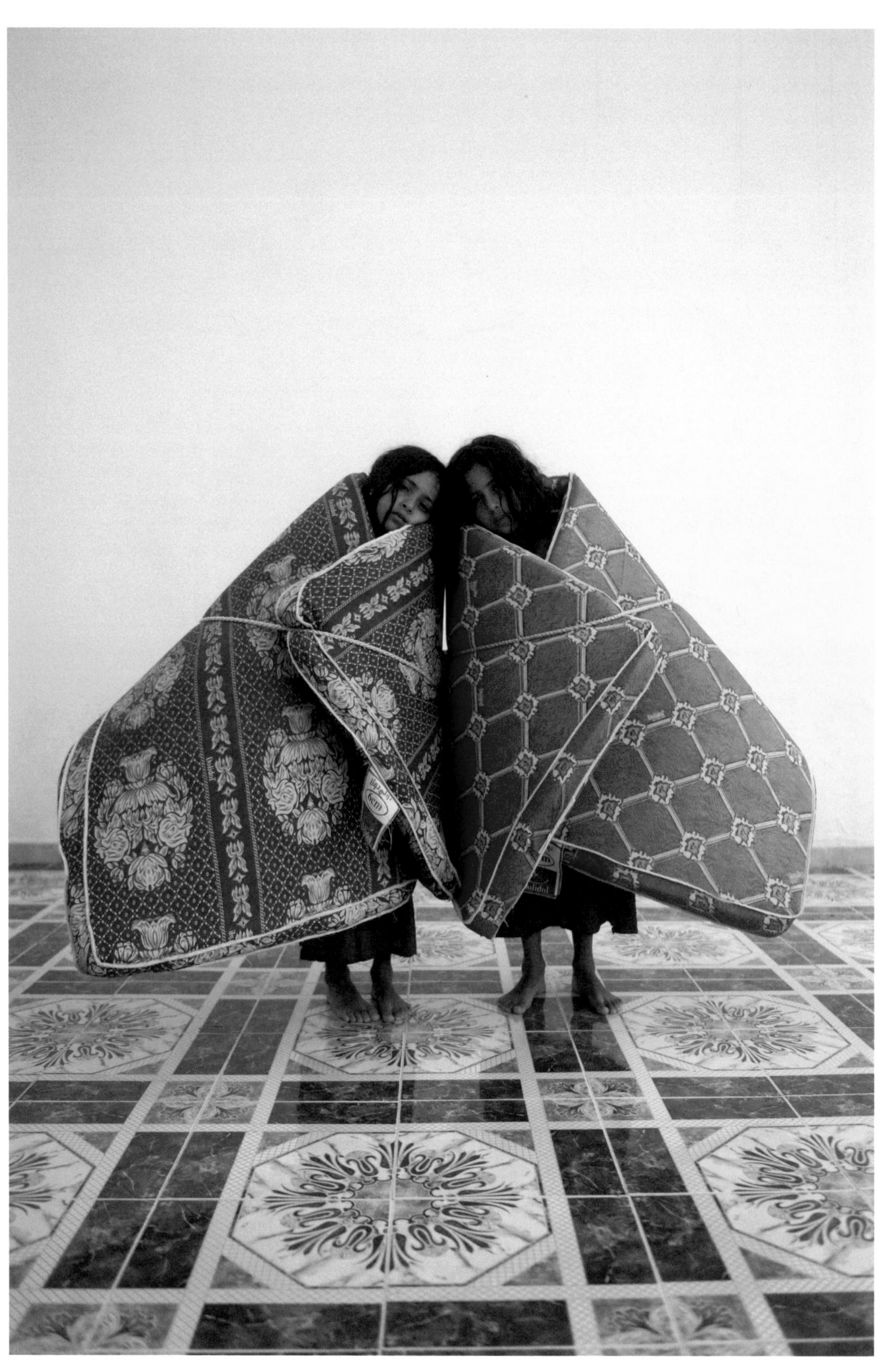

photo Mous Lambarat – Morocco

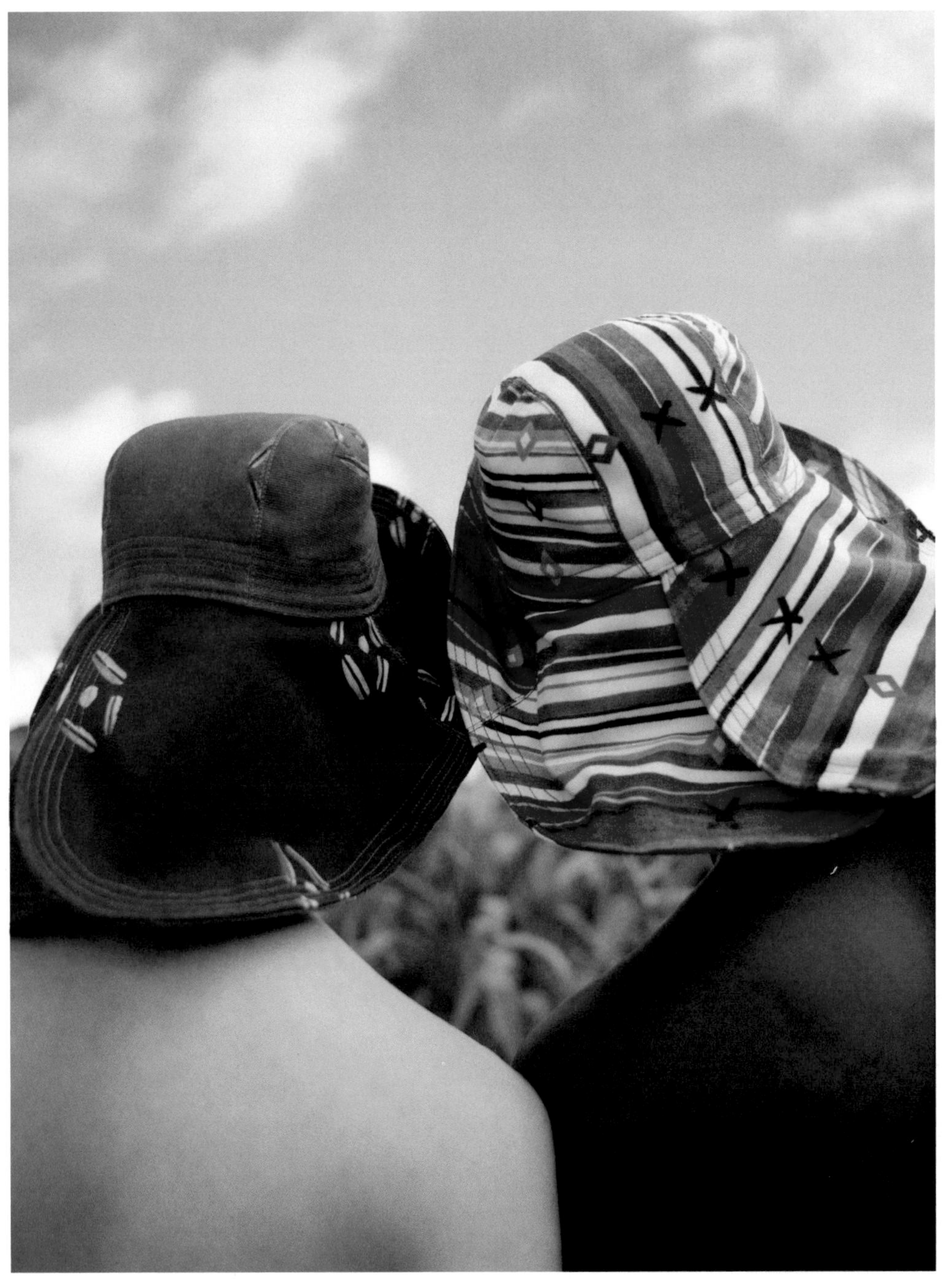

photo Pedro Loreto *design* Ori Rio – Brazil

PROUD & BOUQUET

The abundance of nature is a signature of the south and an heirloom to continuously create with. The tropical and subtropical climates are heaven for exuberant species that create extraordinary landscapes of colour, shape and fragrance that never stop to influence designers, artists and photographers. The sinuous movements of climbing species, intersected by the sculptural features of violent beaks of beauty, by explosive bulbous seedpods and wild grasses, need to be scrutinized in detail to be fully captivated. When the abstract cactus encounters the cut-out leaf, the open-hearted flower and the opulent fruit, design emerges from this garden of earthly delights and creates a style that has seen beautiful patterns bloom over centuries, executed by block printing, weaving and embroidery, depending on the traditions of the various regions. Allowing birds, butterflies and monkeys to inhabit and possess these traditional patterns. Furthermore, nature is captivating as alluring backgrounds and astounding props and make-up. From simple loincloths to elaborate caftans and from a simple leaf to a bouquet of colour, the various botanical gardens will continue to inspire fashion, photography and styling. *L.E.*

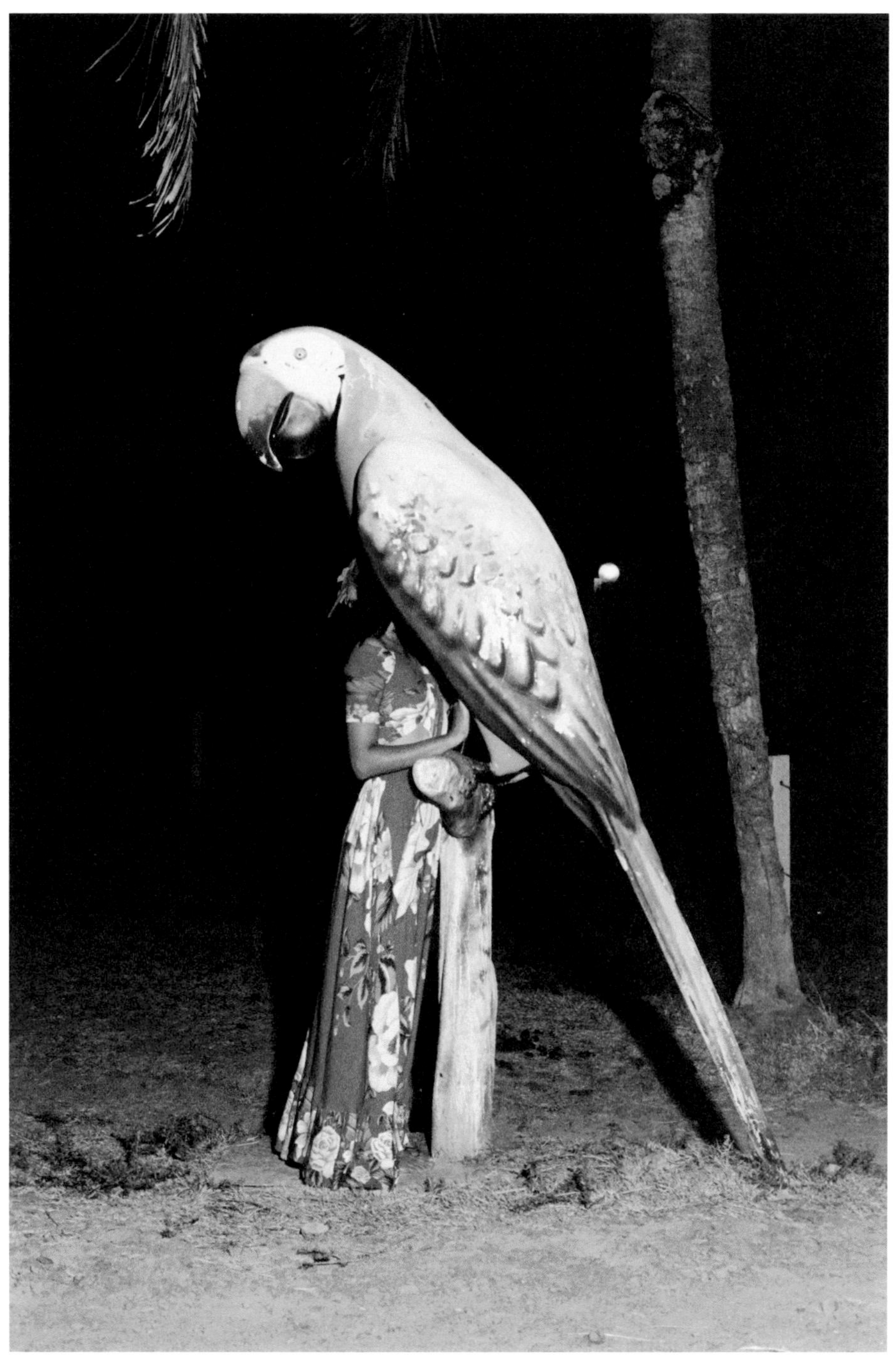

art Atong Atem – South Sudan
photo Raphael Lucena *design* Farm – Brazil

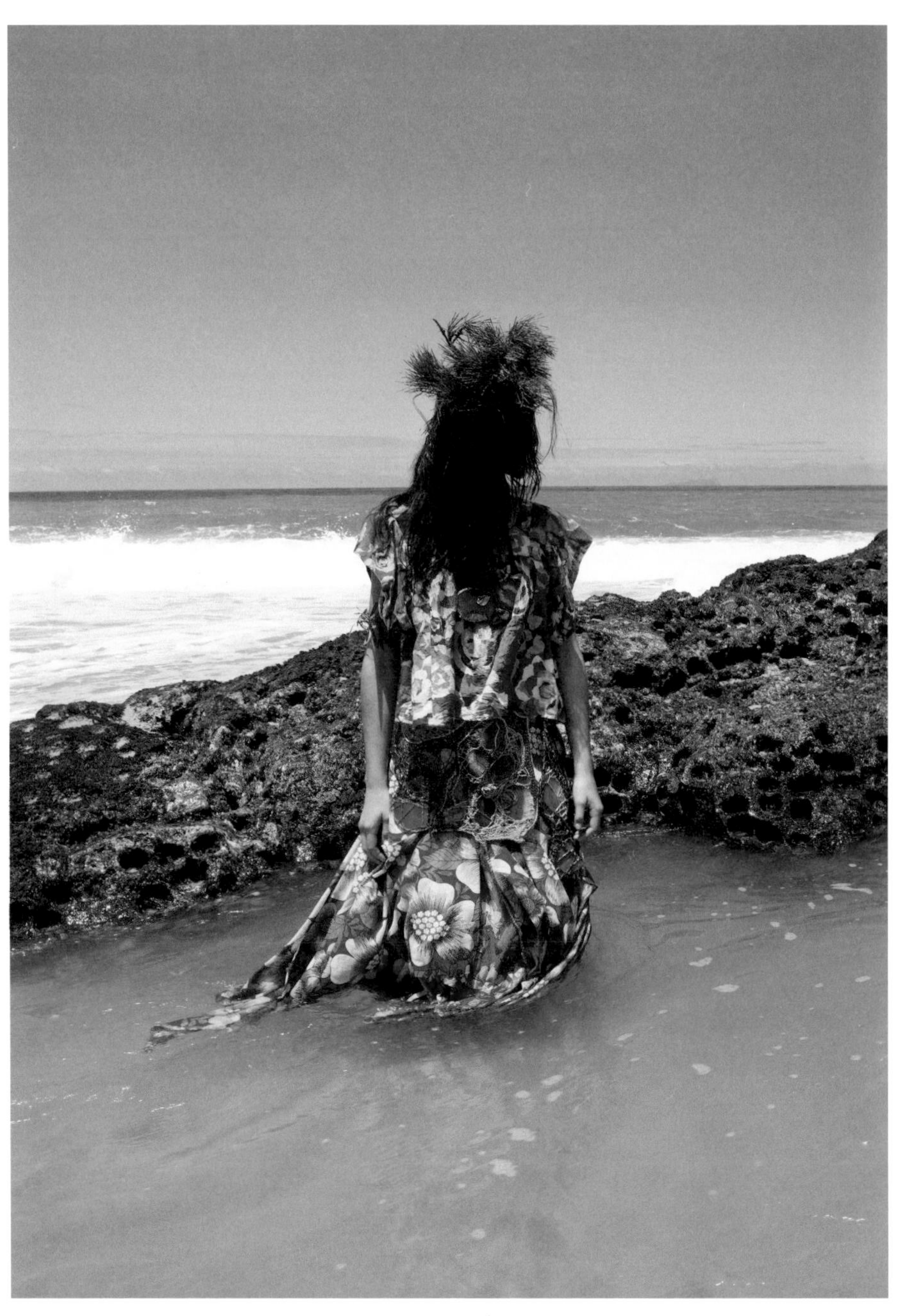

photo Rogério Cavalcanti – Brazil
photo & art direction Francesco Visone – Tenerife

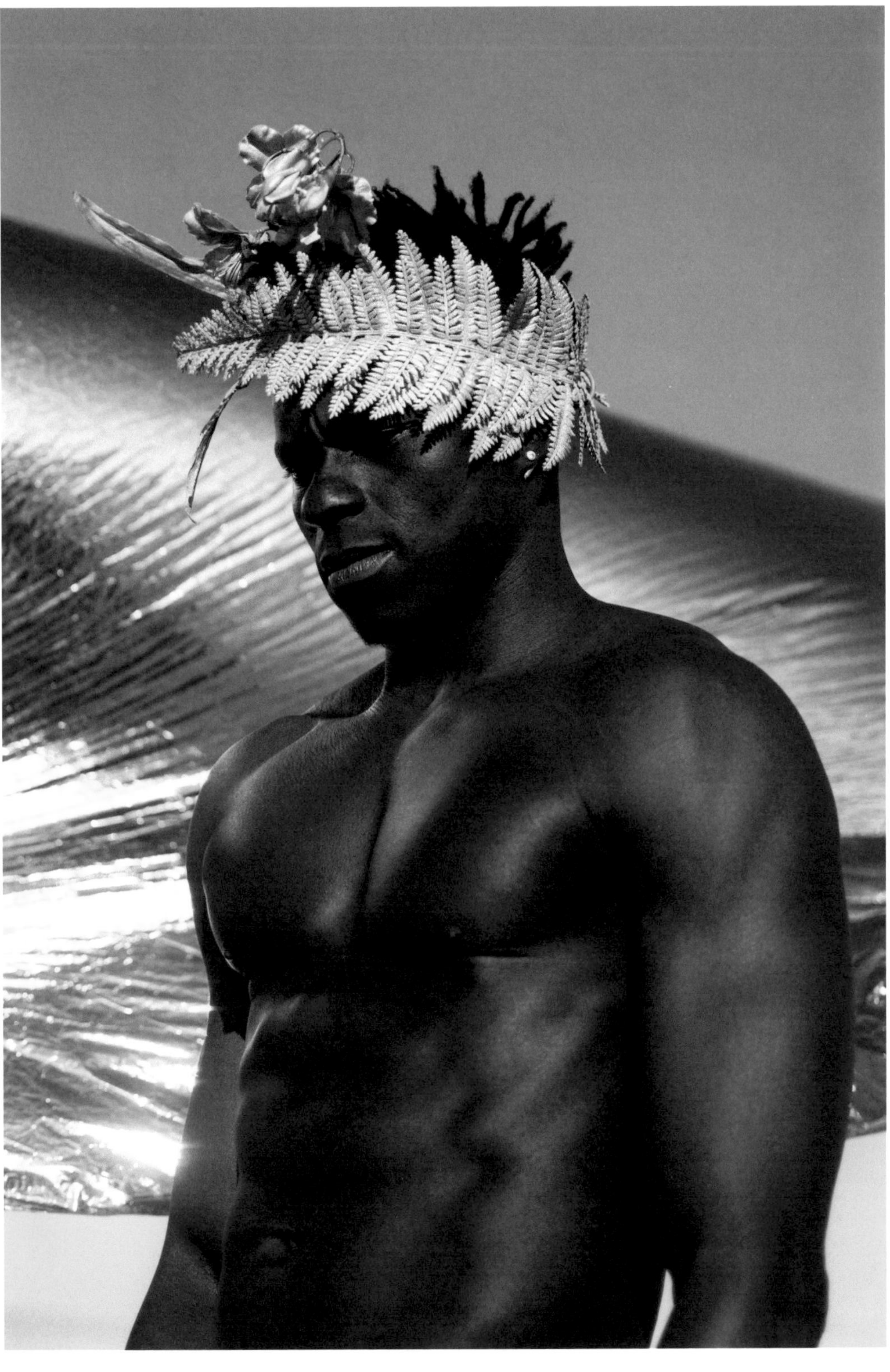

photo Trevor Stuurman – South Africa

photo Aart Verrips *design* Thebe Magugu – South Africa

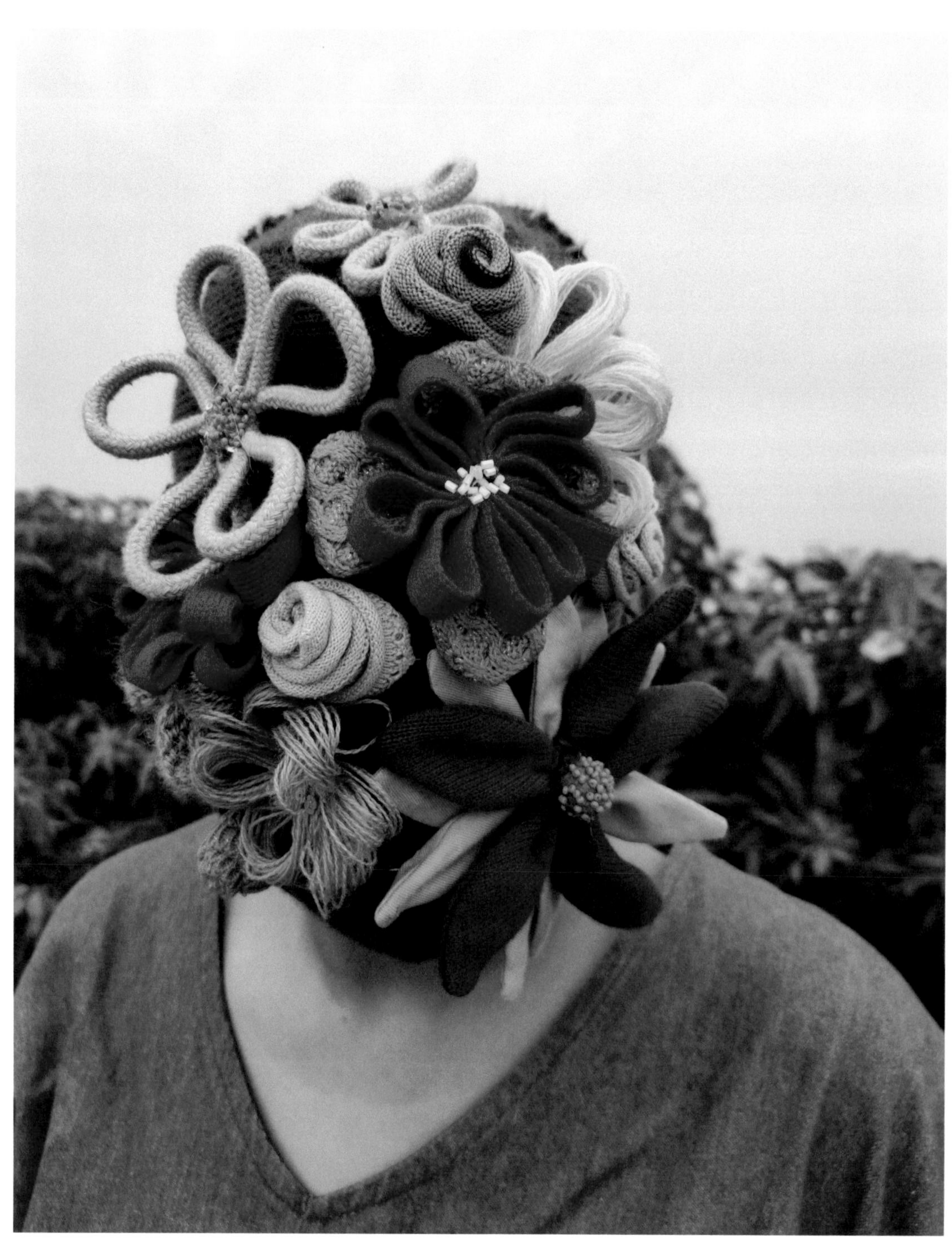

photo B S Kameshwari *design* Deeksha B – India

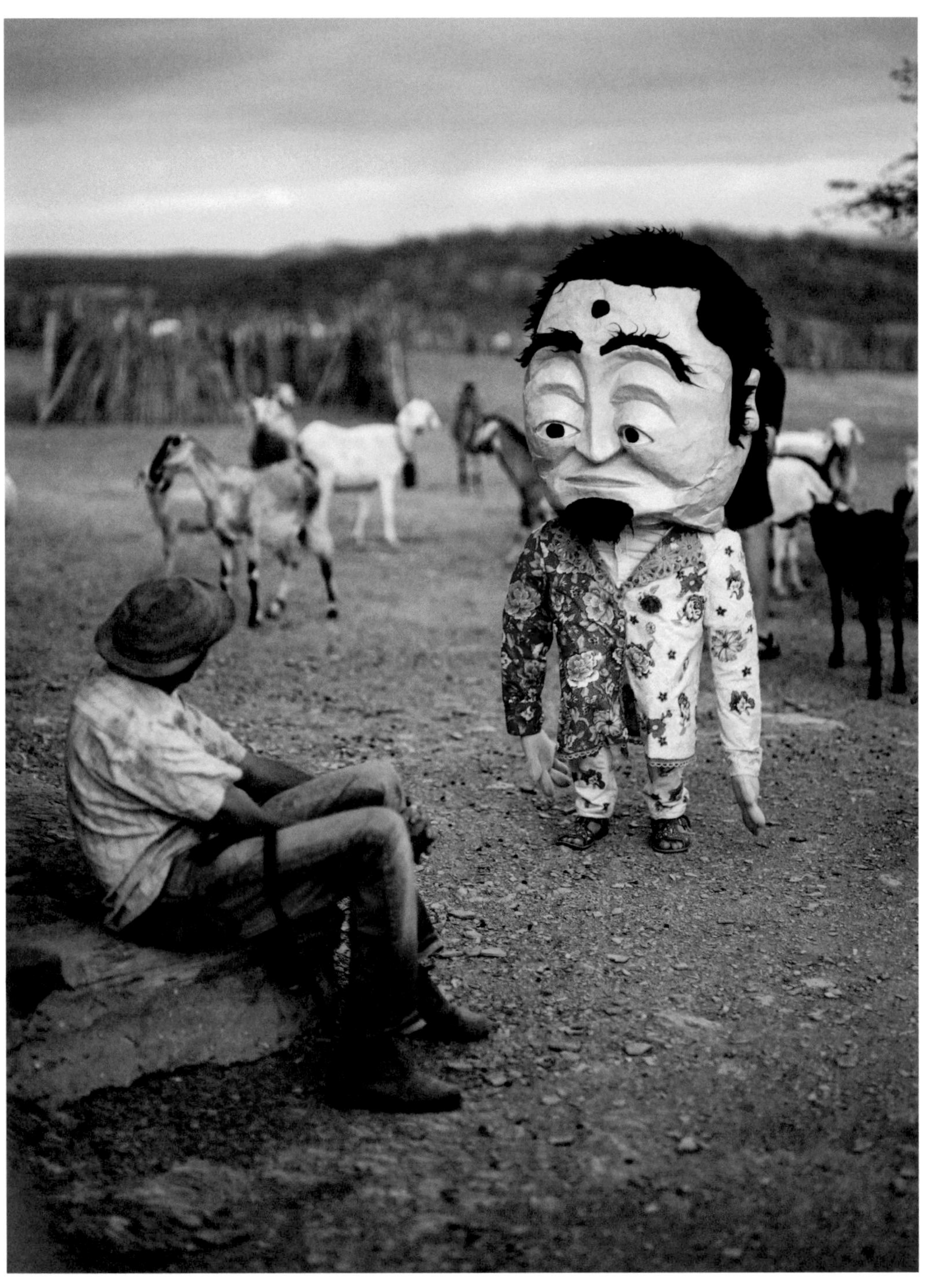

photo Gleeson Paulino – Brazil

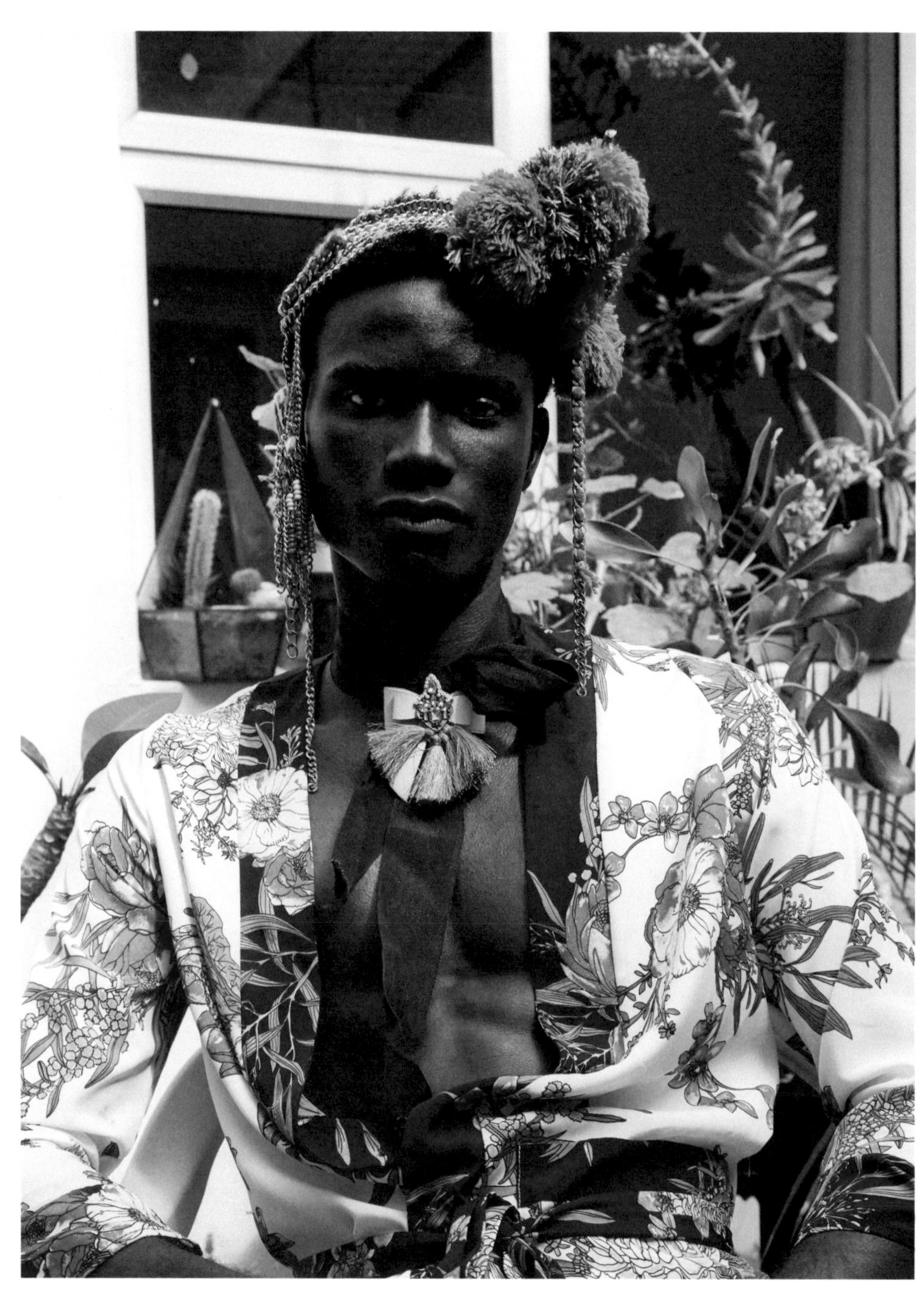

photo Saskia Wegner *design* Shana Morland & Blünke Trotse Tert – South Africa
photo Jamal Nxedlan – South Africa

design Saloni – India
photo Arka Patra *design* Bobo Calcutta – India

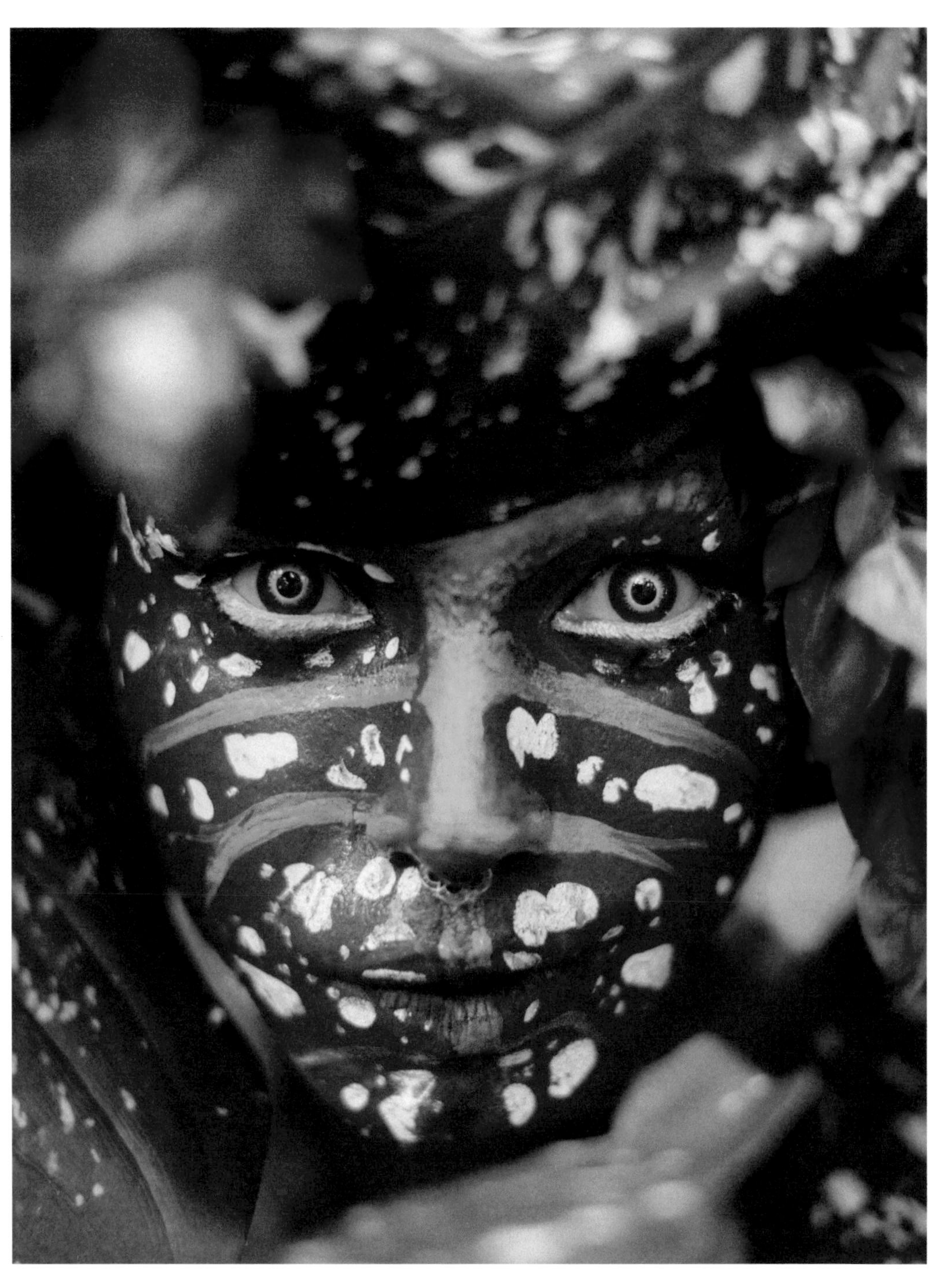

photo Hick Duarte *art* Uyra Sodoma – Brazil
photo Fred Causse *vintage embroidery* – Guatemala

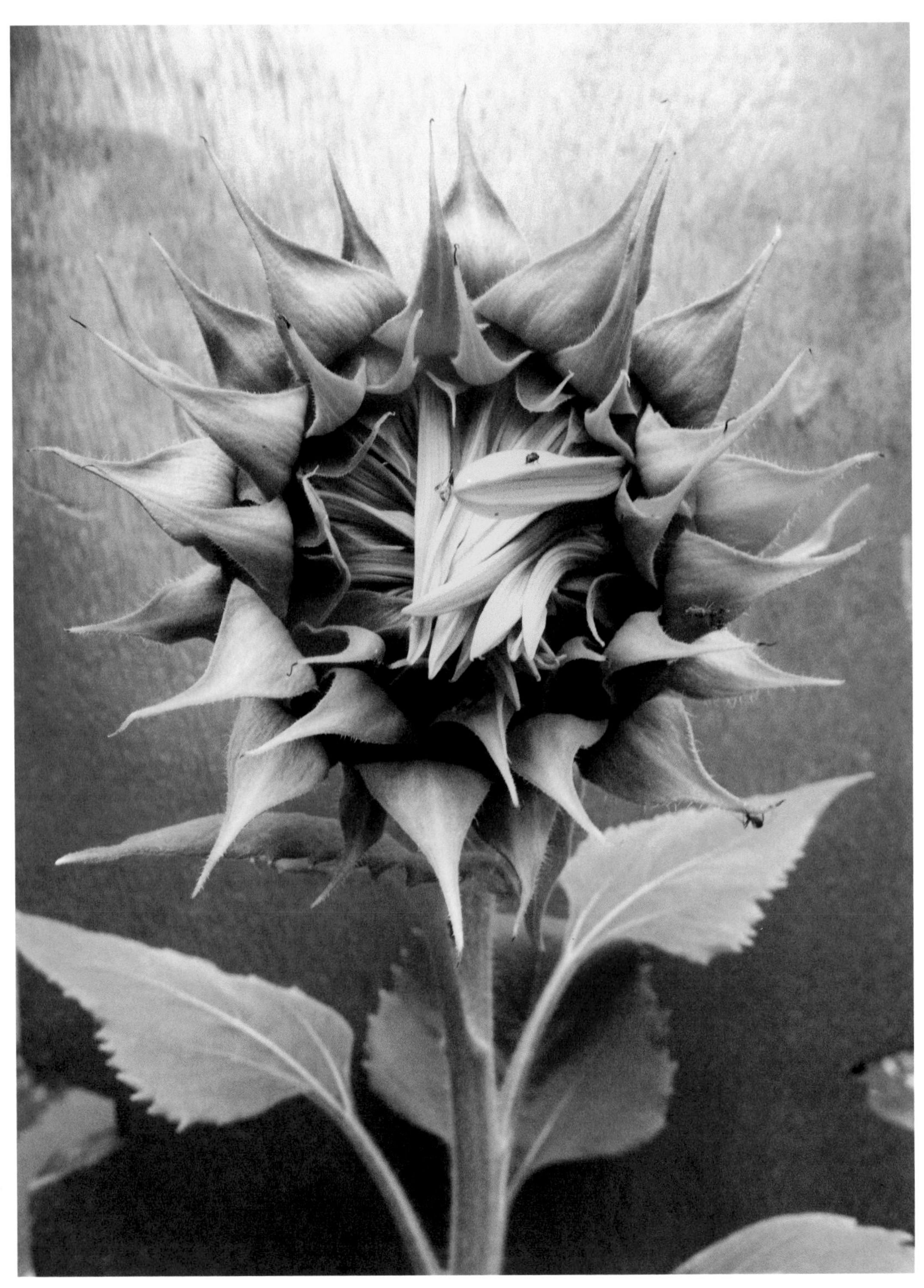

photo Rogério Cavalcanti – Brazil

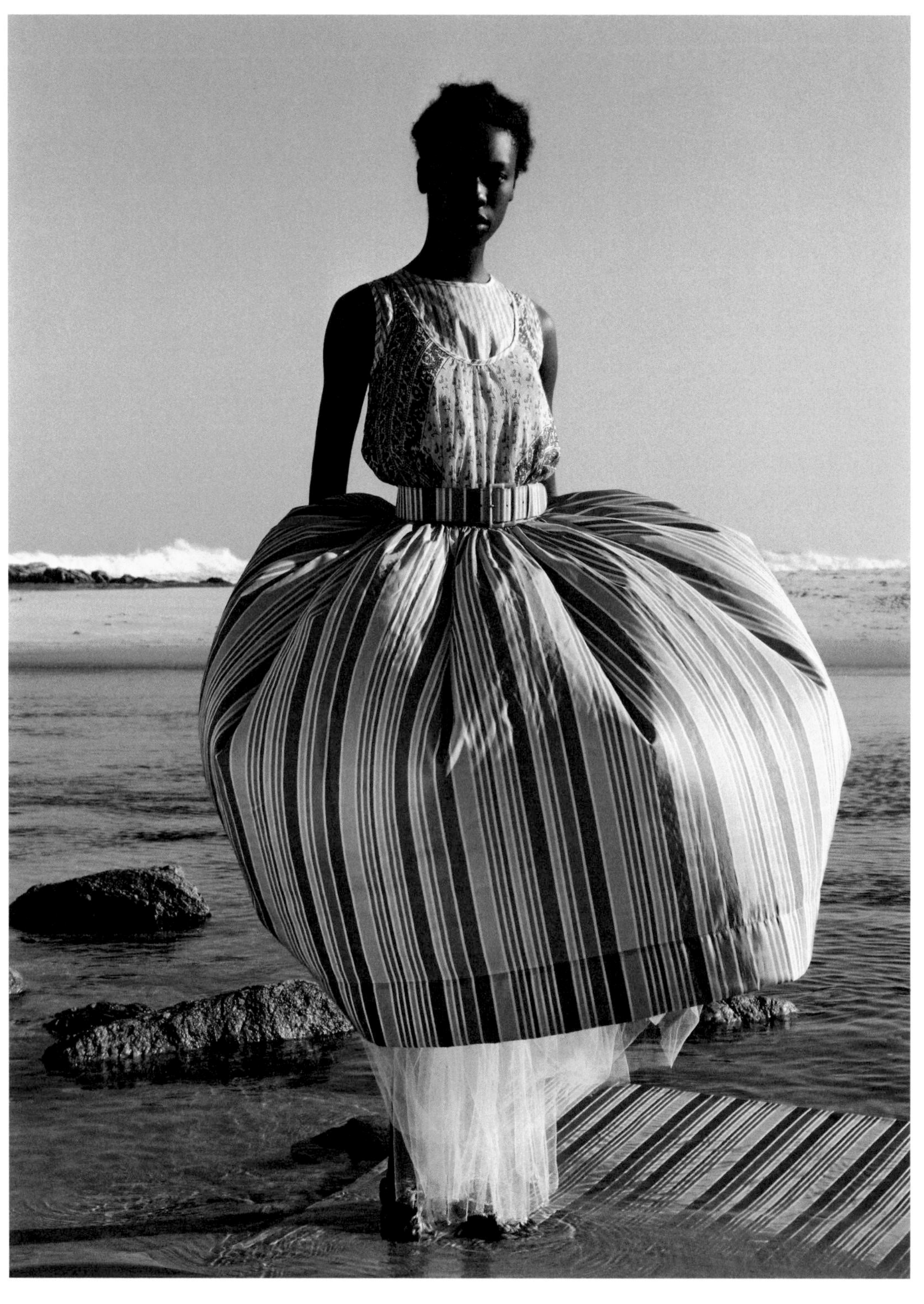

photo Rogério Cavalcanti *design* Diva – Brazil

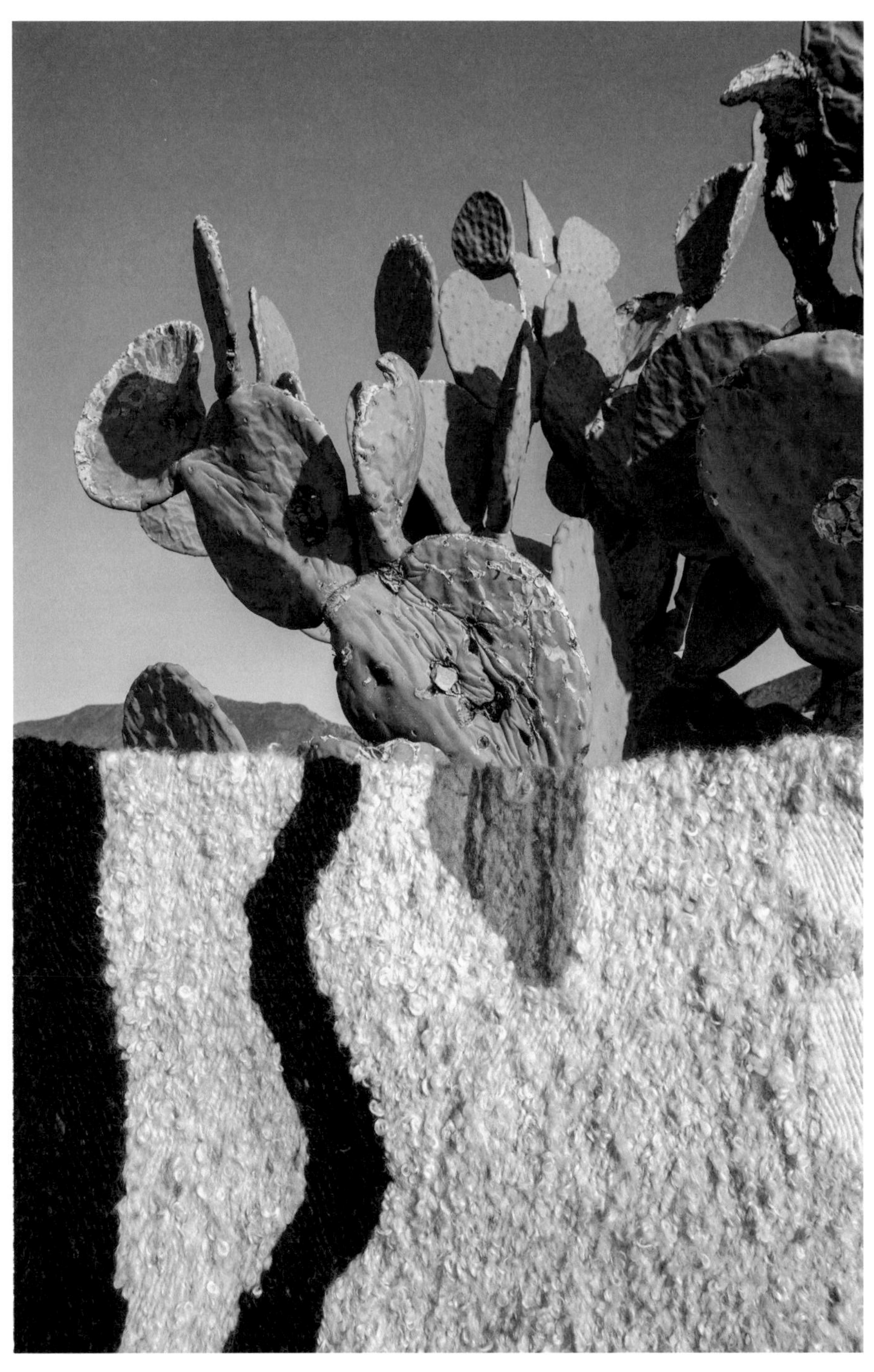

design Frances Van Hasselt *photo* Manesha Smit Mohair – South Africa
photo Gabrielle Kannemeyer *design* Daily Paper – South Africa

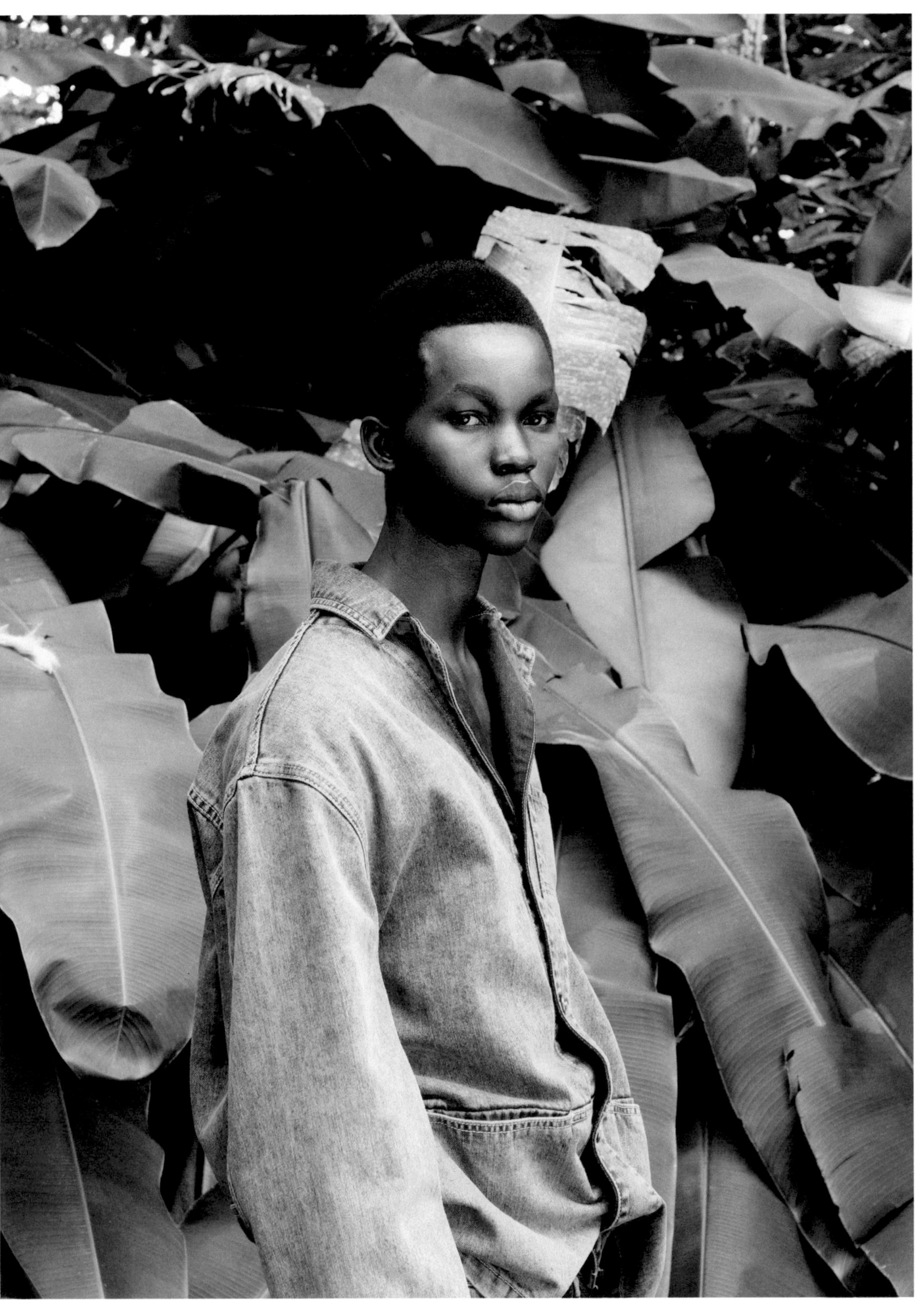

PROUD HOUR

by Modupe Oloruntoba

The ideals of the global north were always unattainable. That's not something I understood in 2011, as I began my fashion design studies in Cape Town. I thought all African fashion needed, all the global south needed, was infrastructure, education and a little more time in practice — we had everything else. I thought the advanced age of technology the world had entered would allow us to close the gap in no time, despite the political, financial and social challenges in our way. I thought we needed to match or exceed the north, and if we worked smart, hard and together, we could. I know now that with my contemporaries we were aiming for the wrong goal. We also know that incredible things are possible for us, in a very different way than we thought. I cannot speak for all of the global south but know that as the world has become more of a village, we've come to exchange views that look and sound more alike than different. One common view is the idea that, because the creative worlds of the global north are more mature, the pain points we experience don't apply — after decades, and in some cases centuries of watering, it makes sense that their grass looks so much greener. We know better now, empowered by digital tools and social media to learn from stories and experiences grounded in reality. While centu-ries of cultural and economic development, excellence in design practice and industry infrastructure have built the north's fashion capitals into immense, credible stores of value, many of our long-held perceptions were still largely unrealistic.

Their world, the one so many of us idolised, is just as susceptible to greed, pride, cruelty and discrimination as ours is. It has incredible peaks, accessible only via heavily crowded paths. Ports of entry can be unjustly difficult to navigate without favour or privilege. The desire to succeed or even just to survive is readily exploited by people ready to go further than most to gain and keep power. In any and all realities, in theirs and in ours, these human problems persist. Pretending they don't is dangerous. Expansive dreams are fuel for much of what we do, but the romantic pedestals we can create with them are a dangerous way we've participated in deceiving ourselves. Another misperception was that adopting the north's forms would always produce its results. The influence of context cannot be overstated; it makes a considerable difference to the rules of engagement. While generations of our designers and other practitioners have been frustrated by the realisation that not everything that works for them will work for us, they have also innovated a path to our present day by pragmatically accepting it. In pointing out these contrasts, it's not my goal to paint a sad picture, but to display a real one — to burst a bubble I believe holds the south back. I remember when the bubble burst for me, standing on a street in London. Looking out and up at the buildings ahead of me, I realised that Vogue House could be one of the buildings at the end of my line of sight, and that Hearst UK wasn't too far away either. It was exciting to be so close to what always felt so far away, and then suddenly, the possibility blended right into the busy street. The excitement fizzled to calm focus. Three years into a career in content production and editorial storytelling, the work was no longer a deified fantasy to me, and from that moment on, neither was the world that helped inspire me to choose it. It remained true that the publishing legacy those buildings are home to is to be applauded and respected, and I was grateful to have learned so much of my love for and knowledge of fashion from their historic titles. It was also true that I was as real as they were, and they were as human as I was.

It's a point many of us in the global south have already come to, as our observations and experiences chip away at fantasy so the more rugged beauty of reality can emerge. We are undergoing a transfiguration. After a northward gaze defined so much of our creative output for so long, our gaze has turned homeward. Our updated outlook casts a new light on everything, from the value we create to the rich heritage we have at times taken for granted. We've changed, and so has our context and position in the world of fashion. More importantly, we've begun to embrace this change, and define not only our creativity by it but our visions for our creativity as well. I see the difference in the widely visible reintegration of indigenous design techniques and principles, organic and unforced. It's in the celebration of original, culture-specific values and symbols, in the design of new symbols by traditional principles. It's even in the choices that are reshaping value chains, as we increasingly choose the pace, substance and inherited wisdom of our ancestors' handcrafts over the insensate efficiencies of an offshore factory line. Fashion's image makers know it too, as it informs an eager push toward a homegrown southward gaze, informed by cultural awareness, empathy, and recognition.

Many global shifts have led us here over time, but two stand out to me: access and fatigue. The increase in access to modern technology and internet connections across the global south accelerated exposure to shared technical, cultural and personal knowledge, expanding our views considerably over the past two decades. As we learned more from the world and woke up to the ways the world had learned and could continue to learn from us, we subconsciously moved away from pictures of creative success that defined winning as north-bound association, validation, acceptance and recognition.

As interaction between our worlds increased, fatigue came into play. We tired of shifting goal posts that never shifted in our direction, and of being the involuntary muse — an inspiring subject, but never a worthy co-creator. We decided we were done with discriminatory scales that didn't fairly measure our outputs and contributions; done with lenses that proved unable to see us as equals, as anything but former subjects of unjust empires. As we tired of the old, we were energised by the new. More and more of us are determined to make the most of the scattered remnants of our predominantly postcolonial and post-conflict realities. We don't ignore the complicated layers, but we recognise the opportunity that living in our time represents and seeks to heal our pasts with our present.

What I believe emerges next, emerges now, is a louder, collective questioning. A new shape of curiosity accompanies this wave of change, moving us to question standards set by imposed tradition and definitions we no longer identify with. While eurocentricity is still prevalent, it's no longer passively accepted by the majority of creative workers. Among others, fashion designers have emerged as leaders in the challenge that our new perspective issues to the status quo.

AS THE WORLD LOOKS
TO THE SOUTH FOR MORE
INSPIRATION, FRESH ENERGY
AND NEW STORIES TO TELL,
WE'LL WELCOME THEIR
INTEREST, BUT DECLINE
THEIR TERMS AND
INSIST ON OURS.

We ask, 'why this?' and we also ask, finally, 'why not us?' Why not our style, our narratives, our priorities, our folk wear, our subcultures? Why not us when this age makes so much more possible? From its fringes to its core, popular culture has always responded to these signals, and the seeds planted by this mindset shift are already bearing fruit in that arena, in explosive waves. The incredible reception that contemporary music from across Africa is receiving on the global stage is a shining example, as is the world's response to artists, architects, fashion designers, and other rising and risen talents across the global south. With no suitable answer to why we shouldn't win, we make bigger, better bets on ourselves, and on each other.

What I believe follows that self-belief is widespread rejection. Slowly, we will more overtly reject imposed perspectives and definitions. We will abandon beaten, crowded paths for curious, experimental exploration. As the world looks to the south for more inspiration, fresh energy and new stories to tell, we'll welcome their interest, but decline their terms and insist on ours. We'll reject the compromises many have felt they had to make to succeed in the old world and push to bring more of ourselves and our priorities to collaboration and trade in the creative workplace. We can even reject the idea that the differences between the global north and south make us direct competitors on opposing sides of an issue, and instead embrace a point of view that invites all of the global fashion industry and its surrounding creative class to dismiss established standard procedure and pull our ecosystem toward necessary change.

The north has undoubted advantages, having invested in professional creativity for much longer with better and more abundant resources, building intricate systems in cultures that often place significant value on their work. Be that as it may, their advantages are in just one system, the one we have, not necessarily in the ones we can create. The world has changed in ways that can generate new options, if we will construct them. They are unlikely to be polar opposites to the present method — every innovation has some echo of the past as nothing is truly new. They can be imagined more like bright new nodes in an existing network which is charged, interconnected and loaded with potential to contribute beautifully to the strength and diversity of the whole. Within current global power dynamics, it may sound like a regression toward idealistic thinking, but I can imagine a future in which the north's model, however well established a monopoly it now seems, will be just one of many systems for creating, sharing and experiencing fashion.

For ourselves, for the health of the planet, and for a world of inspiring creativity we may never see without change, we should dare to imagine divergent ways to work. If our new models imitate old ones, they will repeat the old model's incredibly costly mistakes, with harm done to cultures, natural resources and vulnerable workers. If we can't see new peaks to climb in our local realities, we may need to imagine them, pushing past circumstantial challenges and comfortable but ill-fitting conditions to do that. Echoes of the old mindset persist in strangely common ways, but we believe there is much more room that we are yet to see in the global market and consciousness for our distinct, proprietary creative work. To seize it, we need to expand our vision far enough to recognise a foreign future's potential beyond familiar metrics. It is in our hands to define success with a new plurality.

Once we have, all that's left to do is create these futures, capitalising on the momentum of the renaissance we are beginning to experience. I imagine a rich diversity of ideas on display, finally swinging the world away from the homogeneity first brought on by globalisation. I imagine a better quality of life for every role-player in fashion's value chain, as wealth increases and is more fairly distributed than before. I imagine new definitions of the creative economy that don't just take global south realities into account but originate here and form around them. I see an expanded global fashion conversation in which the creative classes of the south are more than guests at the northern table, but valued and respected stakeholders in a global, distributed network of creativity, trade, and support. This change won't be linear. Individually and collectively, we will experience weather that would tempt anyone to return to familiar postures. But creating change is challenging, worthwhile, rewarding work, it seems a number of us are finally ready to do.

Questions remain, a key question being whether we, the global south, can see our cultural and social diversity as a strength and collaboratively grow its power. I hope for and work toward a future in which we move from looking up at the north to looking around at the rest of the south, recognising each other's value and potential. We have an opportunity ahead of us to offer something different, but also something better, an approach that improves on the present because we turned perceived weaknesses, like a lack of infrastructure, into a future proofing strength in a world that threatens to make the establishment's infrastructure obsolete. I hope that this future offers us the grace and space to make a few of our own mistakes as we imagine ways that fashion can redefine its value to the world.

PROUD & ROUTE

art & styling by Namsa Leuba
– Switzerland / Guinea –

The body of work of Namsa Leuba, a former master student from ECAL in Lausanne, is absolutely essential to understanding the cultural misconceptions of past times and the changing perceptions of ethnicity today in both the north and south. Born from Swiss and Guinean parents, she embodies these perceptions within one person and expresses them in her potent work, cherishing her mixed cultures. For her first series, she travelled to her mother's homeland of Guinea to understand and experience Animism, taking part in rituals and ceremonies, indulging in the invisible yet palpable world of spirits. Her totemic and fetishistic figures are transformed by the young artist using her African ancestry, accentuated and laid bare by her European discernment. This cross-cultural approach is resulting in new concepts for contemporary ethnic photography which is having a huge influence and will continue to do so. Appearing at once primitive and subjective but also suggestive of an inner sense, her subjects stand proud and upright on their found pedestals, incarnating their dress made from waste materials as if it were couture. Projecting their invisible strength. As she continues to alternate her narrative fashion photography with the abstraction of architecture and landscape, she extends her explorations further south with a series of sculptural pictures of children that defy apartheid's past by raising their little fists, defending their Zulu and Ndebele patterns and paraphernalia. The artist is clearly showing us the way, where citations of ancient cultures are allowed to go. *L.E.*

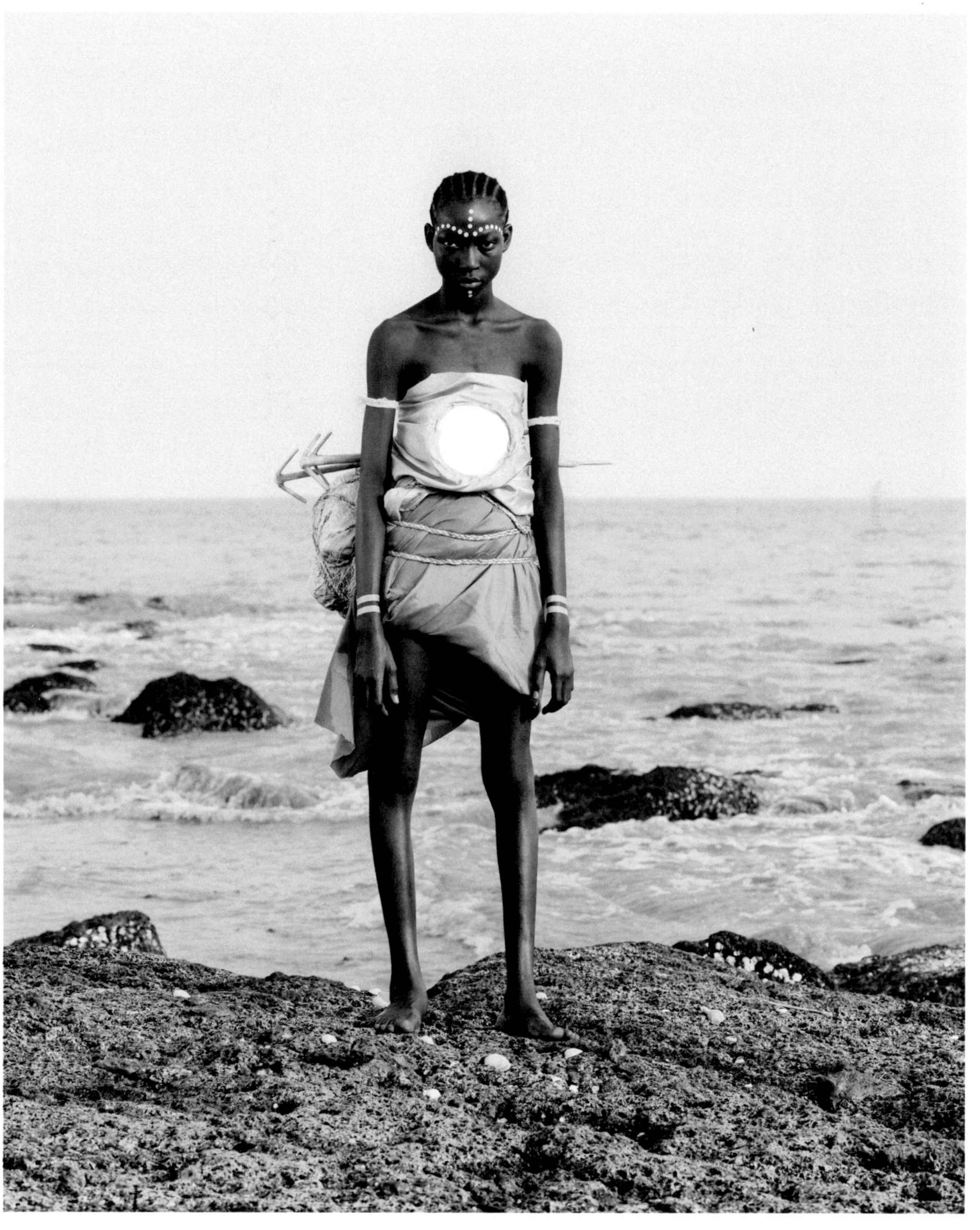

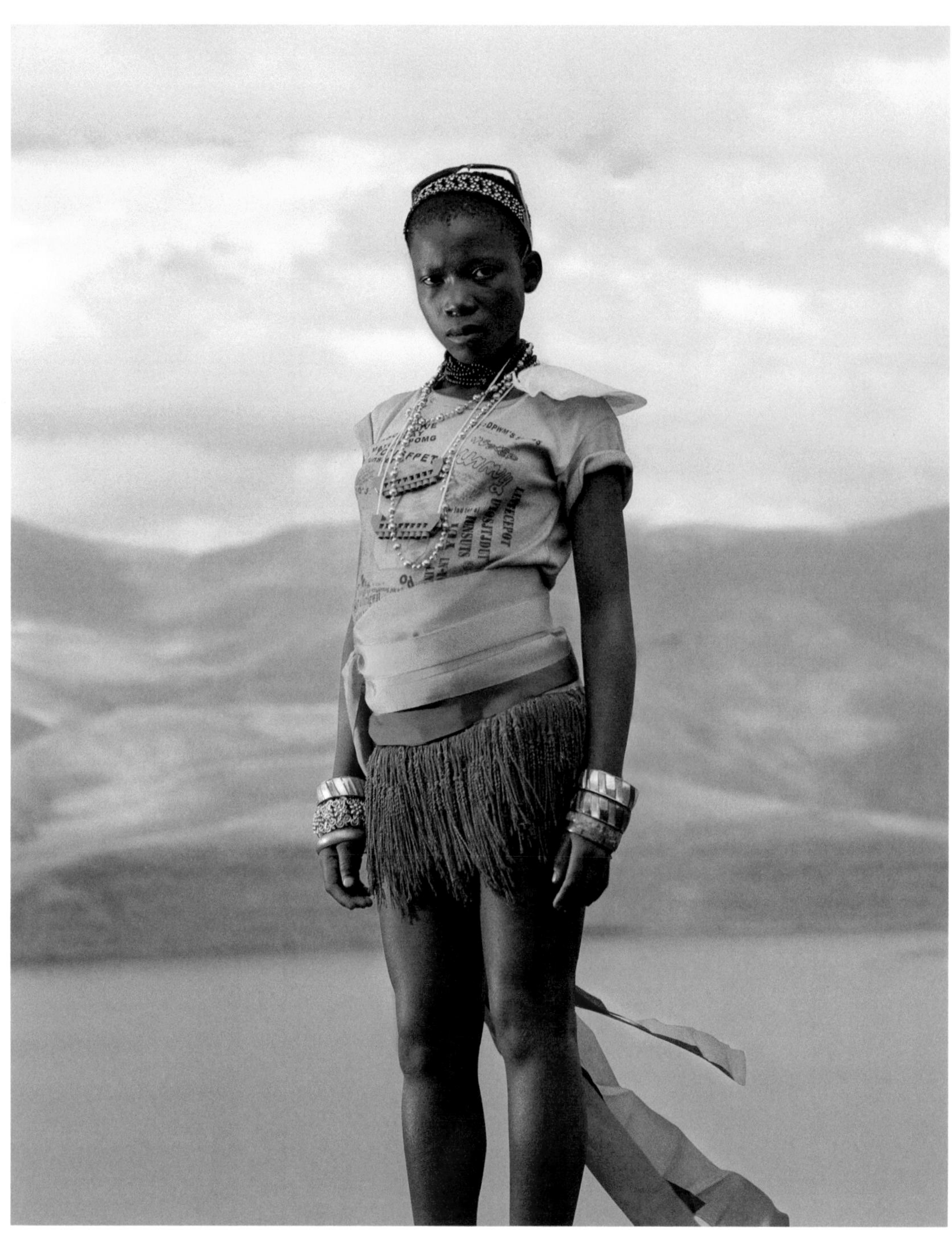

Coca-Cola
J & B
OUP SAVE
CENTRE
Coca-Cola

PROUD & FIBROUS

Dressed in wild constructions to install fear in people, the voodoo masters of Benin are swaddled in straw tents that give them an imposing presence, preventing trouble on dark moonless nights. Whenever there is grass there is tension and clothes. From hermetic rain capes to vibrating dancing skirts to opulent conical robes. Head-to-toe, fibres are shielding humans from heat, dust and water and create opulent forms following the grasses, such as sunhats and sneakers. Employed in building and garments to protect from the elements and project a rooted fringed aesthetic, the power of these unique creations keeps their indigenous character alive. Straw will weave totes, embroider dresses and crochet summer hats, bringing craft to contemporary creation. Although not restricted to the south, it is here that fibres such as raffia start being coveted as a rich material origin, getting more popular as local resources are rediscovered and reinvented by contemporary designers and stylists. Now that hirsute creations are on the rise in the world of fashion, a southern fibrous future is forecast. *L.E.*

clockwise

photo Mous Lambarat – Morocco
photo Eric Lafforgue – image taken in Benin
photo Santiago Baravalle *design* Anikena – Mexico
photo Ruy Teixeira *design* Osklen – Brazil

clockwise

photo Jackie Nickerson – USA / UK
photo Mous Lambarat – Morocco
art Phyllis Galembo / Axis Gallery – USA

clockwise

art Phyllis Galembo / Axis Gallery – USA
photo Jamal Nxedlana – South Africa
photo Jackie Nickerson – USA / UK

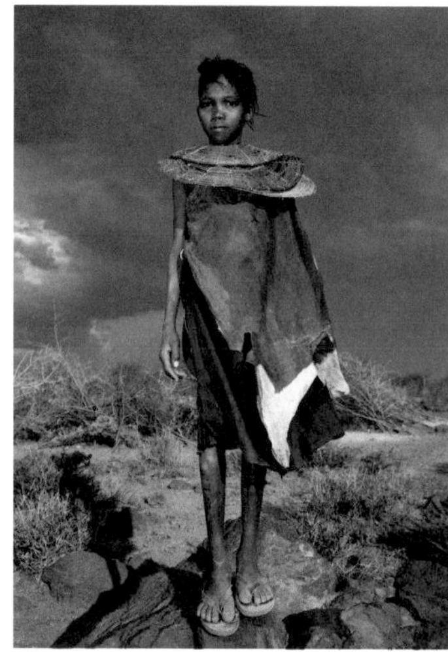

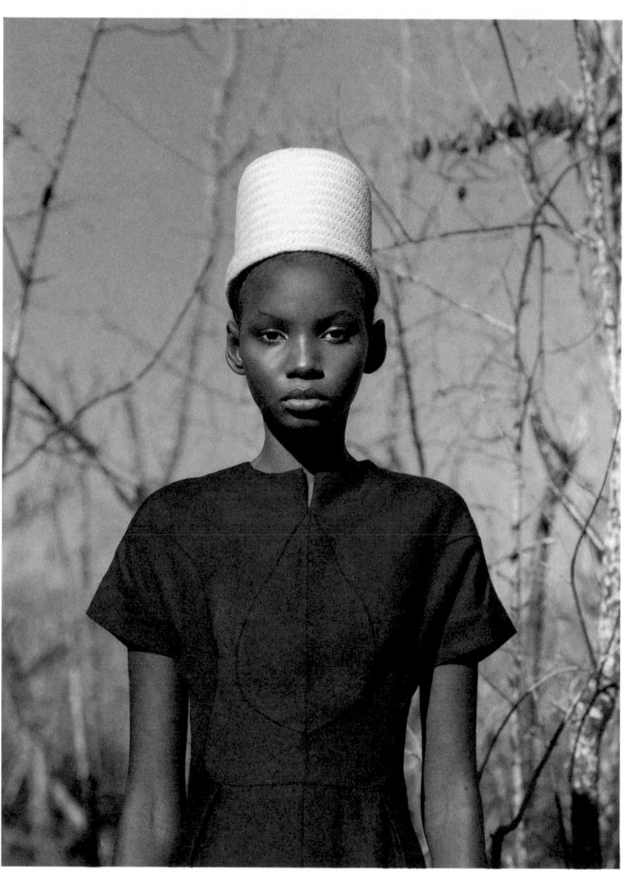

clockwise

photo Eric Lafforgue – image taken in Kenya
art Namsa Leuba – Switzerland / Guinea
photo Bruna Sussekind *design* Helena Pontes – Brazil
photo & art direction Cai Ramalho – Brazil

clockwise

photo Gleeson Paulino / Elle – Brazil
photo Marvin *design* Helena Pontes – Brazil
photo Kenji Nakamura *design* Samuray Martins – Brazil
photo Rogério Cavalcanti – Brazil

clockwise

photo Tinko Czetwertynski *design* Paula Raia – Brazil
photo Rogério Cavalcanti – Brazil
photo Fabrice Schneider *design* Sarah Viguer – France

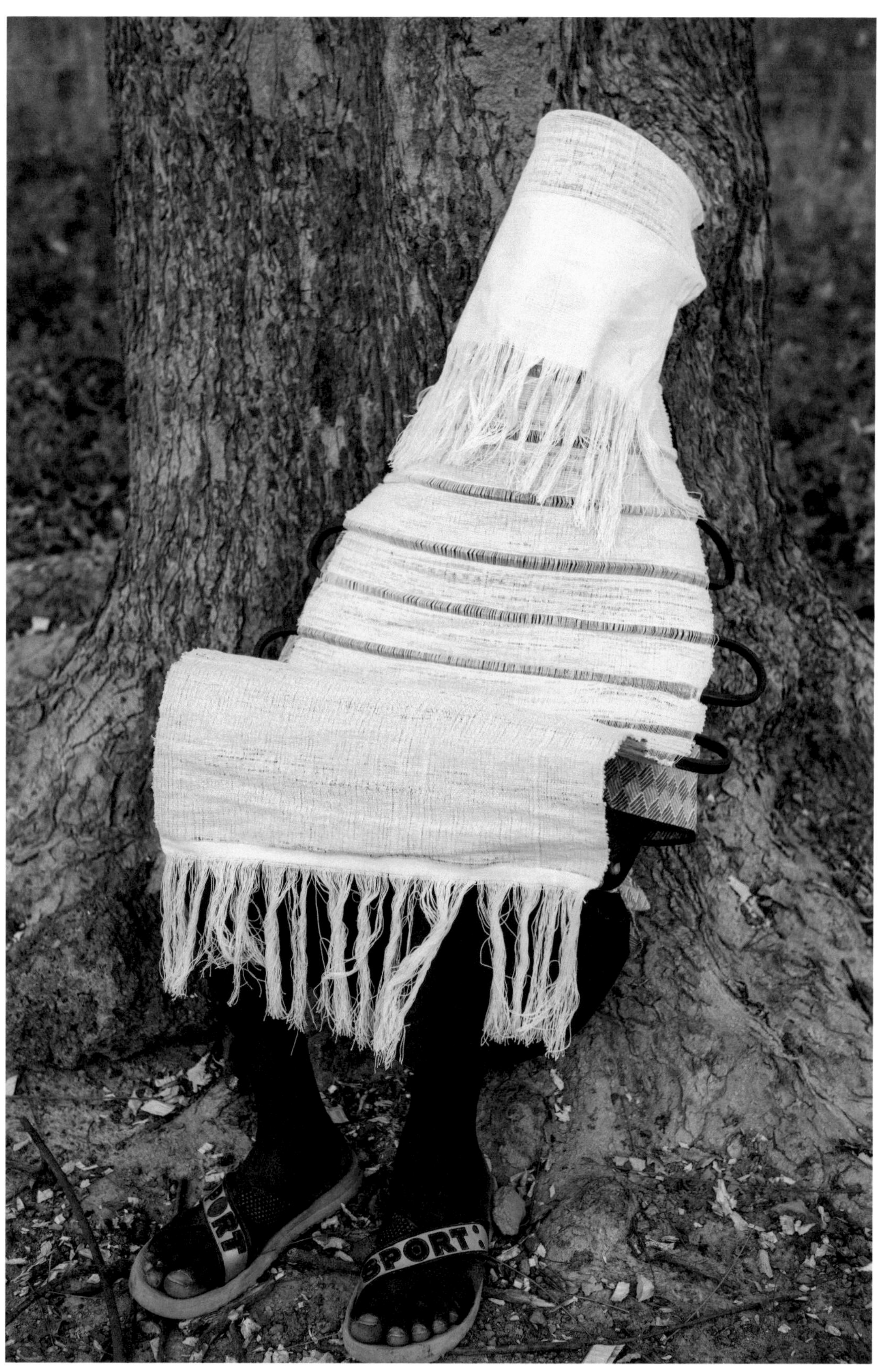
SPORT

PROUD & RIGOUR

◇◇◇◇◇◇◇◇◇◇◇◇◇

When people think of southern style, they rarely imagine minimalism. Bright colour and a wild motif are projected on the different continents, as if the world is divided into the cool north and the hot south, bringing prejudice even to clothes. This ignorance will be repaired by the gifted designers of a new generation that do their homework and discern the roots of rigorous dress in the history of their countries. They pick up the kurta, the huipil and the jellaba, the sarouel and the loincloth, the shawl and the blanket and start rethinking these perfected basic ingredients for future casual fashions, giving them new life with exotic fabrics such as pineapple and abaca, giving banana fibre another life also. This revival of indigenous shapes with their distinctive pockets and plackets and refined finishes, often using ribbons versus buttons, is a benediction for style-conscious individuals that intrinsically know the value original style has in a wardrobe. Rethinking minimalism from the beginning of time. *L.E.*

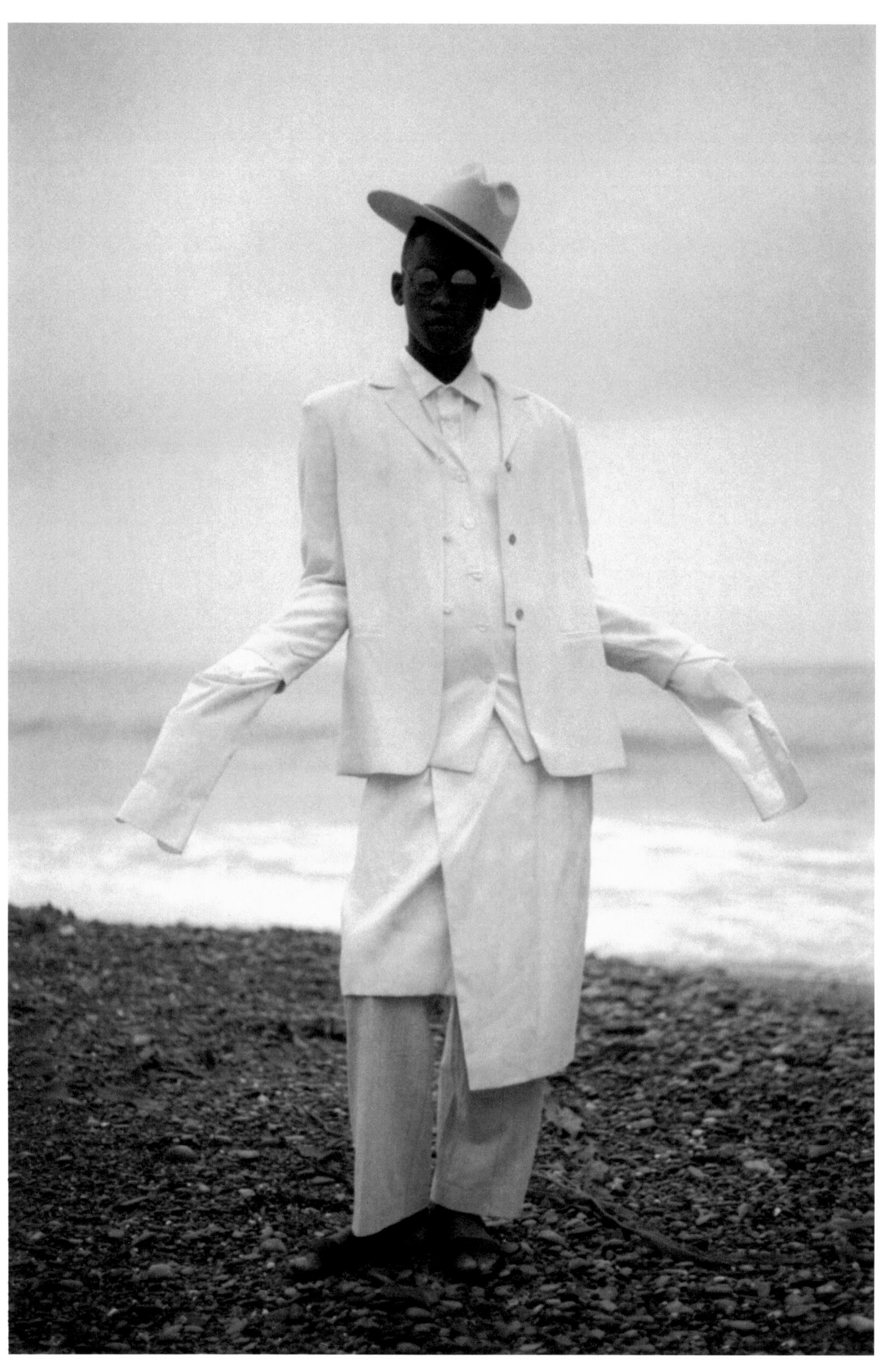

photo Richard Ramirez Jr. *design* Bagtazo – USA

art Edson Chagas / Stevenson Amsterdam – Angola

photo Fleur Bult – the Netherlands

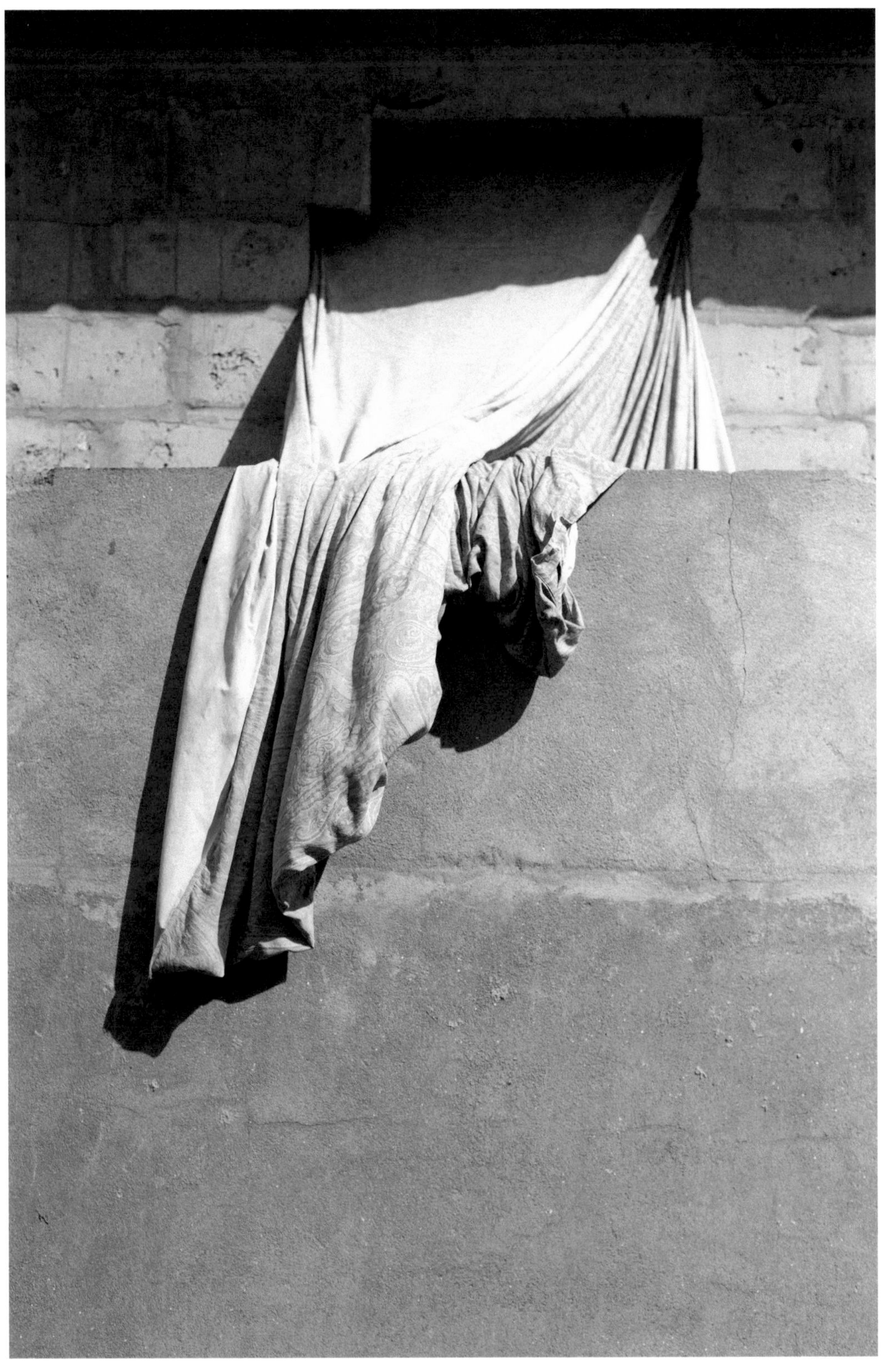

art Edson Chagas / Stevenson Amsterdam – Angola

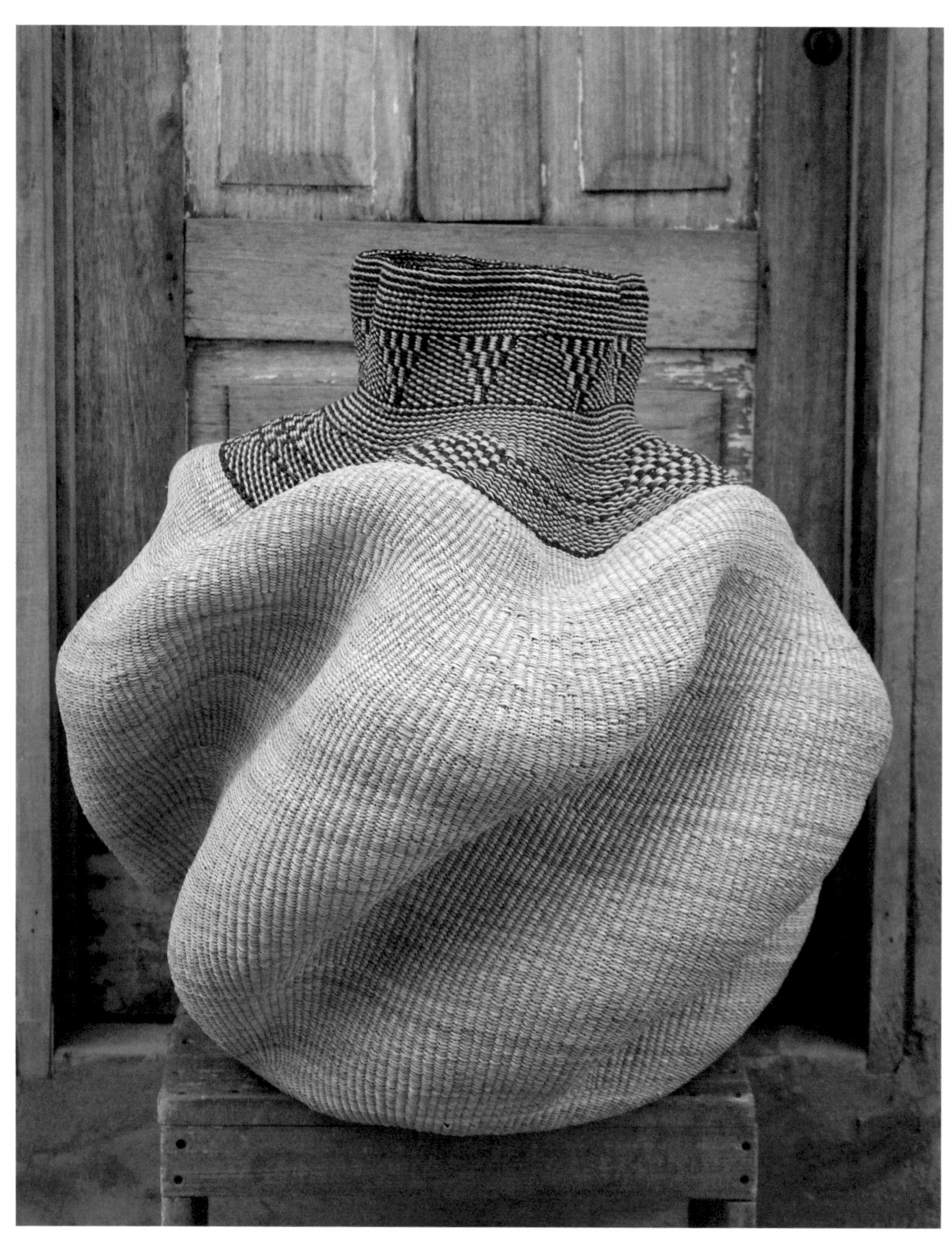

design Baba Tree *photo* Azure Abotizure – Ghana

photo Pedro Loreto *art direction* Flora Velloso – Brazil

photo Daniel Obasi *design* Orange Culture – Nigeria

photo Gabrielle Kannemeyer *design* Daily Paper – South Africa

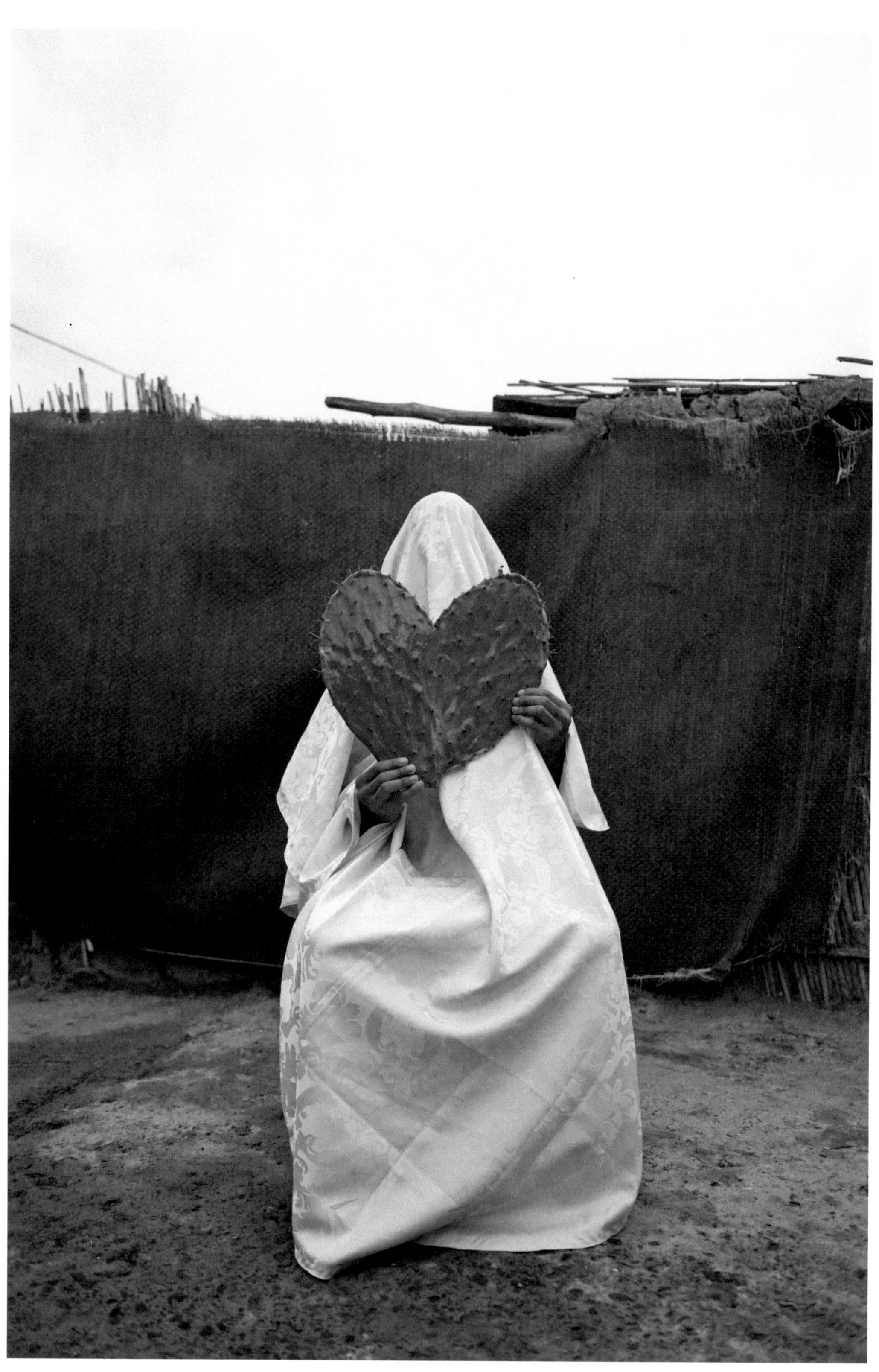

photo Mous Lambarat – Morocco

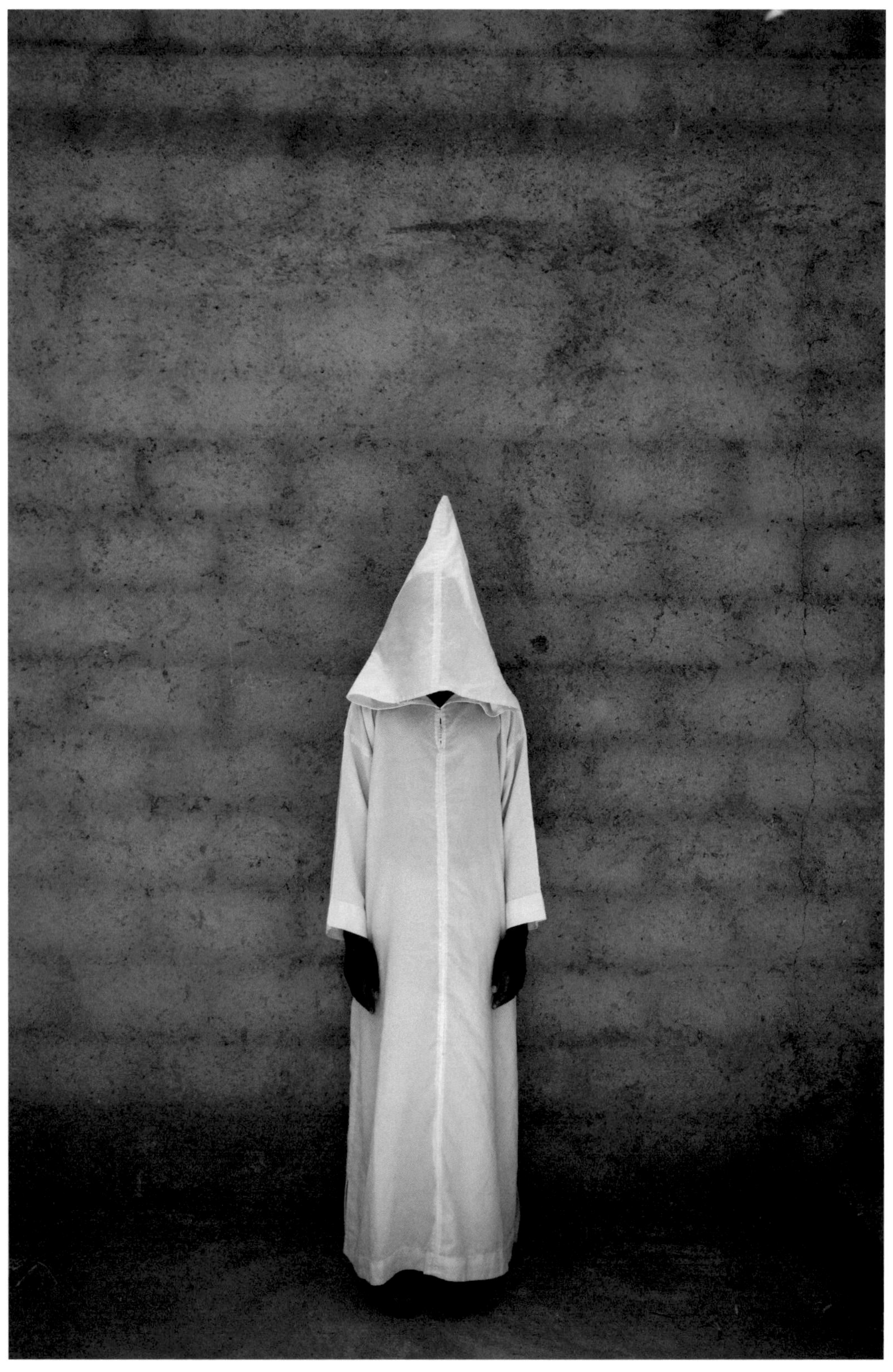

photo Mous Lambarat – Morocco

design Tiaan Nagel *photo* Travys Owen – South Africa

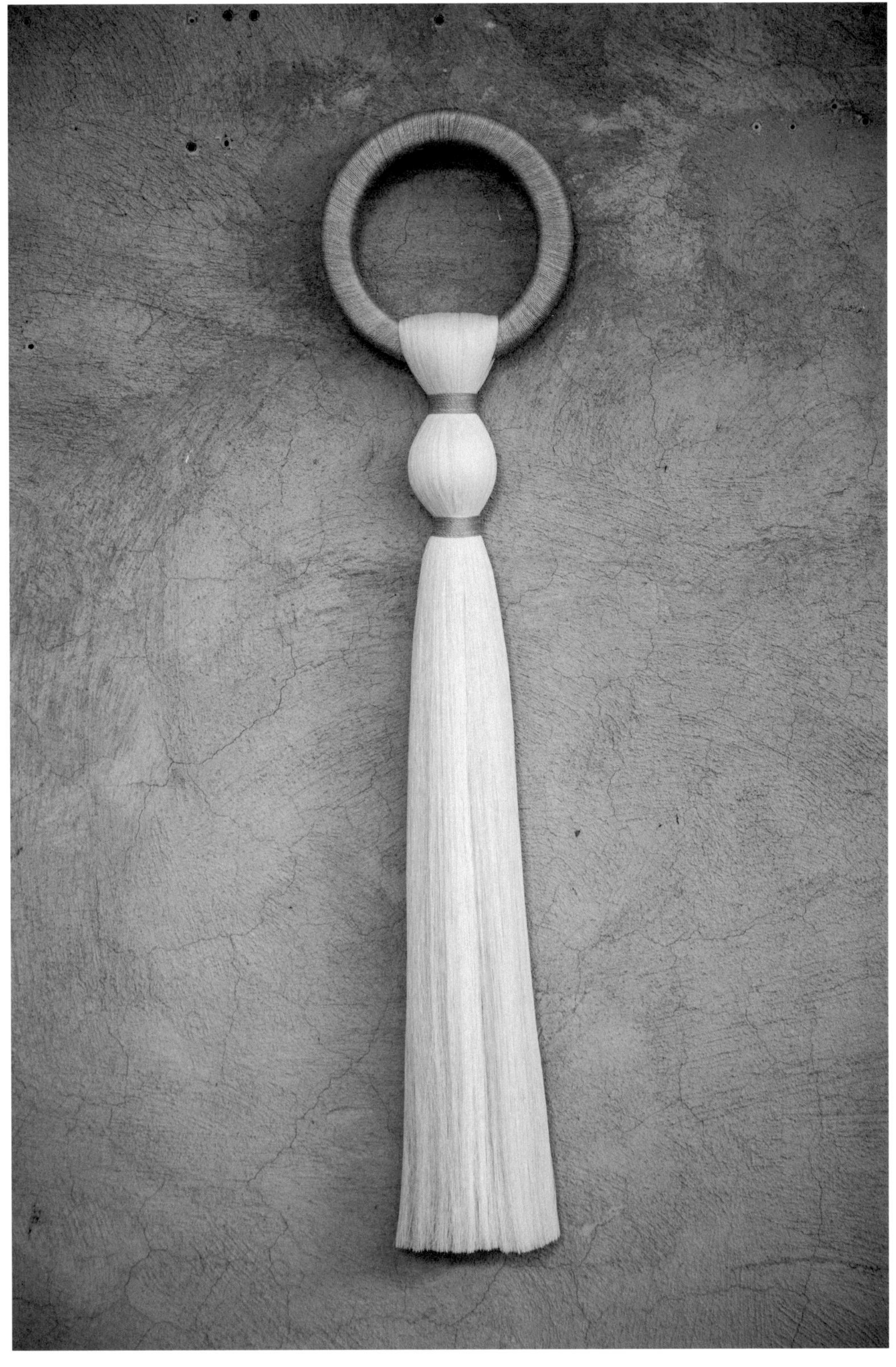

photo Diego Mateos *design* Caralarga – Mexico

PROUD & CLOUD

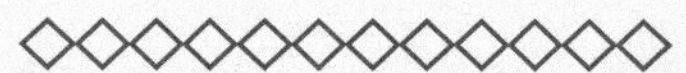

Drifting slowly in the sun-drenched landscape is a cloud of white fringe, a movement of white frill or an illusion of shuddering white dresses, acting as a mirage in broad daylight. Suddenly the colour white boldens under the hot sun, contrasting skin in magnificence. Used in abundance and excessive forms of layering, the white textiles start billowing and breathing, allowing movement to take flight. Used in impeccable poplins, cool woollens, and fine transparencies, from birth to wedding to burial, the colour white has many readings and is related to the most important moments in life, the moments of transition from one state to the other. This is why white clothes are favourite memories for many people. Often related to religion, white is used for celebration, for mourning and for pilgrimage, going from joy to pain to extreme serenity. Ultimately giving peace to the soul. Inspired by floating white landscapes in the sky, dotted with surging birds, the colour white has always represented the ascension to heaven and the right to another, better life, even if in the afterlife. *L.E.*

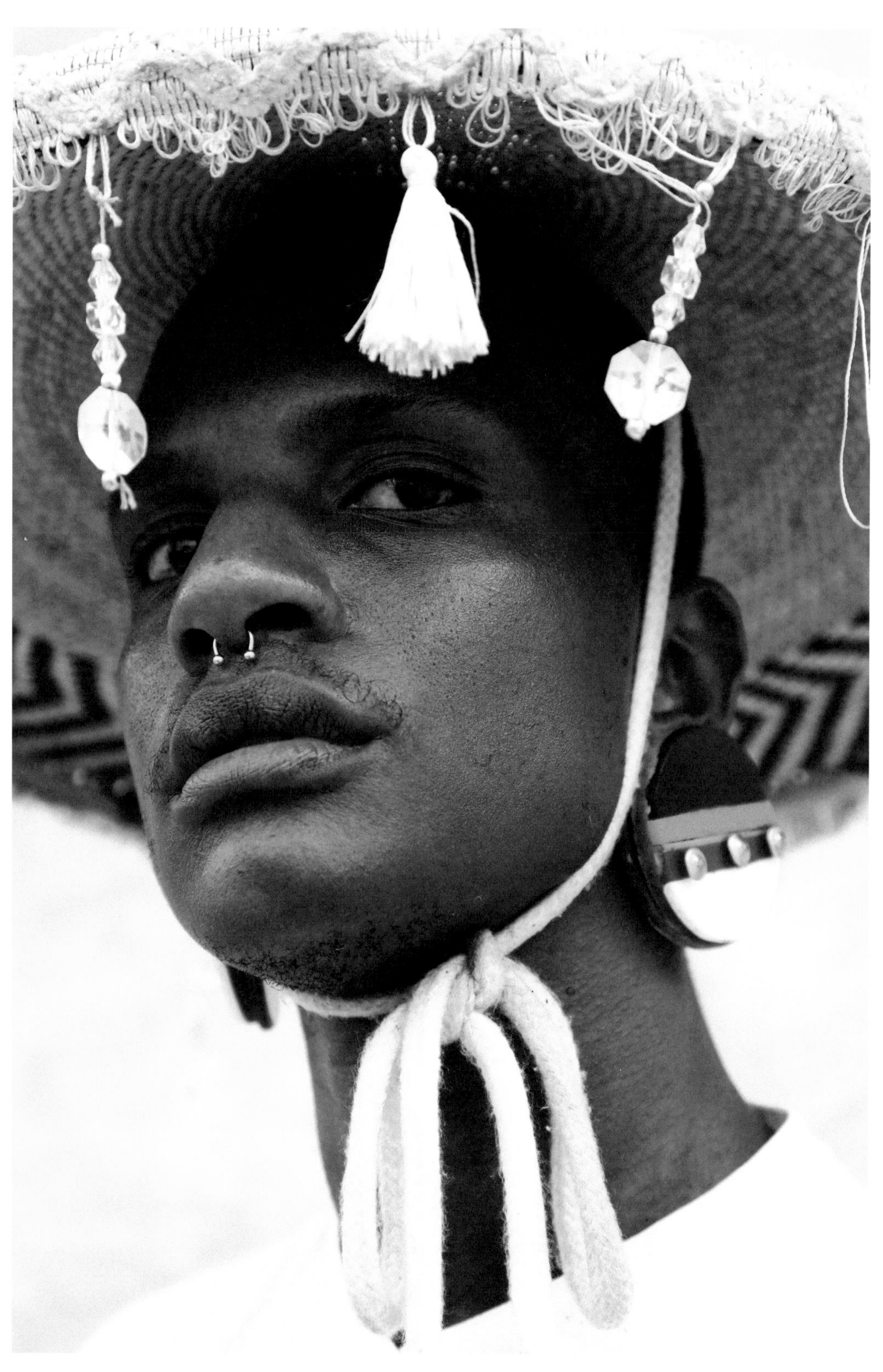

photo Trevor Stuurman – South Africa

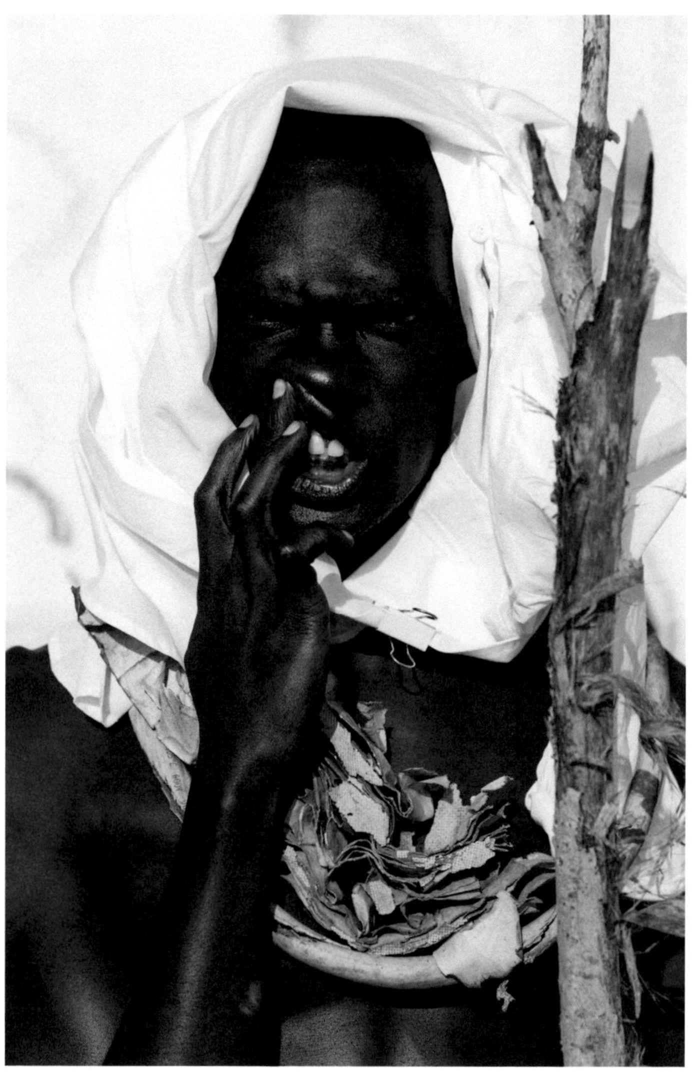

photo Niculai Constantinescu *design* Buki Akomolafe – Germany / Nigeria

photo Niculai Constantinescu *design* Buki Akomolafe – Germany / Nigeria

photo Ruy Teixeira *design* Thais Signorini Costa – Brazil

photo Mous Lambarat *design* Daily Paper – Morocco

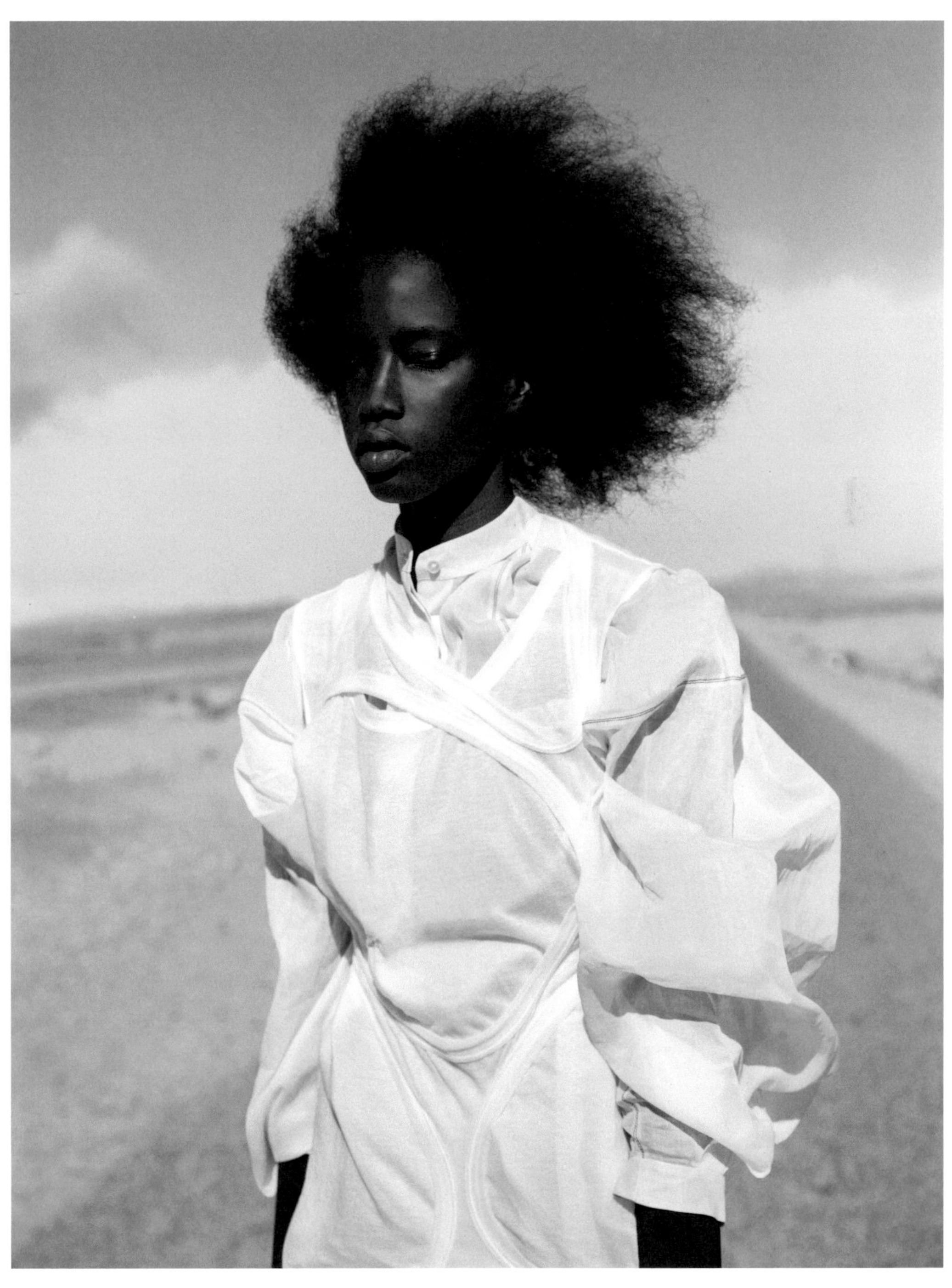

photo Jackie Nickerson – USA / UK

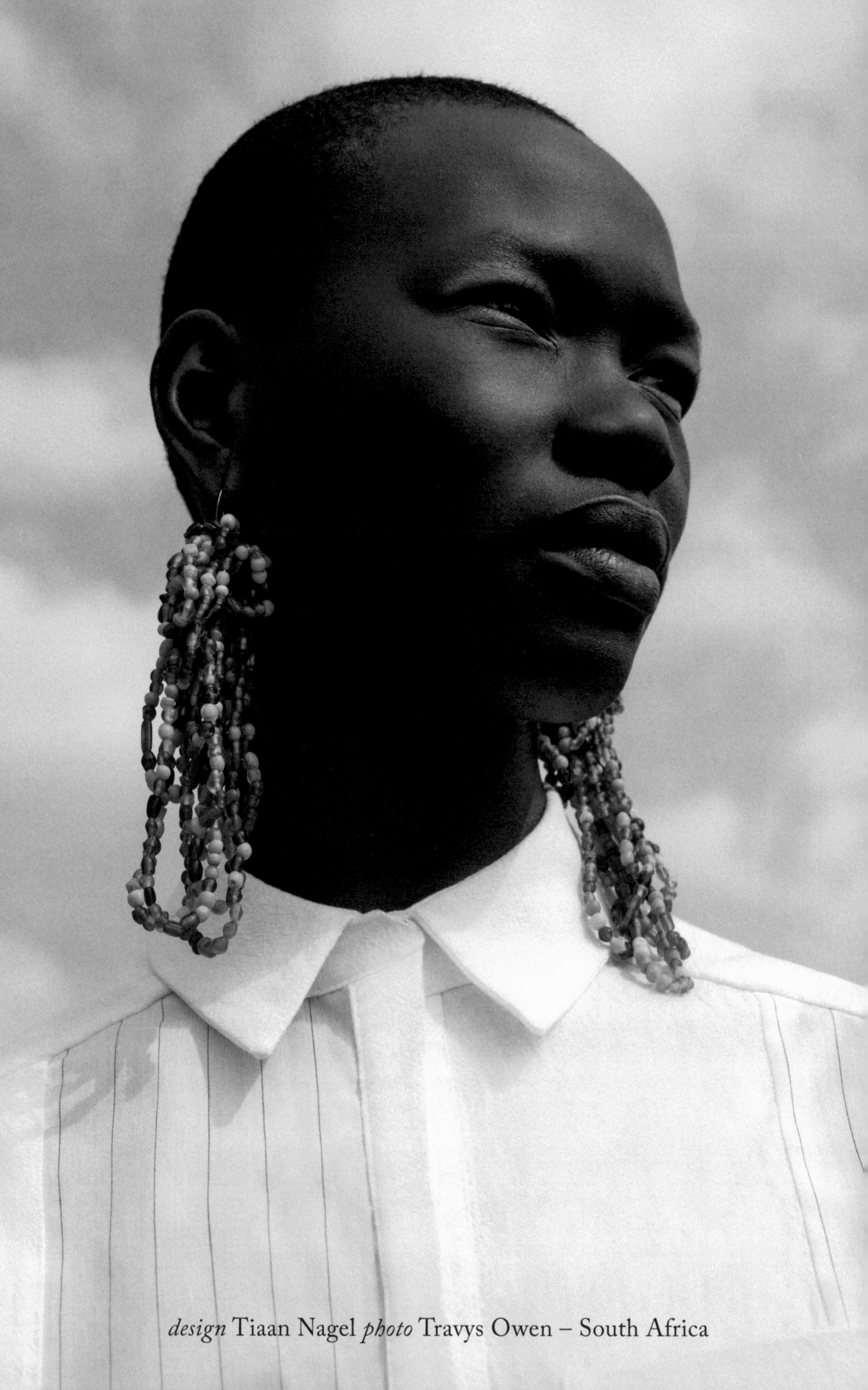

design Tiaan Nagel *photo* Travys Owen – South Africa

photo The Masons / Trunk Archive – UK

photo Kristin Lee Moolman – South Africa

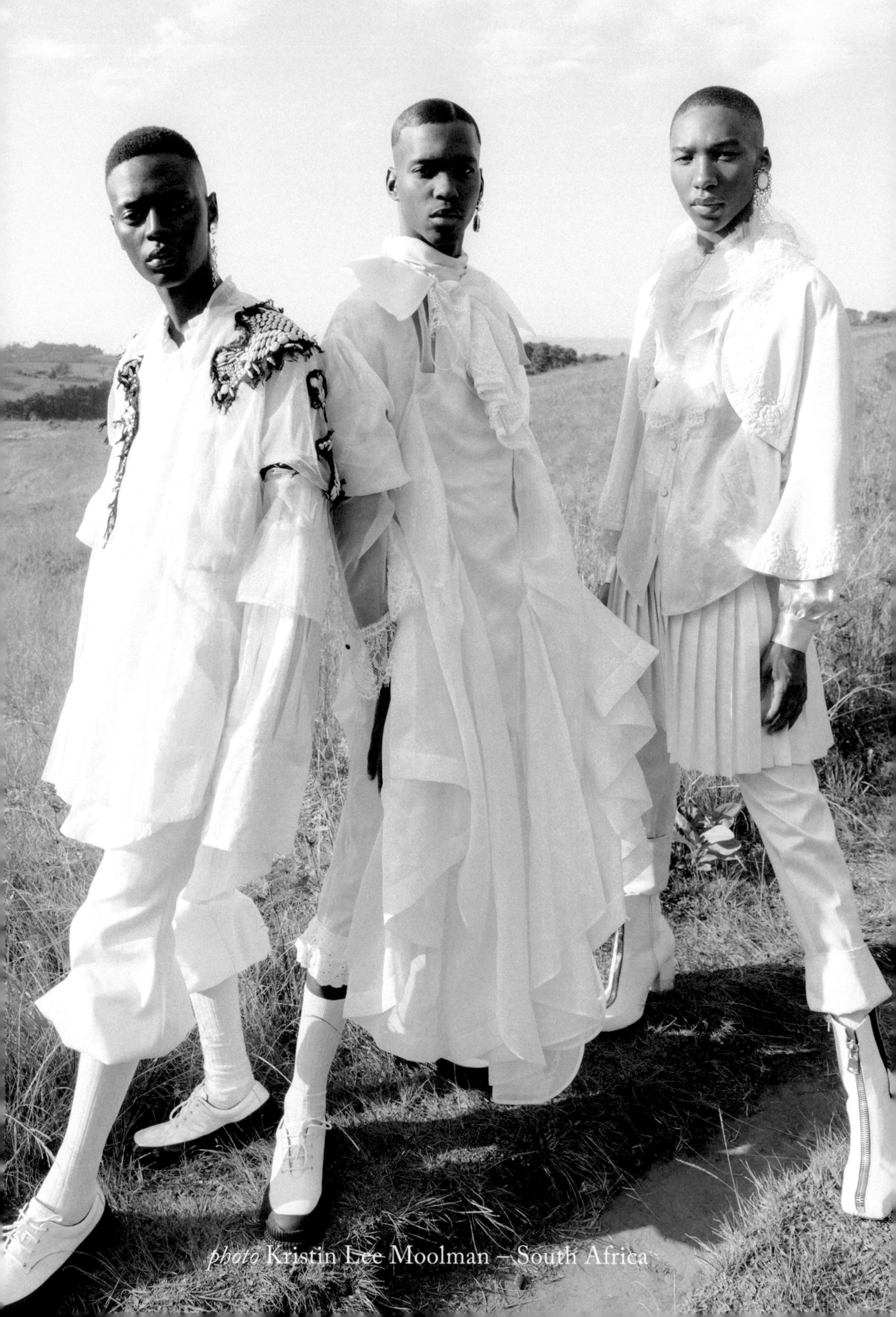

photo Kristin Lee Moolman – South Africa

photo The Masons / Trunk Archive – UK

photo Ricardo Simal *design* Rich Mnisi – South Africa

photo Trevor Stuurman – South Africa

photo Niculai Constantinescu *design* Buki Akomolafe – Germany / Nigeria

photo Trevor Stuurman – South Africa

photo Gleeson Paulino / Elle – Brazil

photo Gleeson Paulino / Elle – Brazil

photo Zander Opperman *design* Rich Mnisi – South Africa

PROUD JOURNAL

by Lidewij Eelkoort

The camera has been a weapon as much as a wondrous instrument since it was introduced through daguerreotypes to most southern countries in the late 19th century. A tool to archive colonial control and, at the same time, a trinket to remember a baby's first portrait. Documenting extreme violence and suppression and proof of the first acts of activism and emancipation. Although the camera itself was not guilty as such, it is certainly an invention that has borne indelible witness to slavery and domination, violence and humiliation.

Remnants of indigenous splendour and abhorrent poverty narrate a layered and complicated past, where western influences reined in local power, without ever completely succeeding in their goals. People would be pictured in western style settings, facing the camera, but their proud disposition was discernible in a straighter pose, a stronger facial expression, a faint disdain for the apparatus and at times visible fear that it might abduct the soul. Hair would be magnificent and body language languid, like Mexican dandies regarding the lens as if staring down the enemy. Their outfits would be composed like a modernist painting with African women posing as men, smoking a pipe, knees wide apart under their ample cloth, signalling power and poise. Their jewellery could blind the camera, when Indian families would outdo their colonial monarch in excessive paraphernalia, showing their resolve of sovereignty. A clear sense of self stares back from the photographic paper with defiance. Being proud certainly is part of the pictures of the south. The stretched body carrying the flag of revolution, the slight smile of an aboriginal artist, the cynical silhouette of a handsome farm hand, all come to mind, sampled from vast global archives.

Contrary to painting, the early photograph was a document that registered the truth, spelling out the promise of transparency and trustworthiness, even when the picture was staged. The camera seemed to be there for the people and could provide proof of the injustices and hardship they were going through. From the annals of humiliation and humanity to the triumph of the self, this transparency was the reason for its popularity, as the art form rapidly conquered the south. And now experiences a revival.

The lens came to Africa from people of the diaspora that migrated back to their countries, going door to door to offer their services, making passport portraits and wedding photos, setting up shop as soon as they could. Making the archives of the future, allowing ordinary life to be captured in their surroundings. This rush of pioneers was followed by explorers, colonial administrators, soldiers and travellers, introducing daguerreotype to several countries, mostly on the west coast. Photography became a method of expression, of correspondence, and allows us to take a fundamental look at the evolution of culture.

Sitters commissioned portraits to capture their social standing, using dress, setting and pose as socio-economic indicators. The camera was frequently used to capture an intimate gathering, a priority of subject over instrument, the group staging their own reflection. Photographers and sitters working in unison developing an aesthetic that was rooted in local artistic trends.

The studio Photographic Souvenir created by the famous Philippe Ayi Koudjina provided material of capital historical esteem while the homemade Camera Box from itinerant Yao August Azaglo registered portraits and passport photos. The 60s saw a radical change in subject matter and approach, when the Rolleiflex would capture youth and dance and fashion, for the first time fixing flirtation on paper. Malick Sidibé established his style in the black and white photography of his time and became one of the most venerated stars of the continent at the same time as Seydou Keïta, who started with a Kodak Brownie Flash when he opened his own studio in Bamako. He didn't need a flash since he preferred to use broad natural daylight. He gave his

THE POSITIVE AND NEGATIVE ROLE OF THE PHOTOGRAPHIC IMAGE IS BEING ERASED BY A NEW GENERATION OF PHOTOGRAPHERS, THAT HAVE LIBERATED THE MEDIUM FROM PRECONCEPTIONS AND OPENED THE LENS ON ANOTHER, STRONGER, ALMOST VISCERAL FORM OF CREATIVITY.

customers objects like bicycles and radios to make them portraits of their time. He used dynamic patterned boubous as backdrops that engaged with the sitter's clothes and cloth to form a kaleidoscopic dynamic. The buoyancy of photographic culture was burgeoning from postcolonial independence. Self-determination emerged as an overruling quality, a characteristic that seems to be at the core of southern photography, even more so today.

The pictures of the southern Americas pay witness to extreme hardship and therefore share a kinship with the other continents that have experienced diasporas, droughts, famine and exploitation. Latin American photography differs from country to country but has several traits in common. In this continent, a sense of self is evident in all subjects, even when they've grown up in remote rural areas. The Argentinian gaucho and the Guatemalan weaver share their pride through amazing handwoven textiles and crowning hats. Burning the photographic paper with desire, the Mexican models exude an erotism that is mellowed by grief. But as the photographer Graciela Iturbide explains, although she notices the pain as well as the beauty, the works seem to ignore poverty and hardship by elevating the subject to another, more spiritual plane, as she only considers the dignity of her subjects.

After the daguerreotype came to life, studios set up as soon as they could in Mexico City, Buenos Aires and Rio de Janeiro, finding clients amongst the rich and famous that could afford such luxury. But by the beginning of last century weavers and workers, maids and miners, as well as anarchists and the avant garde, were posing for their own, much more expressive portraits. The Vargas Brothers pictured a large sample of society ranging from local Indians in fibrous huts to posh Peruvians drinking high tea. Latin America is characterised by enormous diversity and the regional identities are divided by the indigenous world, the colonial experience and the religious core that has influenced photography most. The Cuban revolution, military dictatorships and mass social movements have also introduced a direct anarchistic idiom into the lens on history. Photographers acted as activists and their oeuvre can be considered as a wake-up call against silence. Ideas about *indigenismo*, the movement for Indian reform and search for indigenous genius, was part of the creative research and ethos, as early as 1925. Almost a hundred years later, the same subjects are relevant, and the creative current is similar to the Peruvian textiles of Chambi, the flowers of Flor Garduno, the sun-drenched drapes of Alvares Bravo and the erotism of Tina Modotti, touching on and personalising the rituals in their countries. Often these rituals are religious, dealing with matters of life and death, a powerful photography that is venerating the power of black and white.

In the period after the Great Mutiny in India (1857), photography became a moral weapon when it moved from architecture to public places and from landscapes to people, recording the multiple cultures and dense traditions of the continent. Known as the photographer-prince, Maharaja Sawai Singh the Second of Jaipur, was carried away by the art of photography and founded a School of Arts that taught the principles of photo-making and assembled a collection of more than 6000 images, contained in the museum named after him, with pictures by the emerging talents of that time. In the second half of the 19th century, various Indian photographers opened up studios in Bombay, Delhi and Agra. The successful Lala Deen Dayal was one of the first Indian photographers to be fully acknowledged on the photographic scene, picturing the lifestyles of the rich and famous, as well as clichés of cultured courtesans, unveiling symbols of power and dominance within Indian hierarchy. His aesthetic eye had such elegance that he accumulated sumptuous commissions, managing four studios at the time around India. He became the court photographer for the sixth Nizam of Hyderabad and was given the ultimate appointment to become court photographer to Queen Victoria. Accused of perpetrating the colonial vision, choosing opulence versus oppression, his work is nevertheless crucial in recording the grandeur that dominated the 19th century, a grandeur that is distinctly Indian and is devoid of any British bourgeois influences other than Mulligatawny soup.

In the early 20th century, the most renowned photographer of her times was a handsome female reporter from Gujarat called Homai Vyarawalla. She managed to still the private attractions between famous people, seducing them with her own agile and alluring presence, and recording important funerals and dignitary visits as well as the travels of Prime Minister Nehru. She set the bar high for other women to follow in her footsteps. It was finally the artist Sheba Chachhi that picked up the challenge and started in the 80s to document activism and feminism by staging portraiture with her subjects, recording anti-dowry protests and female ascetics, organised in large scale installations of images, sound and light.

Although successful in covering major tragedies, the real contribution of Pablo Bartholomew was the intimate way he chronicled the lives of friends and loved ones. His work celebrates the trials and tribulations of relationships, love and loss, the intimacy and the challenges of growing up in the

70s. Contemporary photographers like Kushai Ray and Sohrab Hura continue to look inward and document relationships and relatives as intimate journals, vulnerable testimonies of an India coming of age, gaining post-independence while still hugely influenced by currents from the west. Their act of making photographs can be seen as therapy to come to terms with their deep societal concerns, soul-searching contemporary generations, recording mundane family matters, picturing boredom, happiness and sadness.

The personal and the intimate remain characteristic of contemporary South Asian photography and sets it apart from the other continents and communities, bringing people together and documenting the interaction with subjects that are flirting and languid, as if arrested by heat on a full summer's day. The aesthetic erotism introduces a rare intimacy in fashion photography, where the strong bond of the models brings the bond of all people to the fore, whether gender fluid or sexually inclusive and hints at a new era of modelling and casting, selecting awareness over physical beauty. The positive and negative role of the photographic image is being erased by a new generation of creative minds, photographers, stylists, hair artists and designers, that have liberated the medium from preconceptions and opened the lens on another, stronger, almost visceral form of creativity. Distinctly different from the north, the south has found its own voices that echo and complement each other across oceans with many character traits in common. Concerned with life and death, rituals and religion as well as roots and blooms.

First comes the act of casting, with wild cards like boys impersonating women, soft and sensuous choices with gender-fluid personas, or examples of another, almost eerie alien beauty. The models are never modelling, the stylist doesn't seem to style, the pictures will not look like stills, the vibrant energy is difficult to contain. The stillness seems to be stirring.

The ease with which backgrounds are chosen is astounding, at first it looks like anything goes, but the horizon is tilting like a jacket, the cloud a pattern to complement the face, the desert an extension into abstraction and the mountain fills the void as colours clash and coordinate. There is a sense of space, lands are vast and there are often oceans and boats, like oblivious memories of shared pain. Houses are dilapidated, flowers opulent and trees are ancient, throwing expressive shadows onto white sands. Roots are deep, therefore. The work is reaching out to a global platform, exploring the political and the aesthetic, trading the exotic for a more universal and powerful point of view, bringing the south to the centre of the world.

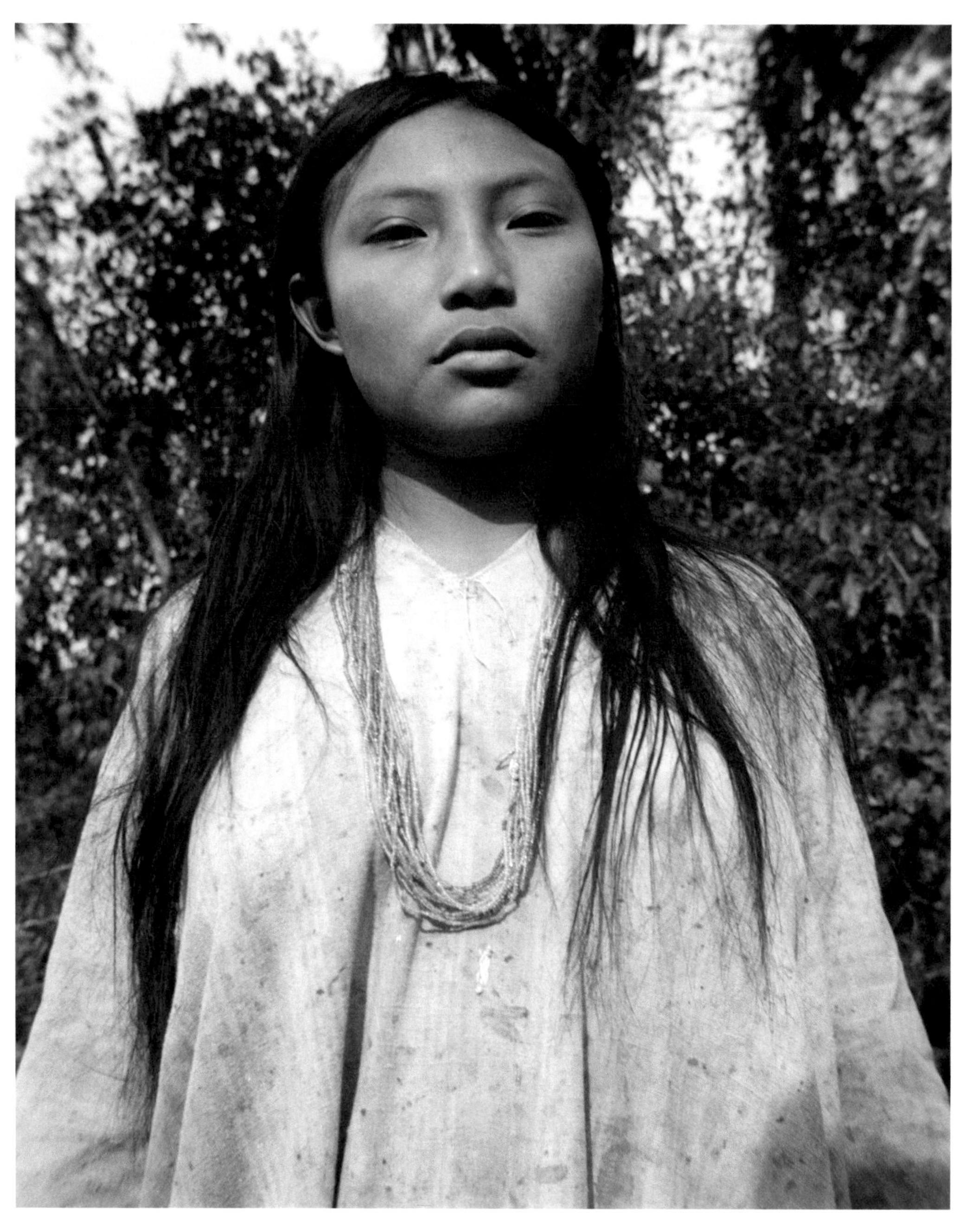

photo Manuel Álvarez Bravo, *Margarita de Bonampak* – Mexico
photo Rudi Geyser *designer* Lukhanyo Mdingi – South Africa

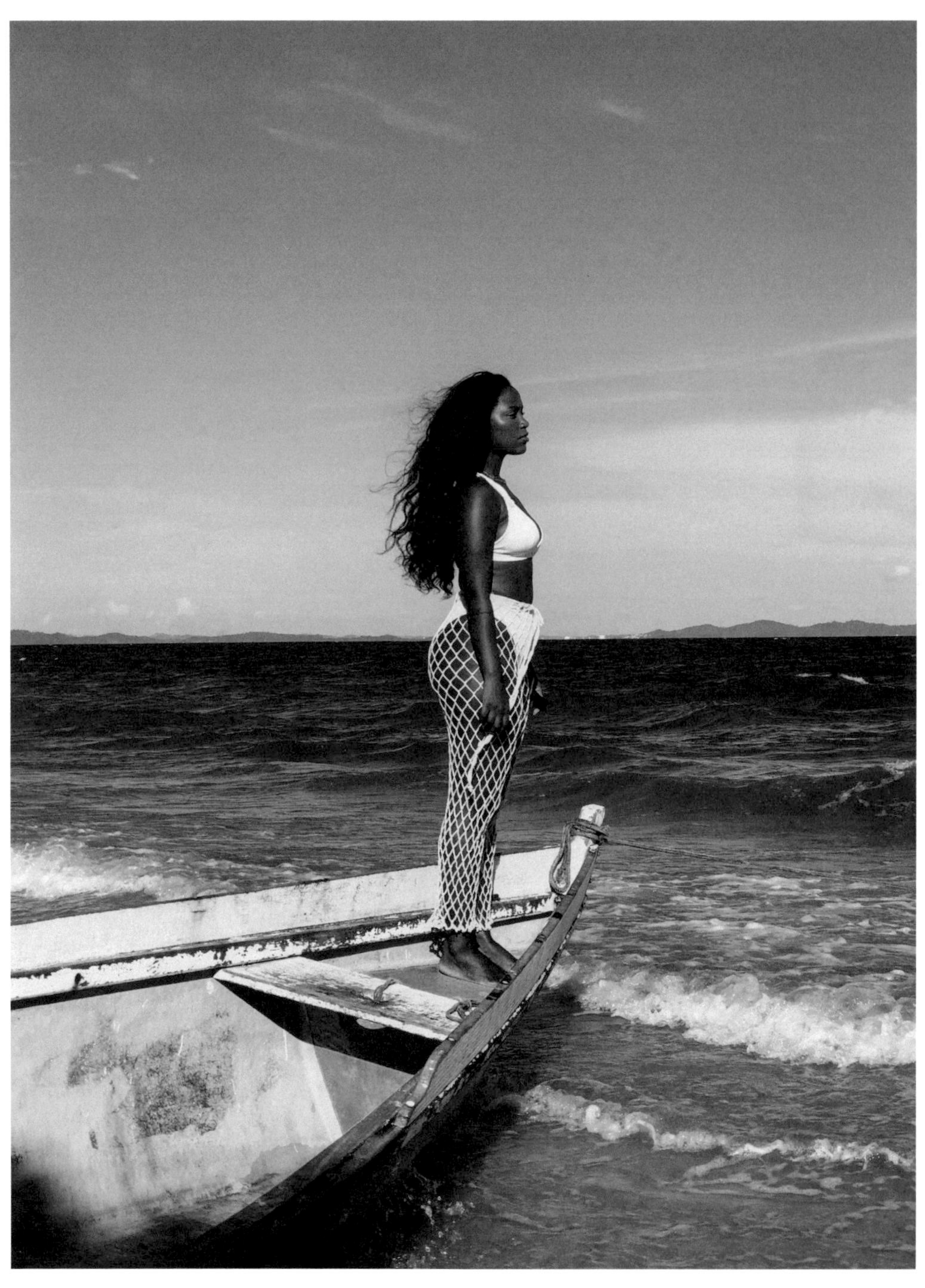

photo Gabriela Cajado *design* Cajá – Brazil
photo Graciela Iturbide, *Vendedora de Zacate* – Mexico

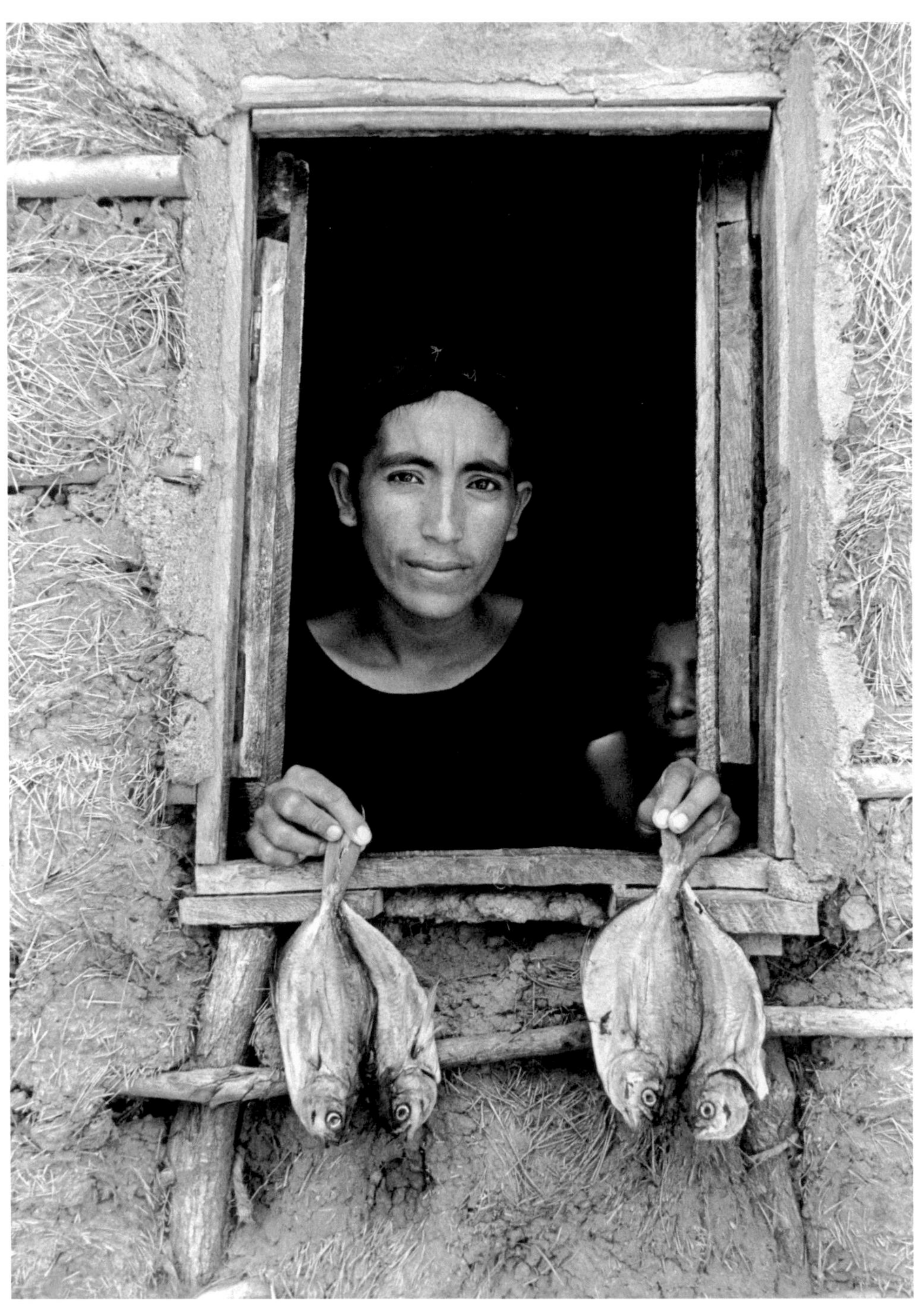

photo Graciela Iturbide, *Serafina* – Mexico
photo Graciela Iturbide, *Cuatro Pescaditos* – Mexico

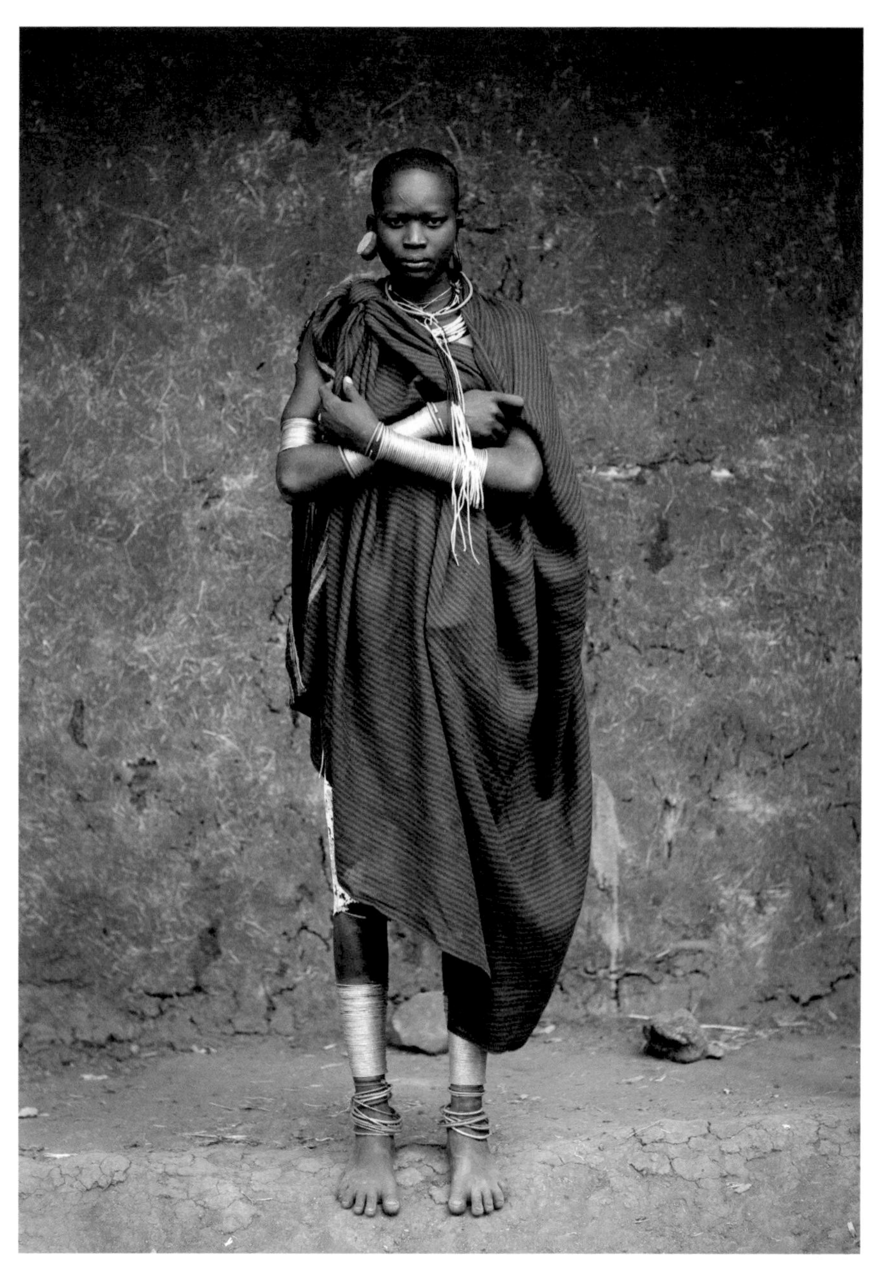

photo Eric Lafforgue, *Miss Nashure* – image taken in Ethiopia
photo Jackie Nickerson – USA / UK

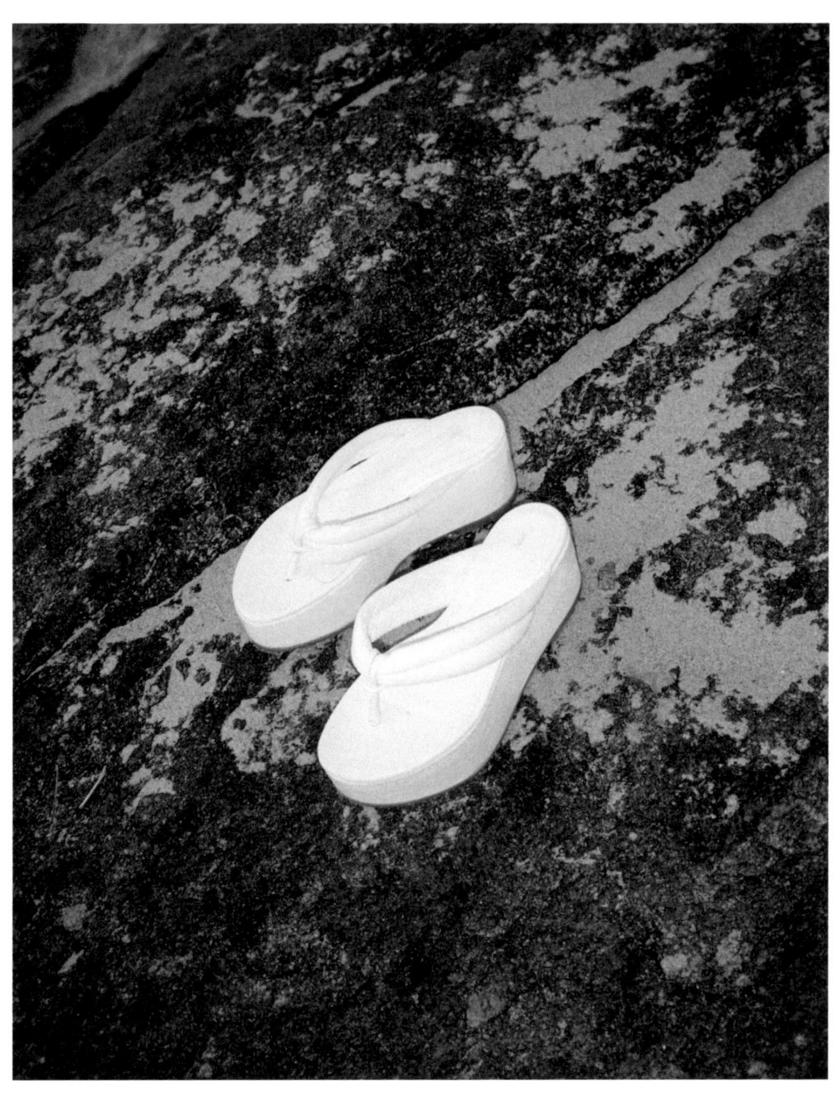

design Pége – Brazil
photo Graciela Iturbide, *La Ascensión* – Mexico

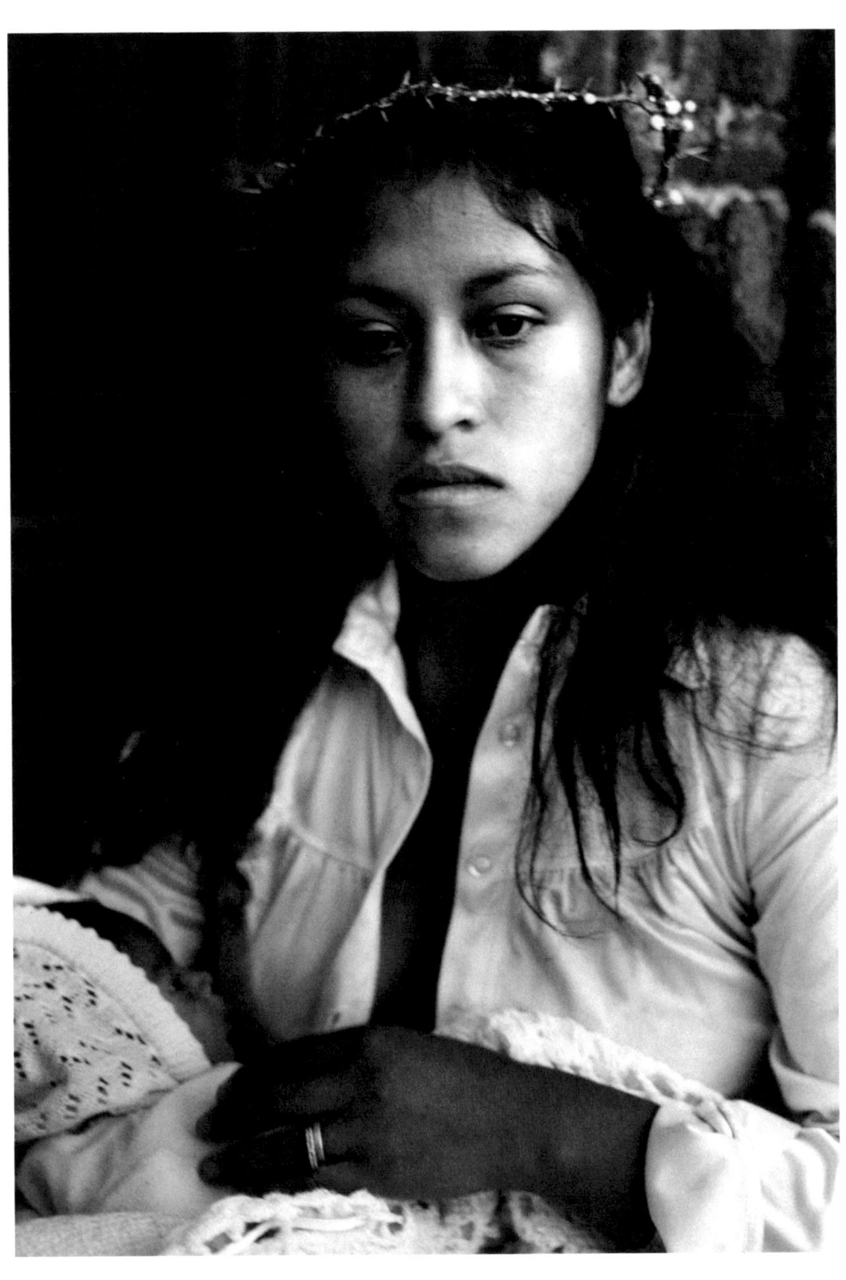

photo Graciela Iturbide, *Madonna* – Mexico
photo Vaishnav Praveen *design* Kaleekal – India

photo Tina Modotti, *Woman with Flag* – Mexico
photo Ashish Shah *design* Raw Mango – India

photo Jaipur City Palace Collection – India
photo Sawai Ram Singh II – India

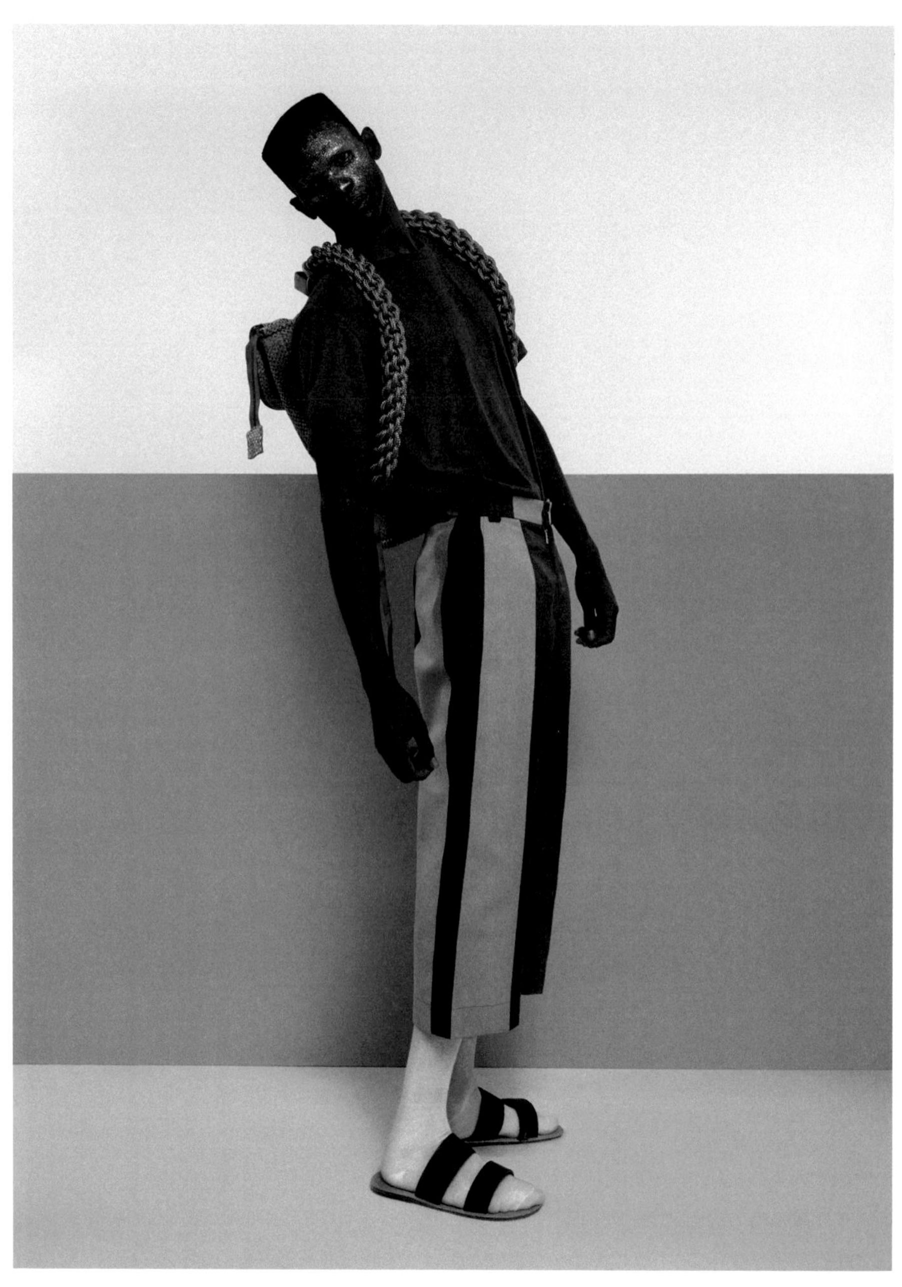

photo Travys Owen *design* Lukhanyo Mdingi – South Africa
photo Leah Gordon, *Mulâtre* from the *Caste Portraits* – Haiti

MULÂTRE

photo Eric Lafforgue – image taken in Ethiopia
photo Joseph Moïse Agbojelou / Revue Noire Paris – Benin

PROUD & FLOUNCE

As the little black dress implies, most of the time the colour black is related to minimalist perfection with maximalised impact. From mourning to celebrating, the colour black has navigated mental minefields and established symbolisms. First black was for the poor and the widowed, as a colour of pain, related to pure forms of suffering. Then the dark colour started its ascent by assisting working women, tailoring their basic uniforms and worked its way up by being used for cocktail dresses as the perfect backdrop to precious pearls. From there the sombre tint set the tone for punk paraphernalia, and gothic clothes keep on telling its very romantic stories till today. But in the south the colour is also a protest against all rules, when black is espousing coloured skin, bringing black into the realm of activism and revendication, designing friction by frills, protest by pleating, while teasing public opinion with tulle and feathers. Almost threatening dresses stir up and destroy scenarios of colonial rule, volumes point to religious exorbitance while the stirrings of nonbinary clothes illustrate a fluid future world, veiled in layers of black. *L.E.*

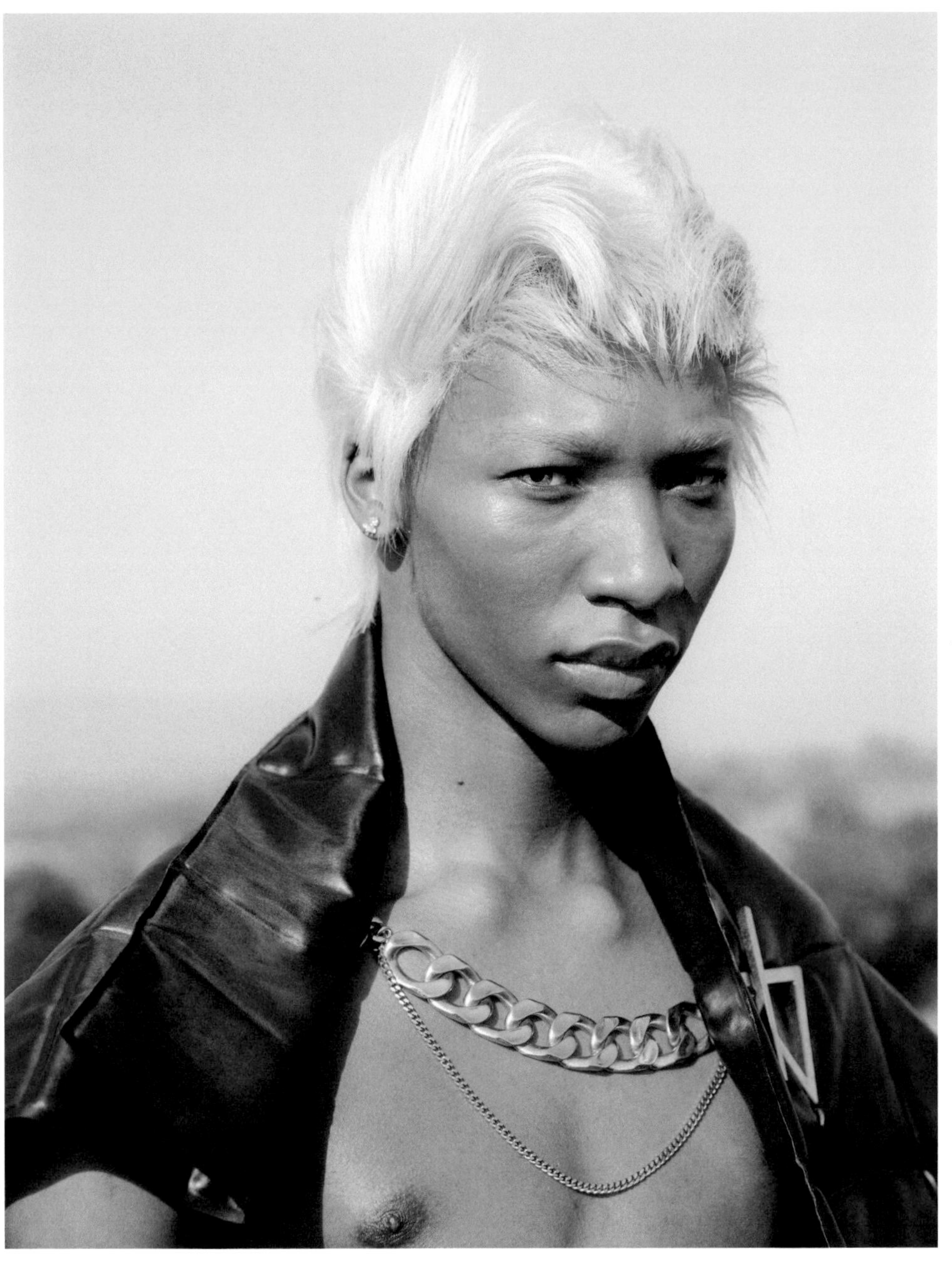

photos Kristin Lee Moolman – South Africa

photo Erdi Doğan *design* Hatice Gökçe – Turkey
photo Cecilia Duarte / Elle – Brazil

photo Jamal Nxedlana – South Africa
photo Cecilia Duarte / Elle – Brazil

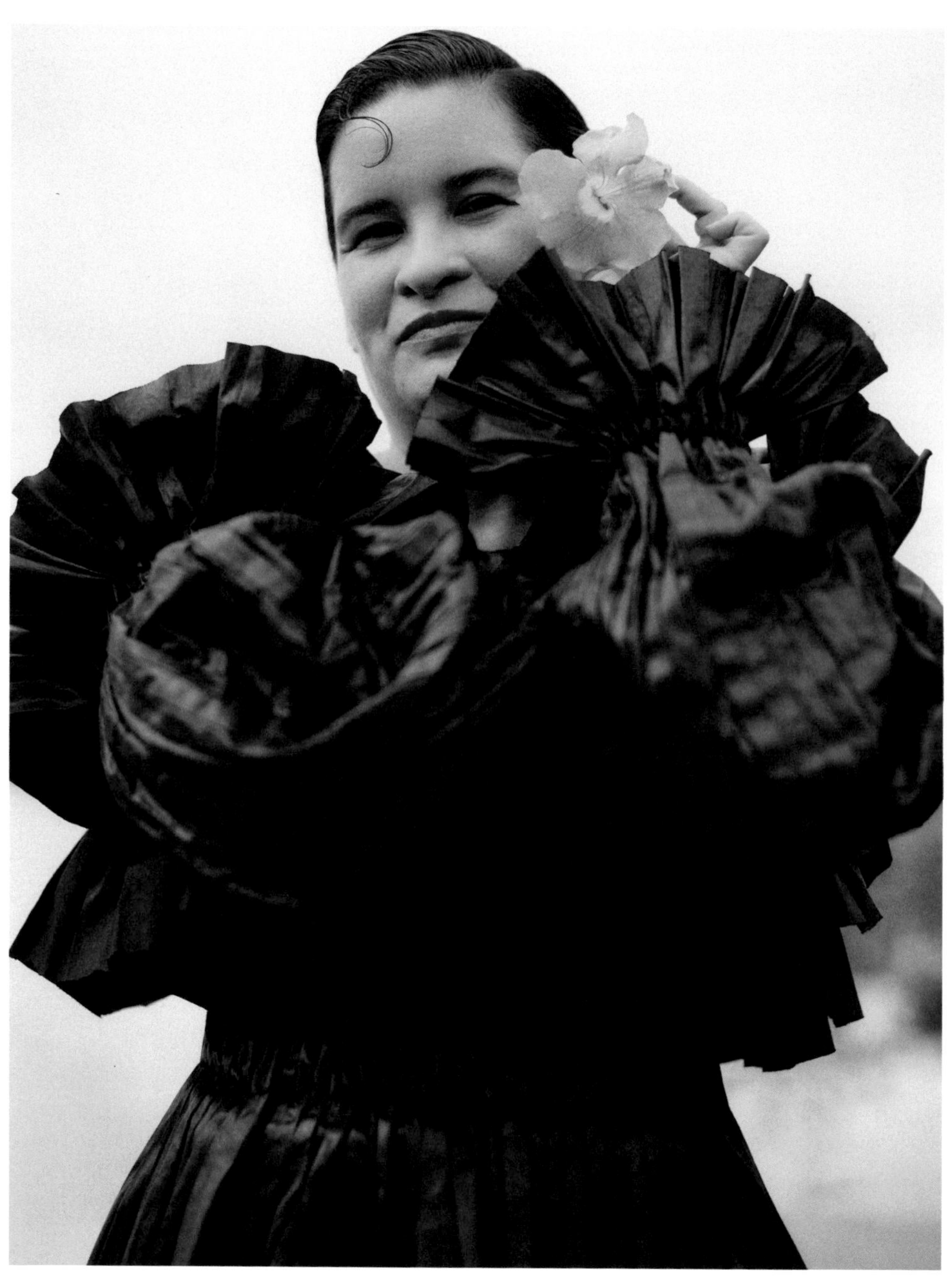

photo Hick Duarte *artist* Dionéia Ferreira / Vogue – Brazil
art Tamary Kudita – Zimbabwe

photo Mous Lambarat – Morocco
photo The Masons / Trunk Archive – UK

photo Celine van Heel – Spain
photo Trevor Stuurman – South Africa

photos Kristin Lee Moolman – South Africa

photos Kristin Lee Moolman – South Africa

PROUD &
& AUROUS

Related to the gods and power, gold has been the preferred metal to work with, crafting idols and objects and elaborate jewellery in all southern parts of the planet. Found in streams and mined from the earth as shiny desirable nuggets, gold has spoken to the human imagination from the first day it was found and has never stopped inspiring trading and design. Gold became part of every social culture, as its lustre and beauty and great malleability made it amazing to work with. The metal was compared to the sun as it never tarnished or eroded, it would forever shine. Creating wealth, upon being designated as money. Gold's early expressions are ornamental and linked to deities and dynasties, expressing awe amongst the early civilizations. Mayan culture, Egyptian pharaohs and Indian rulers all venerated the iconic metal as their own way of branding. Today the metal of metals captures creative young minds, turning skin into opulence, converting leaves into jewellery, tinting cork into lingots, transforming cardboard into fashion and fashion into contemporary gods. Perpetuating the legend by recycling its power. *L.E.*

photo Mariana Maltoni *design* Casa Geração Vidigal School – Brazil

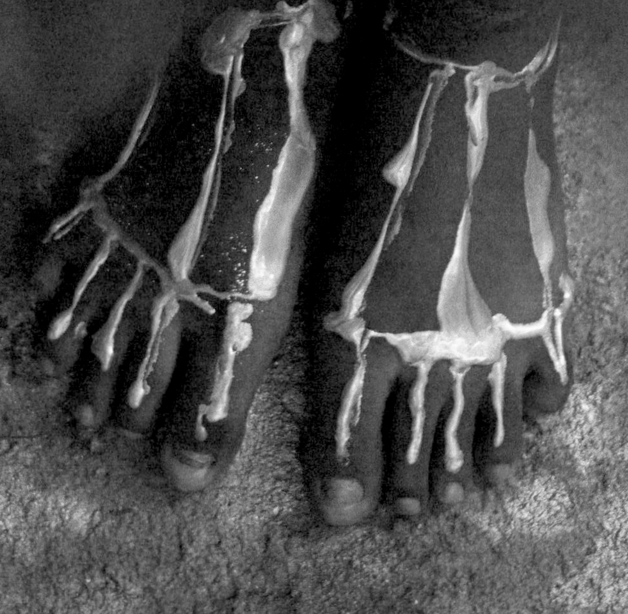

photo Mariana Maltoni *design* Casa Geração Vidigal School – Brazil

photo Mariana Maltoni *design* Casa Geração Vidigal School – Brazil

photo Demian Jacob – Brazil

photo Rogério Cavalcanti – Brazil

photo Rogério Cavalcanti – Brazil

PROUD & TOUGH

photography by Neville Trickett
– South Africa –

The proud and tough carrot-picker girls go through very physical and hard discipline. In the vicinity of Durban, working in dire conditions from great heat to damp cold, they spend their days together, dedicated to delivering the goodies. They have decided to bond as a group of joyful gay girls that incarnates masculine archetypes, dressing in drag and make-up. This daily role play is almost humorous, but one feels a keen sense of hierarchy and restraint. This is serious business. From tough butch to two-spirited souls, their aim is to accumulate as many textiles as possible within each potent outfit. Dressing up every day in layered skirts over rubber boots topped with towels, channelling their fashion sense. For those who love textiles their dress is to die for. The genius that eternalised this amazing group of ferocious females is the über-gifted Neville Tricket, a venerated household name in South Africa's design community. Although a recluse, living with his creative family up in the hills, he is famous beyond the borders of his country. His talents include forecasting and foraging and collecting and curating, making sense of the times we live in, creating beauty out of literally everything he encounters. Designing, merchandising, transforming, painting, photographing; the expansive sky is the limit of his imagination. His life is solely dedicated to creation. He dresses like a model, walks like a hermit, talks like a prophet and drinks like a sailor, connected as much to the world as to the land of his farm. He is very much loved. *L.E.*

LOVE WAVE

KAIZER

JEANS

GANDER

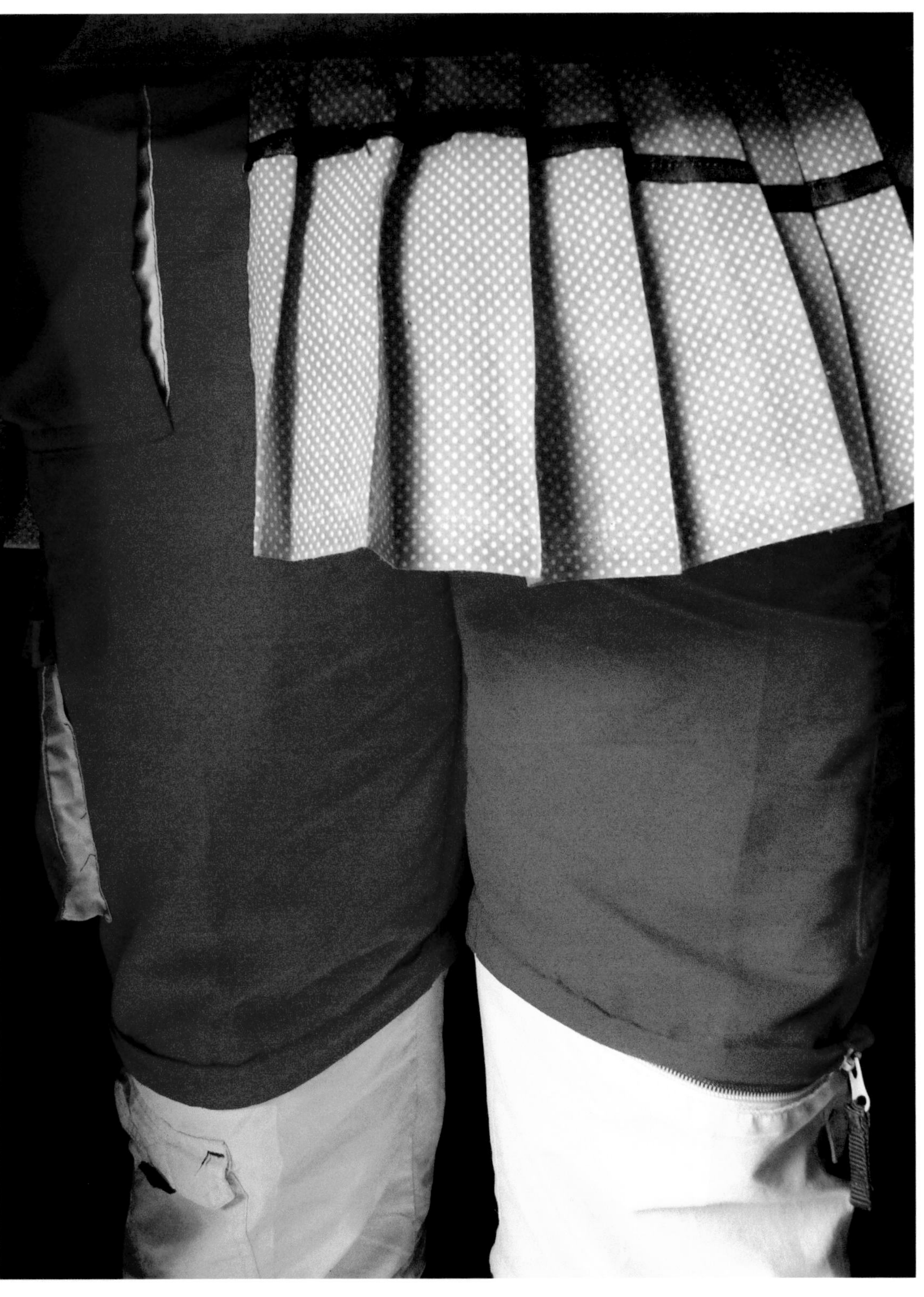

PROUD & HONOUR

photography by Jackie Nickerson
– USA / UK –

Born in the north but transformed by the south, the work of Jackie Nickerson stands as a milestone in the development of photography from southern Africa and has reached monumental proportions. Her subject matter of farms and scraps seem to become more pertinent every day. Her eye is distant and discerning but emphatic in its embrace of the human condition, laying bare the beauty and hardship in labour and harvest and second-hand clothes that are brought together with innate taste on amateur models. Western junk becoming sublime southern style. Trained in fashion, she chose an alternative path for her own itinerary and it is in the south that she crafted her famous series *Farm* and *Terrain*. She continues to be spellbound by an attraction to the natural environment and a repulsion for certain living conditions, a dichotomy where the use of plastic needs to be eliminated but is crucial to food production, where farming is punishing but needs to be harvested for food, where a changing climate is making this even more traumatic. Nickerson is passionate about such questions and continues to address these dilemmas with poignant beauty, so as to share pride and pain. Her models stand strong and even elegant under their challenging conditions. Ultimately, she comes back to fashion, which she nourishes with her acquired aesthetic of wear and waste, influencing style, forever changing the ways clothing might be designed. *L.E.*

PROUD & GENEROUS

It may come as a surprise, but most southern countries experience extremely cold nights and snow-covered peaks on their mountains. Suffering periods of cool rain and storm, inducing shivering moments. Although southern people rarely anticipate low temperatures, the way of building and layering and dressing helps sustain the quality of life through these short periods with heavy walls, open fires, quilted covers, blanket wraps and knitwear. The south therefore has an amazing and rather unknown history of felting, knitting and crochet, using the local flocks of goats and sheep as yarn providers and local plants and trees as natural dye colours. Freely customising their sweaters. These ancestral household chores have grown into powerful contemporary brands that make knitwear their core culture and expand their creations with wild stitch variations and multi-coloured yarn fantasies. They make knits not only cuddling with wrapped crafted details, but also sexy, adding skin to their endearing allure. This product seems the perfect southern platform to also keep northern countries warm. *L.E.*

photo Valentina Minette Escardó *design* Gaia – Uruguay
design FVH x LM Mohair Knitwear Collection
photo Jacobus Snyman – South Africa

photos Bruno Ilusorio *design* Gaia – Uruguay

photos Ryan Wijayaratne *design* Amesh – Sri Lanka

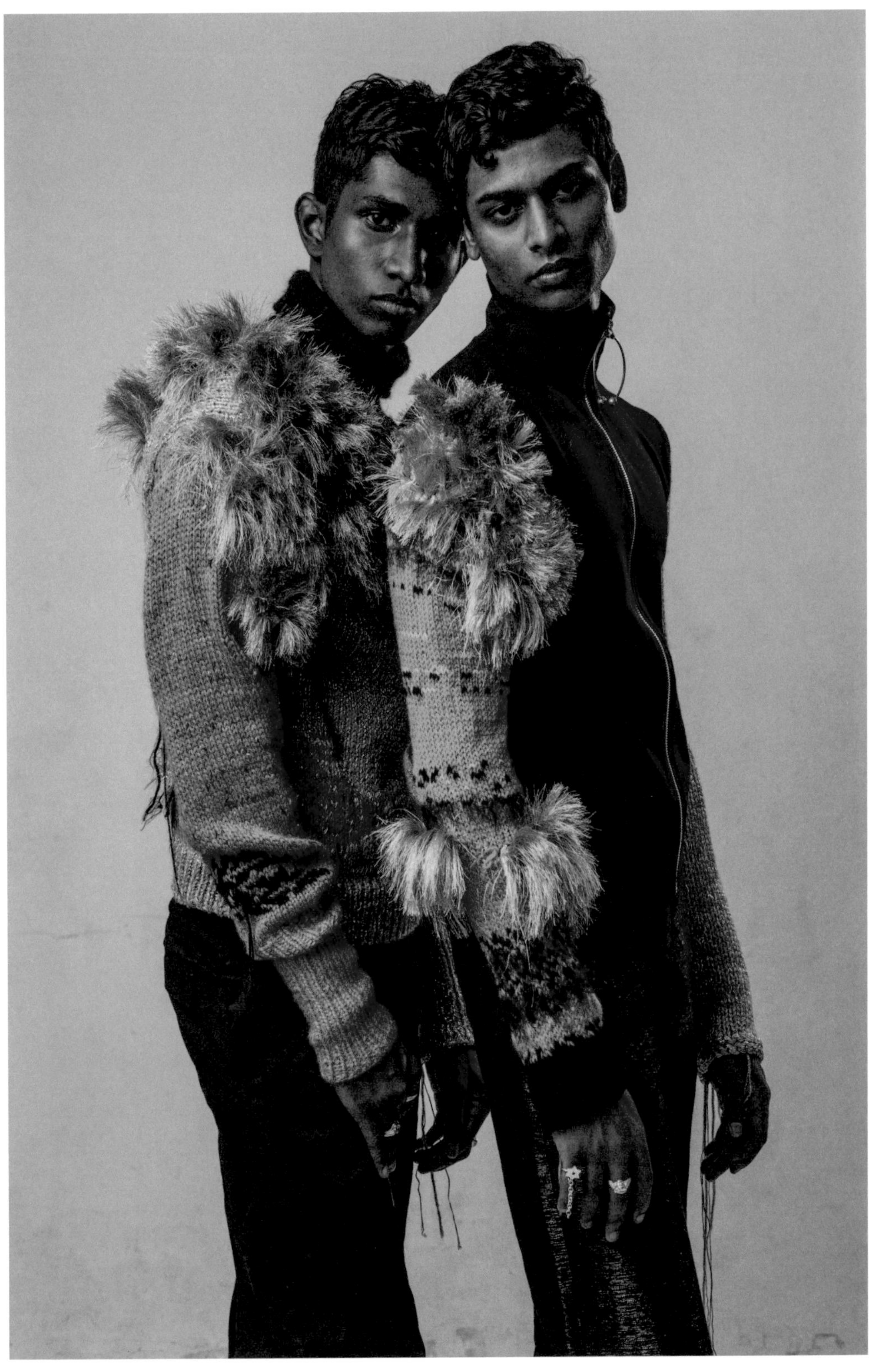

photo Bruna Castanheira *design* Anselmi – Brazil

photo Bruna Castanheira – Brazil

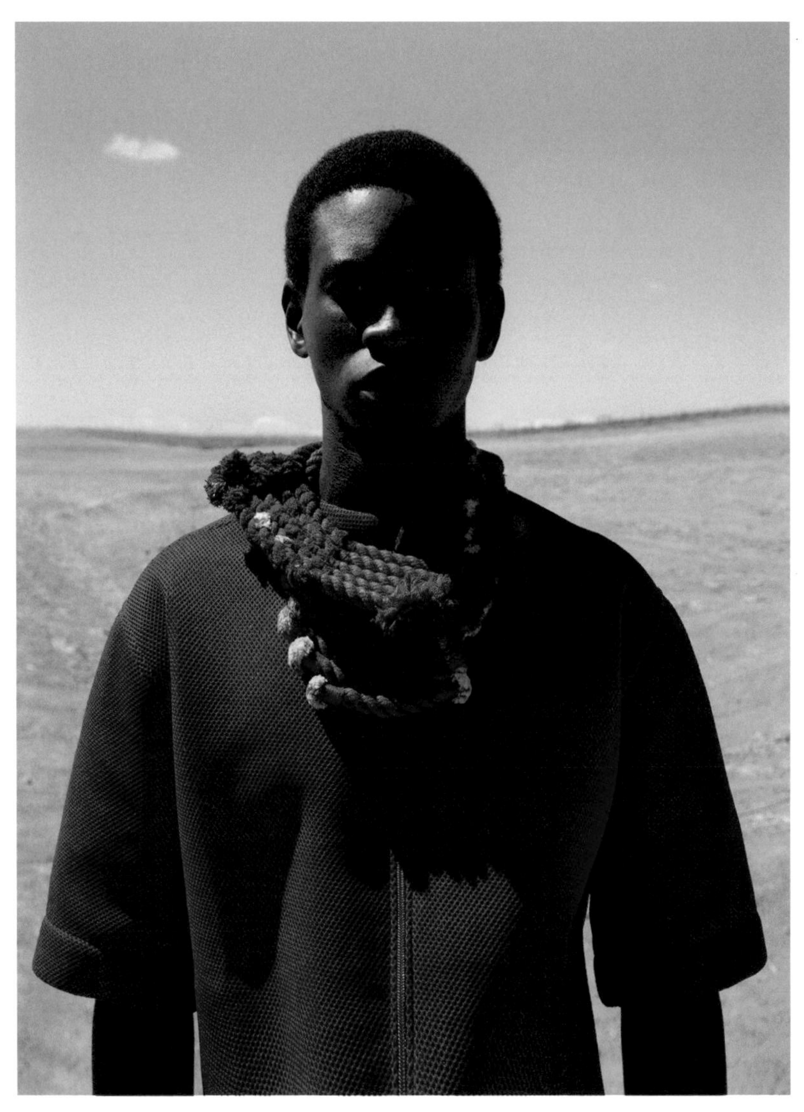

photo Travys Owen *design* Orange Culture – Nigeria

photo Tenzin Lhagyal *stylist* Pandey Akanksha – India

PROUD & COUPE

Nothing is able to bring people together like football. The Dutch are welcome in all countries in the world, celebrated by taxi drivers because of the legendary Johan Cruyff. Doors will open upon hearing the names of Real Madrid and Manchester United and discussion comes easy with *foot*, as it is called in France. In all southern countries young boys can be seen taking a shot at makeshift goals made from clothes or sleeping dogs. In all alleys juniors train their strategic tackles at nightfall. In all regions people wear their favourite clubs on their hearts as a badge of honour. World cups become tribal feasts with painted masks and instruments like vuvuzelas driving the audiences crazy. This ongoing fascination with football has spawned a generation of casual clothes that take the brilliant colour codes and heraldic images to another level of design. These sweatshirts and trainers are reaching ever more people in even more remote regions, pushing up the fever to yet unknown extremes. A southern style that echoes the north but is outdoing it in its exuberance. Winning the game. *L.E.*

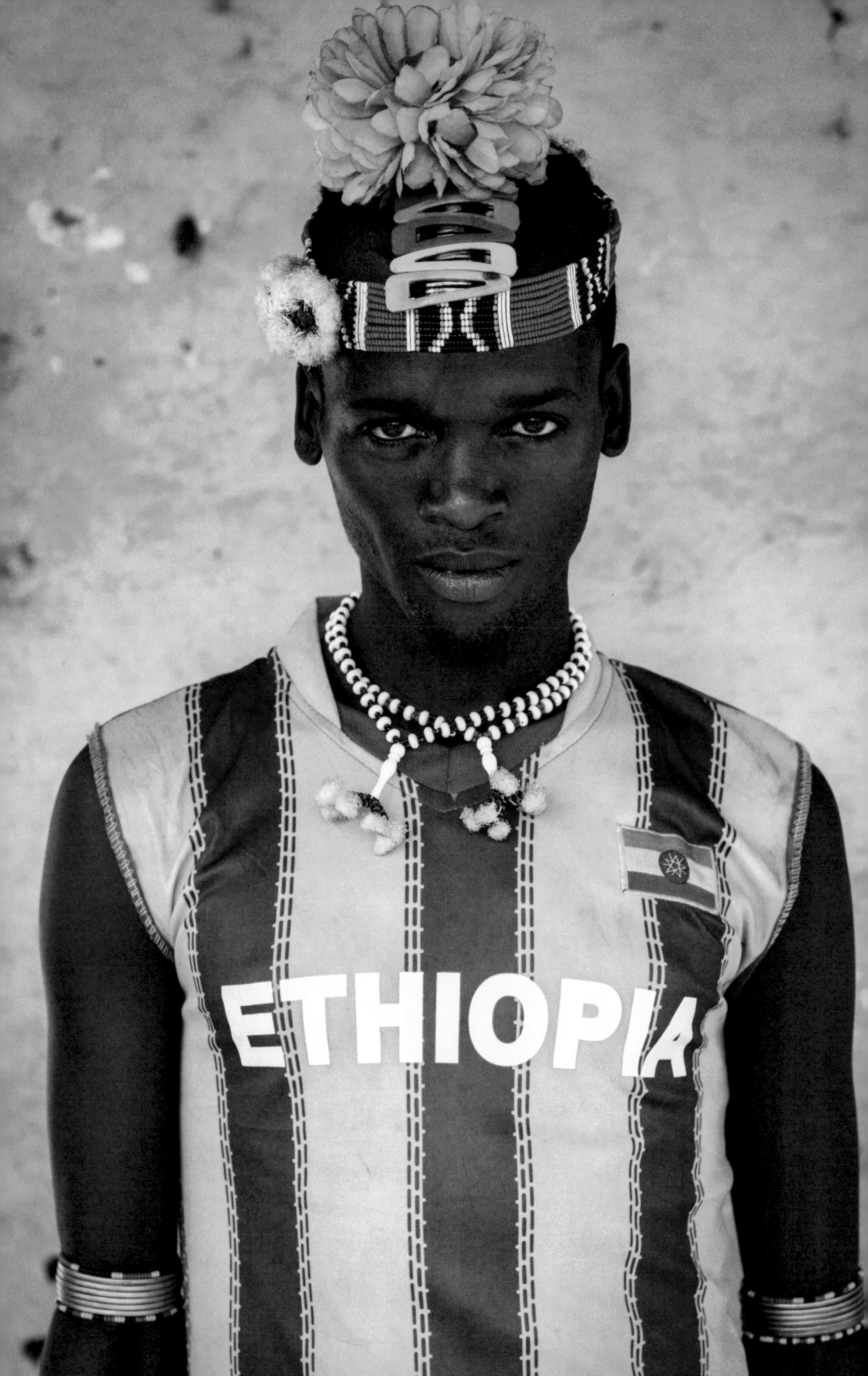
ETHIOPIA

photo Eric Lafforgue – image taken in Ethiopia
photo Duke Quarshie – Ghana

SAMSUN
BARCLAYS

photo Eric Lafforgue – image taken in Ethiopia
art Hassan Hajjaj – Morocco

SAMSUNG

photo Eric Lafforgue – image taken in Benin
photo Kevin Mackintosh *design* Daryl McGregor – South Africa

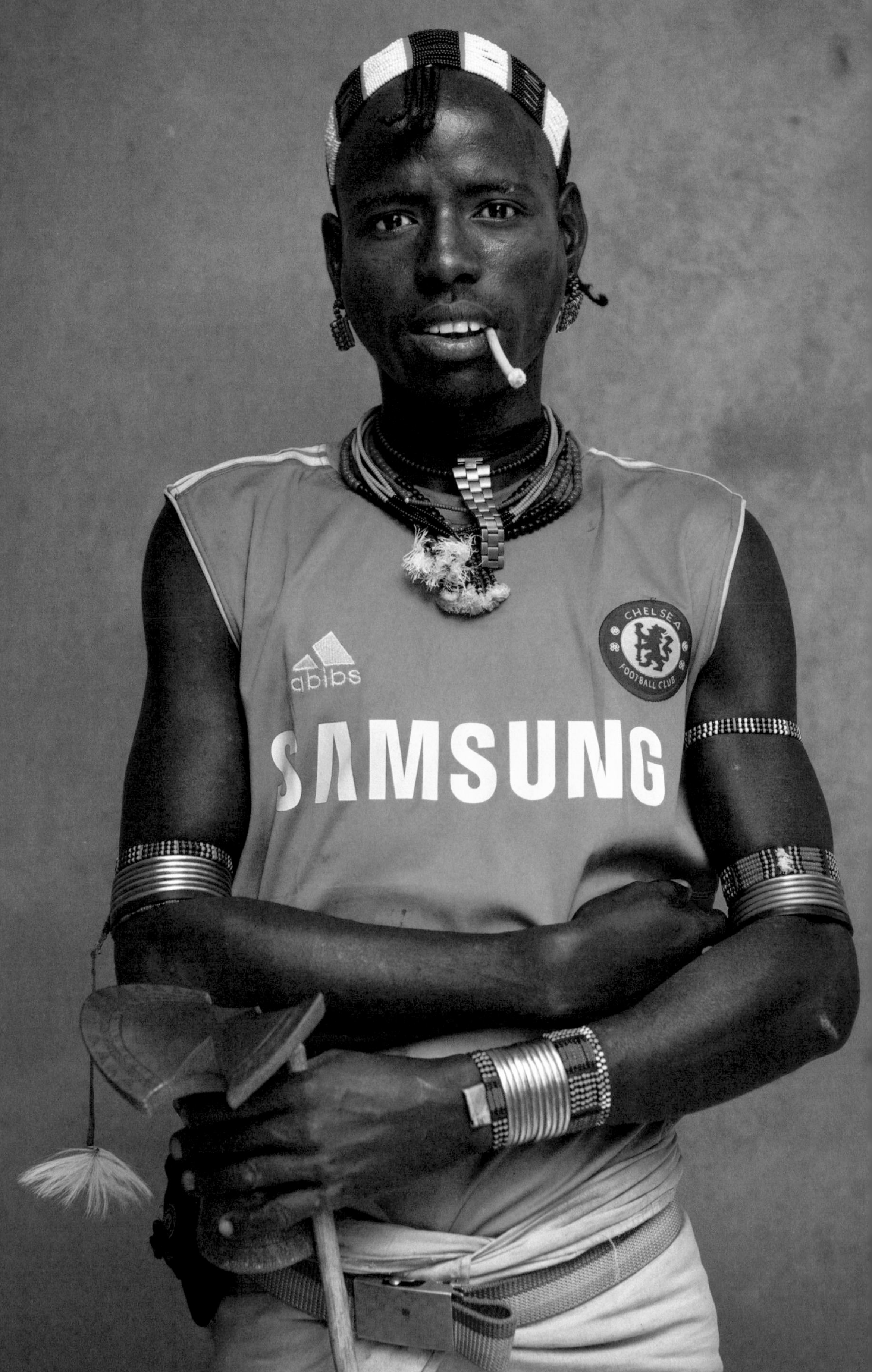
abibs
CHELSEA
FOOTBALL CLUB
SAMSUNG

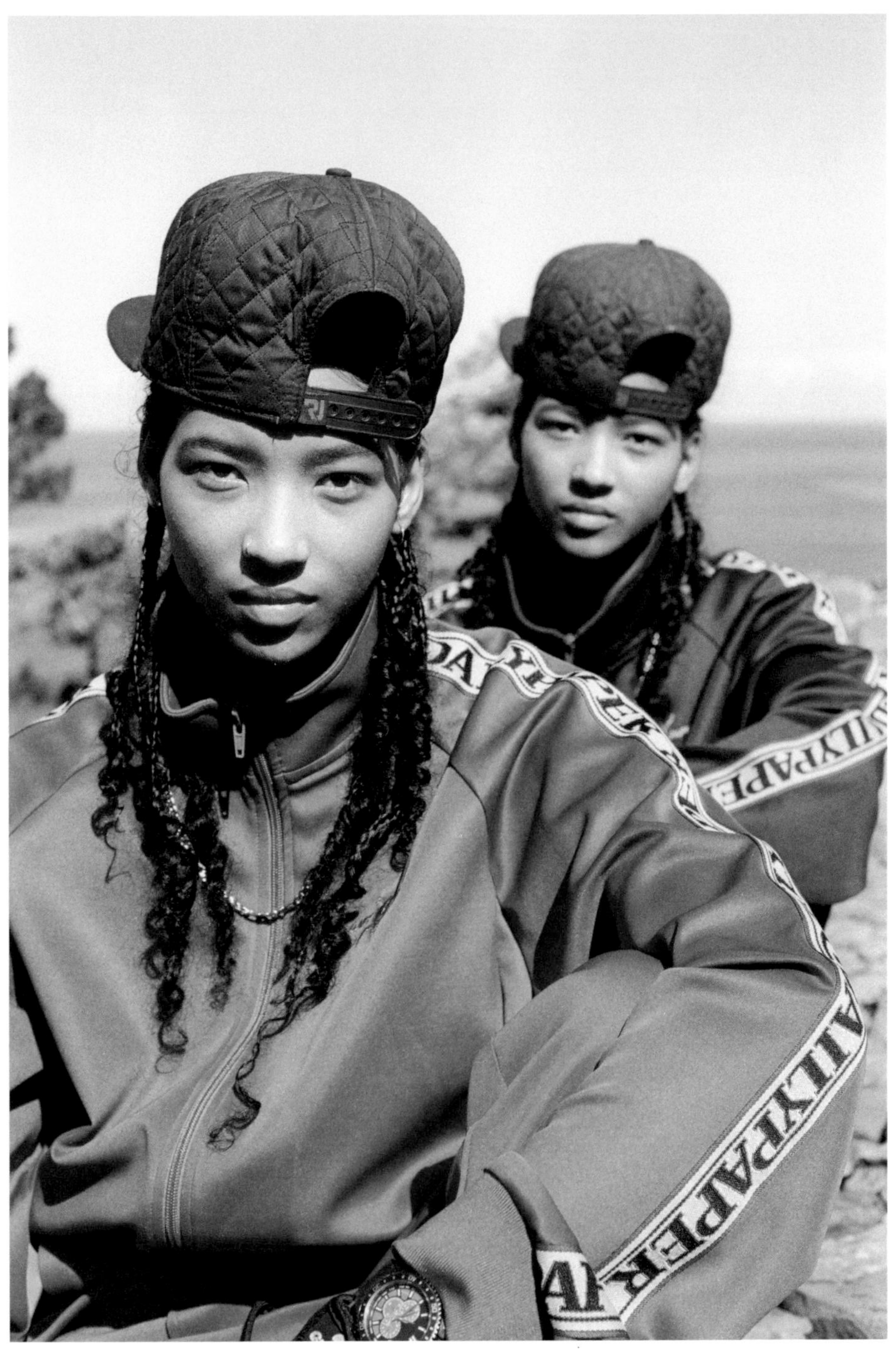

photo Eric Lafforgue – image taken in Ethiopia
photo Haneem Christian *design* Daily Paper – South Africa

PROUD & FAMOUS

Initially invented as a nomadic tool to separate the subject from its background, the animal from its environment and the tree from its landscape, the idea of photos enfolding people in cloth resembling their clothes has made pictures throughout the history of photography. Possibly the most famous ones are by Irving Penn with his series of portraits made in Cuzco, where the *Man with Burlap Sack* sits in front of an unruly burlap textile used as backdrop. But when Seydou Keïta brings the patterned boubou background into his frame the device becomes a norm of greatness and the echo of his irresistible work becomes a school. His legacy is enormous and the effects infectious, the recipe gets reinvented and reincarnated with great vision and personal forms of citation. From loosely recalling the African master to making the images as thrillingly perfected and as intricate as a geometric Escher. The backdrop can be a carpet or a curtain, as long as the colours are in an animated dialogue with each other. Sometimes the pattern takes over and descends from its background to become a contemporary product, flip-flopping the now famous rules. *L.E.*

art Leonce Raphael Agbodjelou / Jack Bell Gallery – Benin

photo & art direction Marianne Marplondon – UK

art Hassan Hajjaj – Morocco

art Cecilia Paredes – Peru
photo Rogério Cavalcanti *design* João Pimenta – Brazil

art Omar Victor Diop – Senegal
art Hassan Hajjaj / Zezo – Morocco

photo João Bertholini *design* Isaac Silva / Havaianas – Brazil

art Omar Victor Diop – Senegal

art Thandiwe Muriu – Kenya

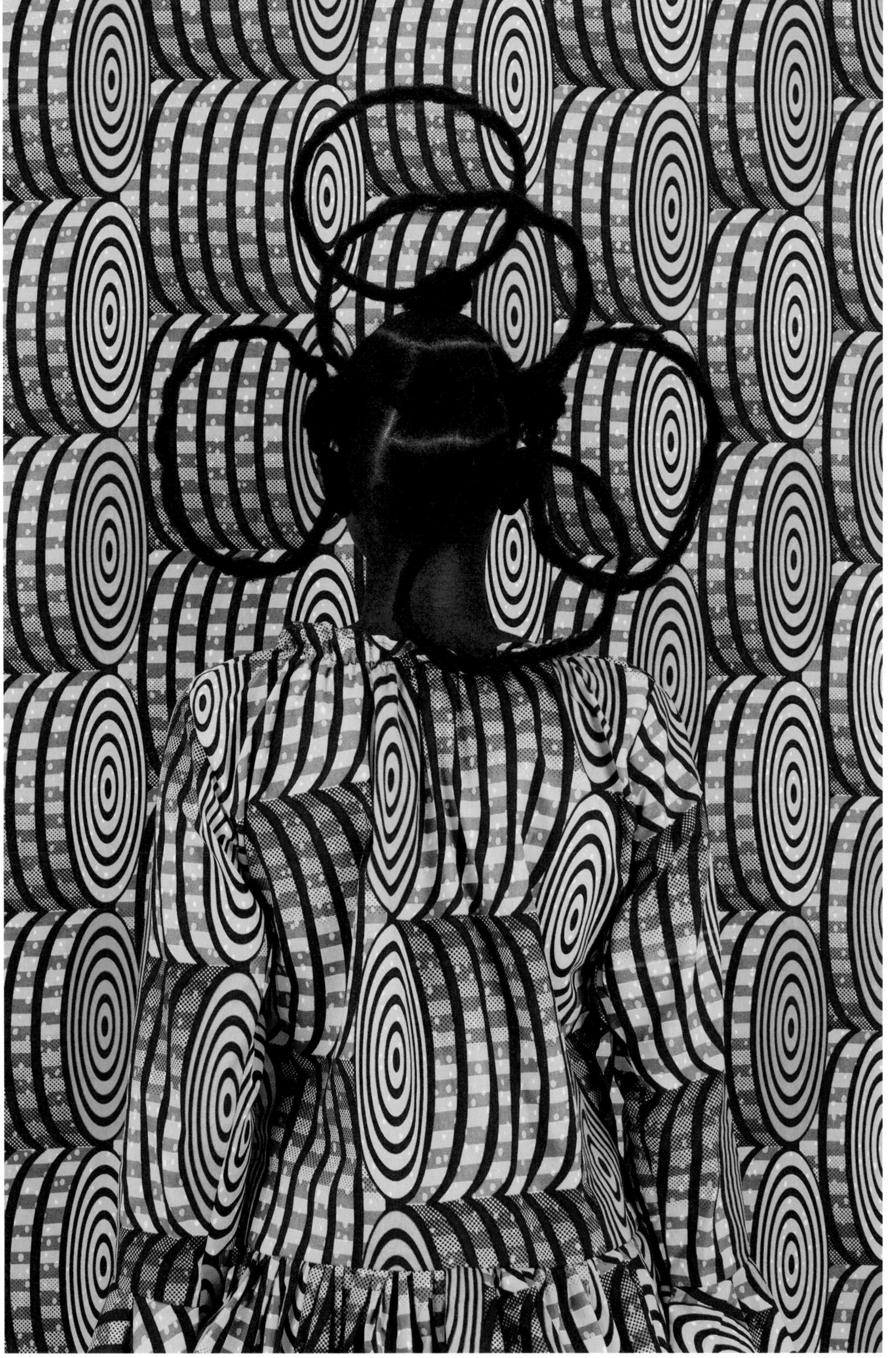

LUMINOUS SOUTH

by Keith Recker

introduction

Through the lens of words, sculptor Richard Serra's 1967-68 text-piece *Verb List* explores his options for acting upon his materials. *To roll, to crease, to fold*, he begins. Passing through a total of 108 verbs *(...to mark, to expand, to dilute, to light...)* he finishes with *to continue*, leaving the door ever-open to inventive exploration of the substances we engage with every day.

The touchpoint between humankind and colour often seems to work in exactly the opposite way. Colour works on *us*, not the other way around. It digs into us, it opens our emotions, it floods us with sensation. It encircles us with meaning, it lifts our experience, and grounds us with its unique gravity. It fires our emotions. It distills and expresses facets of identity in ways both physical and metaphysical. We are colour's raw material.

Our very selves are what it makes with us, no matter where we come from. No matter who our foremothers might be. No matter where we've been or where we think we're going. Colour speeds along the optic nerve, driving information from the outside world deep into the frontal cortex where it reverberates in all the ways human brains are capable of. We soar with the yellows of sunlight, and the brazen blues of noonday skies. We soften with the celadons and indigos of water. We burn hot with ember reds, and warm ourselves gently with translucent apricot flames. We rest in the dark green shade of trees.

What we experience in and with our bodies entwines with our thirsty, adaptive imaginations to spin threads of association, of poetry, of symbolism. From its deep position within us, colour becomes a language we speak without words, in vocabularies that vary not only from culture to culture, but to some degree from individual to individual.

The radiant colour languages of our world draw us into conversations and quips, manifestos and myths, homilies, songs, and fairy tales. Because the thousands of cultures gathered under the rubric of the *global south* each express a discrete u niverse of meaning unto themselves, each has its own lexicon of colour. In their distinctness, they have much to show us about the myriad ways colour operates upon us all. In their overlaps and synergies with each other and with their far-flung global neighbours, they state and restate the human story. It is time to become fully fluent in all the mother-tongues of colour so that we can allow it to broaden and deepen its work within us, ever-fresh and ever-ingenious. So that we can better see each other.

to speak, to proclaim, to identify

Full-throated colour asserts itself, standing proud and speaking loudly. By announcing ownership of the most outspoken zones of the spectrum, textile traditions like West African batik fearlessly command our attention. For the last two centuries or so, the bold patterns of wax fabrics have expressed themselves in complex combinations of saturated tones, often punctuated by jolts of acid green or hot red-orange and structured by outlines of black or deep indigo.

Drawing upon its roots in an earlier age of intercontinental commerce between Africa, Asia and Europe, West African batik continues to reinvent itself. Some printed designs reappropriate important woven traditions like Kente cloth and its golden yellow messages of princely power and authority. Others proclaim individual wealth and status with depictions of cellphones and airplanes bound for faraway destinations. Still other patterns identify personal details: a bird escaping from a cage, for example, tells the story of flying free from a troubled love. In other words: *It's complicated.*

In knits, creatives like South African designer Laduma Ngxokolo juxtapose earthier tones against resolute brights to deliver messages about Xhosa culture — and to breathe life into modern clothing designs with meaning and a sense of identity. Based in traditions surrounding young men's initiation into adulthood, Ngxokolo's work also channels some of the communicative energy of local women's beading motifs, which often telegraph messages about not only their wearer's status but also her feelings.

to heal, to strengthen, to nourish

The oldest gods, male and female, established life on earth out of sheer imagination and will. In the creation story of Australia's indigenous peoples, Mother Sun's first steps on the bare earth bring forth plants and flowers. The Mandé people of Mali and neighbouring countries describe how the progenitor of all, Mangala, creates a series of seeds that develop into the world, the directions, the winds, and eventually people.

Dark, fertile earth tones and the dry grassy greens and dusty serpentines of nourishing plants express our innate appreciation of the building blocks of life on Earth with an essential and broadly spoken language of colour. Ancient Egyptians acknowledged the dark silt of the banks of the Nile as the nourishing, life-giving foundation of green crops and healthy foods. For the ancient Maya of Central America, jade strengthened its wearers with a link between life on this plane and the next. In Haiti, Gran Bois, a deity in the Vodou pantheon who hides deep in the green woods, is sought after spiritually for his knowledge of natural healing substances. The magic of green promises to sprout within us and bring us a renewed sense of life.

to shelter, to shade, to protect

We cannot always strive. Our bodies cannot always take the full heat of day or the harsh winds of the storm. We need the hushed, purpled shadows of shelter to survive. But we need more than protection from the elements because we are more than our bodies: our souls need shade, too.

Running unseen beneath the distinctions of family and clan, country, and position, beyond relationships and obligations, we are merely, tenderly human. We are personal and intimate and individual. Fragile. Parched for refreshment and renewal. Sometimes we need to withdraw to the dappled green of a forest hideout and cloak ourselves in dark patterns of leaf and shadow to breathe easy once again in the rhythms of nature.

COLOUR DIGS INTO US,
IT OPENS OUR EMOTIONS, IT
FLOODS US WITH SENSATION.
IT ENCIRCLES US WITH
MEANING, IT LIFTS OUR
EXPERIENCE, AND GROUNDS
US WITH ITS UNIQUE GRAVITY.
IT FIRES OUR EMOTIONS.
IT DISTILLS AND EXPRESSES
FACETS OF IDENTITY IN
WAYS BOTH PHYSICAL
AND METAPHYSICAL. WE ARE
COLOUR'S RAW MATERIAL.

When we re-emerge, can the nut-browns of tannin-rich mudcloth made to camouflage hunters render us invisible as we walk the paths required of us? Or will it be the deepest shades of indigo that cool and preserve us? Can the healing talismans and charms attached to West African hunting tunics protect us from the world? Can the tarnished silver amulets of Tuareg folk medicine, etched with spells and symbols, coax us towards healing? Can tiny, tarnished bells and chimes scatter the bad spirits that sometimes lurk in the distant corners of our minds?

to share, to remember, to fulfill

In the cocoon of home, in the private space where the inner self can let go, we can be vulnerable. We can relax into the soft blues, faded pinks, and off-whites of vintage findings. Much-laundered Kantha patchworks, made in Bengal of bits of used saris and held together by fields of running stitch, wrap us not just in tender, supple fabric, but also in memories of who wore the cloth before, and what satisfactions and cares they experienced.

A subtle patina of use mellows the colours of cross-stitched flowers embroidered long ago with skills known today by relatively few. In these blooms, we glimpse the imagined gardens of earlier generations. Perhaps we trim them with old crochet techniques like the ones mastered by the women of Bamako's Cooperative Djiguiayasou, where soft African cotton yarns are turned into trims and pom fringes. Or we join them with swaths of Richelieu lace painstakingly handmade in the beautiful hills above Jacmel, Haiti, by women whose great-great-great grandmothers passed their immaculate craft down to the daughters who still wear lace on special occasions.

In the spontaneous, creative recombining of heritage textiles, we assemble their intimate memories into fulfilling ways of being and sharing ourselves.

to dream, to explore, to wonder

In the Sierra Madre mountains of Southwestern Mexico, the Huichol people's ritual Dance of the Deer caresses humankind's wishes into the skin of loving Mother Earth. Then the ceremony deepens with Grandfather Fire, who, sometimes with the help of peyote, illuminates the exploration of the dark spirit world where everything we know transforms in shifting and expanding geometric patterns and glowing sparks. What the inner eye dreams is more alive than life itself, and hallucinogenic gradations of turquoise and cobalt form shimmering contrasts with waves of reds and red-oranges. Huichol yarn-paintings and bead-covered objects channel some of this journey into the waking world. They remind us to treasure the shared, interconnected energy inherent in all things.

Just as the shaman connects humankind to other worlds, the Huichol artist describes and documents the imagined and the experienced, asking us to wonder whether augmented reality is new, or whether it has always been with us in some form. Makers of beaded Vodou flags and cotton appliqué Yoruba banners do the same within the symbol-systems of their spiritual traditions. Peru's Shipibo-Conibo people trace the lines of energy running between all living things onto their textiles and clay pots. When the spirit-world is so strongly expressed, is there anything left to design?

to beautify, to adorn, to glow

Archaeologists tell us that the oldest tool for beautifying face and body was very likely red ochre. Our distant forebears probably dusted and painted red onto skin so that bodies glowed with the symbolic fire of life. Some ancient peoples added thick layers of pure red ochre to graves, where earthy reds again deliver the heat of the lifeblood of humanity. The pulse of red ochre beats its primeval rhythm in Neolithic statuettes like the Woman of Willendorf: its limestone was covered in deep red earth pigment over 20,000 years ago. Red's revered link to fertility and the unfathomable mysteries of conception and birth still warms us with its energy.

Today, Himba women of Namibia apply red ochre to hair and skin as the ultimate mark of beauty and femininity. Red is also very much a colour of love and celebration in South Asian weddings, shedding an auspicious glow on everyone involved.

Gold plays a role here, too. Its untarnished glow adds luminosity and reflection to the body. Building from gold's many messages of luxury and beauty (along with some less admirable impulses), jewelry announces prestige, demonstrates wealth, and in some cases signifies that the wearer is adored, putting them a step closer to ancient deities of Egypt and India whose flesh was said to be made of the rare, yellow stuff.

Flowers are also ancient adornments, though how ancient we cannot know. Their fleeting beauty leaves behind few traces for archaeologists to read. But the tender white jasmine blossoms entwined in the long braids of women in India spring from millennia-old traditions, as do crowns of pink dahlias and orange marigolds in Central America, and a full spectrum of blossoms, leaves, fruits, and grasses used by the Surma people of southwest Ethiopia's Omo Valley. Their colours speak to the beauty of the present moment, here only for a vivid instant.

to celebrate, to enjoy, to delight

Holi, India's springtime festival of love and good's triumph over evil is celebrated by an explosion of joyous colour. Pigments of every hue are thrown about in streets and public spaces, happily colouring the clothes, skin, and hair of celebrants of this holiday. This spontaneous layering of colour, free of the boundaries of composition or design, anticipates the exuberant spring reflowering of the natural world. Traditionally, people aren't the only creatures to get the colourful treatment: elephants are painted in vibrant flower-patterns on the eve of the festival. Garlands of orange marigolds and red hibiscus flowers also lend their delights.

The link between colour and spring flowers runs deeply and sensually within us: pistils, stamens, buds, and panicles subliminally remind us of our own erogenous zones, and our own fertility. Ancient Minoans revered the early-flowering wild crocus as a springtime symbol of the potent return of fertility to the earth. Their saffron-bearing stamens were highly valued as a dye and a spice... and also as an aphrodisiac whose fragrance and exhilarating yellow-orange colour delight body and soul with the deep energies of earth.

to divert, to subvert, to redefine

In an echo of Sigmund Freud's observations about humour and the subconscious, colour often plays a role in the juggling and re-ordering of points of psychic tension to divert and amuse us. Sometimes a bright flowered tunic cut from the kitsch material usually seen in tablecloths at roadside taquerias provokes a smile, as an invitation to pull up a chair and have a beer with a stranger disarmingly decked out in 1950s brights.

Sometimes a little fun is had with more serious matters. Economic and class divisions are poked fun at when the utilitarian faux raffia usually seen in weary red, white, and blue tote bags democratizes a flowing, well-crafted formal garment: nudged to reconsider the rules, luxury benefits from this finger in its eye. Similarly, a flowery women's headscarf tied demurely under the chin of a man slyly revises ideas of masculinity with sardonic jewel tones, just as a felted brown fedora on a powerful woman's head asserts a new sense of authority. Here, the sly immediacy with which colour can convey its meaning helps us work these reconsiderations into our very being. Colour is one of the ways change makes itself tangible and visible.

A stealthy deployment of the vocabularies of colour has the element of surprise in its favour: workaday colours conceal the message until the time to reveal it has arrived. Subversive brights, on the other hand, forthrightly declare a no-shame zone for re-defined identities and passions of all sorts. The rainbow is, happily and wonderfully, yoked to new purposes.

to heat, to ignite, to warn

When change goes too slowly, when we feel overlooked or squashed, our feelings cannot be contained forever. We boil over in heated floes of cyan and hot pink: raw colours telegraph the jagged nerves of prolonged frustration. Orange plays an important role here, too. In Incan symbology, orange, like ordinary people, is sandwiched between the golden yellow of divinity and the red of royal authority. In its brightest tones, orange ignites with the pressures of negotiating a passage between gods and kings, like a deeply human revolution worn on our sleeves for all to see.

Venomous reds and poison greens also telegraph danger and frustration. Combined with other super-brights in insect motifs, snakeskin patterns, or in unnatural depictions of natural elements, these colours have the eccentric strength to signal a rejection of the status quo. Their strange neon hues proclaim a personal sort of autonomy, lighting a very individual path forward — one that is freshly invented with every step taken.

to tempt, to seduce, to touch

Not every feeling is best expressed in a loud voice. We may need to whisper about love, particularly when it tempts us to cast aside tradition. Our lives online are weakening already weak old barriers, allowing for attraction and passion to spark beyond the old fault lines of family, society, marriage, and religion. The old ways may need to be sidestepped in the name of desire. In-between, yet-to-be-named colours are conjured up to allow 21st century lovers to establish a private space where new relationships can be forged on their own terms: onscreen courtships, new gender expressions and sexualities, new equalities between partners, new life paths that look little like those previously forged by parents and grandparents. What we need are seductive, original tones of smoked turquoise, dark berry, shadowy orchid, pearl gray, madder pink and peachstone… all iterations of the careful, tender, nuanced shades that flourish at the intimate, private edges of consciousness.

to gather, to include, to belong

Colour can signal belonging, as in the 2005 flag of newly independent South Sudan, where black represents its long-oppressed people. Among the Maasai of Kenya, red is the colour of community, a marker of shared identity. Colour is equally capable of dividing us, however. In Cambodia during the Pol Pot era, for example, a red-checked *krama* indicated alliance with the regime in power, while green checks were placed around the necks of traitors. As identities and senses of belonging shift and change, as they have done throughout human history, colours are deployed in fresh, untested ways. Clan colours and heritage crafts live side by side with the saturated, high-contrast hues of beloved sports teams or international brands. Logo-ed swag is deployed alongside traditional tailoring with recombinant, hyper-original genius. A techno green football jersey worn adjacent to traditional beaded jewellery in red, white, and black energizes both with new relevance, and gathers aspects of the past into the space of the present. The ubiquitous indigos of denim telegraph a broad message of shared habits, electrified by a sense of openness and inclusion. Everyone has access to the symbol systems of sport, commerce, and online life. All they have to do is want to join in.

to ennoble, to sanctify, to elevate

Leaders, kings, queens, and presidents, north and south alike, are ennobled by red's ancient associations with authority. The traditional monarchs of Nigeria, for example, express their symbolic power in elaborate robes of red, intensified with strands of massive red coral beads. Red is also a sanctifying colour with its sacred references to purifying fire, the deities of destruction and creation, the blood of martyrs, and the lifeforce which fuels humankind and animal alike. Gold as a signifier of status is never far from these dialogues about heavenly and earthly power. Emerald green, amethyst purple, lapis blue, the sheen of pearls, and the sunlight of citrine also elevate both the mighty and the holy.

Whether laden with jewels and gold or draped in hand-worked tapestries of beads and sequins, the chosen few are splendid indeed. We can hardly look away from the magnificent drama of India's ancient *theyyam* celebrations, where low caste performers wrap themselves in elaborate red costumes to personify the most powerful gods. Similarly, ceremonies of the West African Yoruba religion and its close sibling, Haitian Vodou, use intense languages of colour and shine to present the gods here on this earthly plane so that they might be seen and experienced by those who wish to know them.

to mourn, to contemplate, to continue

Lomassa, Mali's Bamana name for darkest blue-black shade of indigo, means *divine blue* — a reminder of the powerful darkness from which we come, and to which we will return. Its interstellar depth launches us into soulful contemplation about aspects of the human soul that can never be fully articulated. Whether we find comfort or unease in its presence depends on our own intuitions and suspicions about the nature of eternity.

If we suspect that our being is merely material, whitened bone serves as a sort of *memento mori*, as evidence that what we leave behind is lifeless. Even worthless. We wrap ourselves in the black of mourning in the face of this dark thought.

However, if, supported only by faith and poetry, we feel that what is most important about us lives on after death, absolute black can suggest the vast and perfect potential of the original void, out of which the first gods and goddesses crafted the world. Our species has been trying to describe this moment of creation forever. We draw with charcoal, paint with lampblack, write with ink, dye with logwood. The flares of dark emotion that flicker across the flame-kissed surfaces of raku vessels speak in their own way to the mysteries of life and death, trying to trace the difference between what is blessed by fire and what is destroyed by it.

This is the black of magic and of power, the black of priestesses and shamans who plumb the depths of the time before time. For answers. For miracles. For a way to continue.

PROUD & COLOUR

◇◇◇◇◇◇◇◇◇◇◇◇◇◇

Just as the word photography encapsulates the ancient Greek terms for drawing and light, we can describe the impact of light on colours that are illuminated by the sun, desert and river, jumping into the photographic frame with a ray of yellow or a bolt of blue, a zest of orange or a shudder of red. Otherworldly colours that are packed with visual energy, expressing a sense of exaltation and underscoring the excess of the garments' volumes: these pigments seem to be designed to billow in monumental shapes. An impossibly blue sky forms a backdrop of deep colour that cannot be found in the northern hemisphere. Such vividness can only be conceived and cultivated within a southern context that embraces bold blooms and recognises spices from birth, smelling and tasting colour as much as observing it. With brightness also comes brown and white as accents to appease and embrace the power of the pigments that dominate creativity and give their striking character to fashion design and photography. *L.E.*

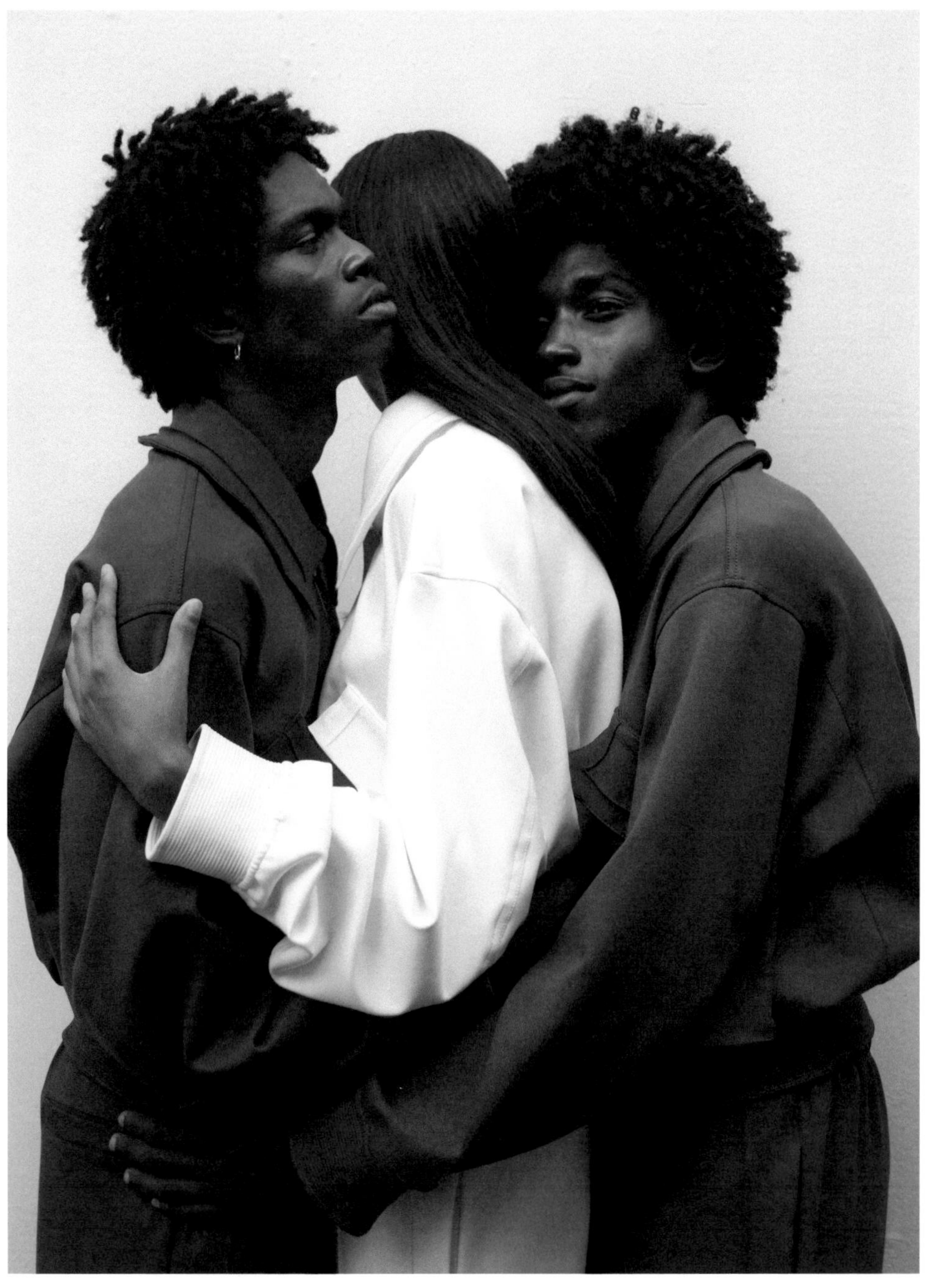

photo Tinko Czetwertynski – image taken in Ethiopia
photo Luca Oliva *design* Misci – Brazil

photo Koto Bolofo *design* Daryl McGregor – South Africa
photo Mous Lambarat – Morocco

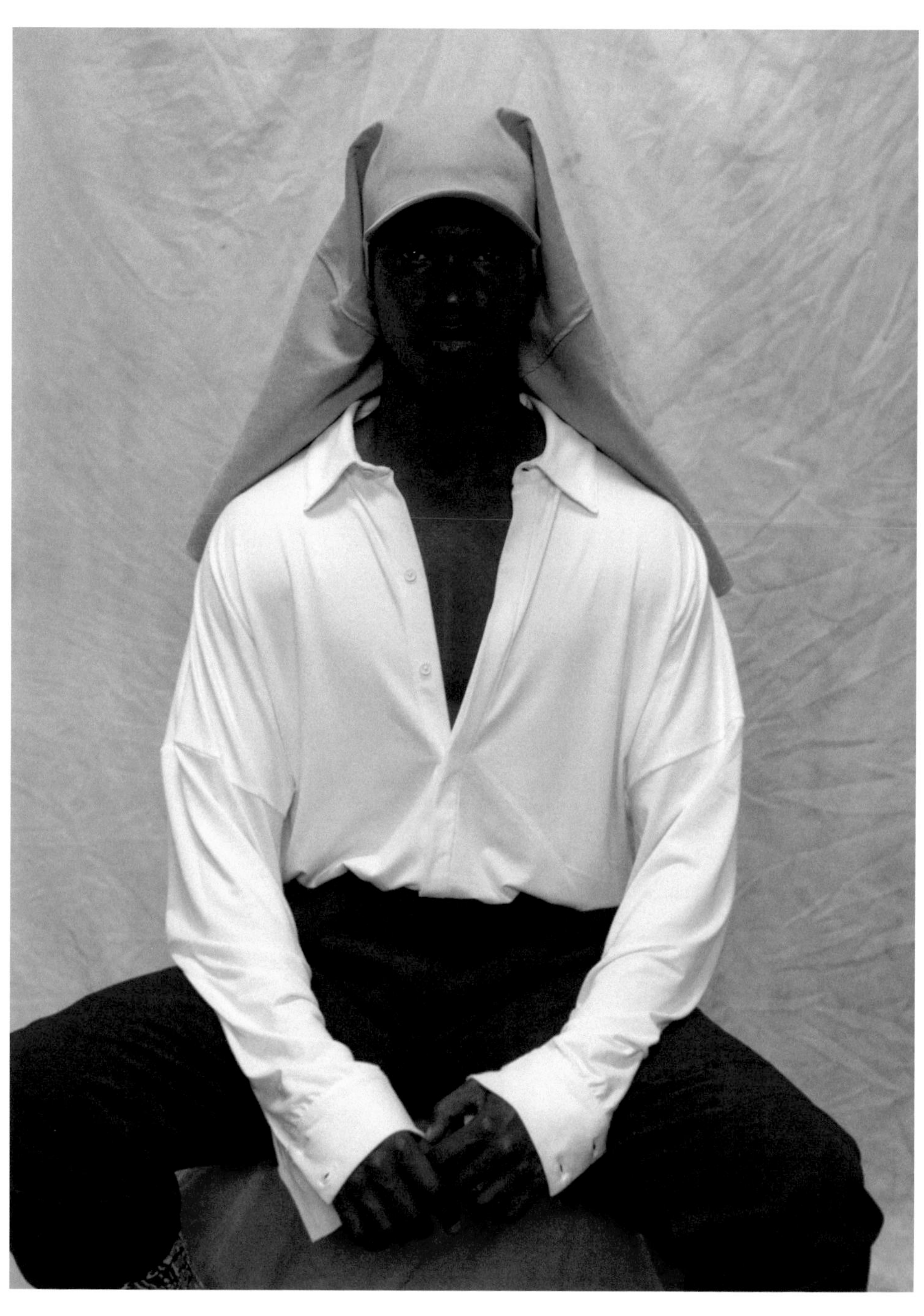

photo Jaime Rubiano *design* Esteban Cortazar – Colombia
photo Gabrielle Kannemeyer *design* Daily Paper – South Africa

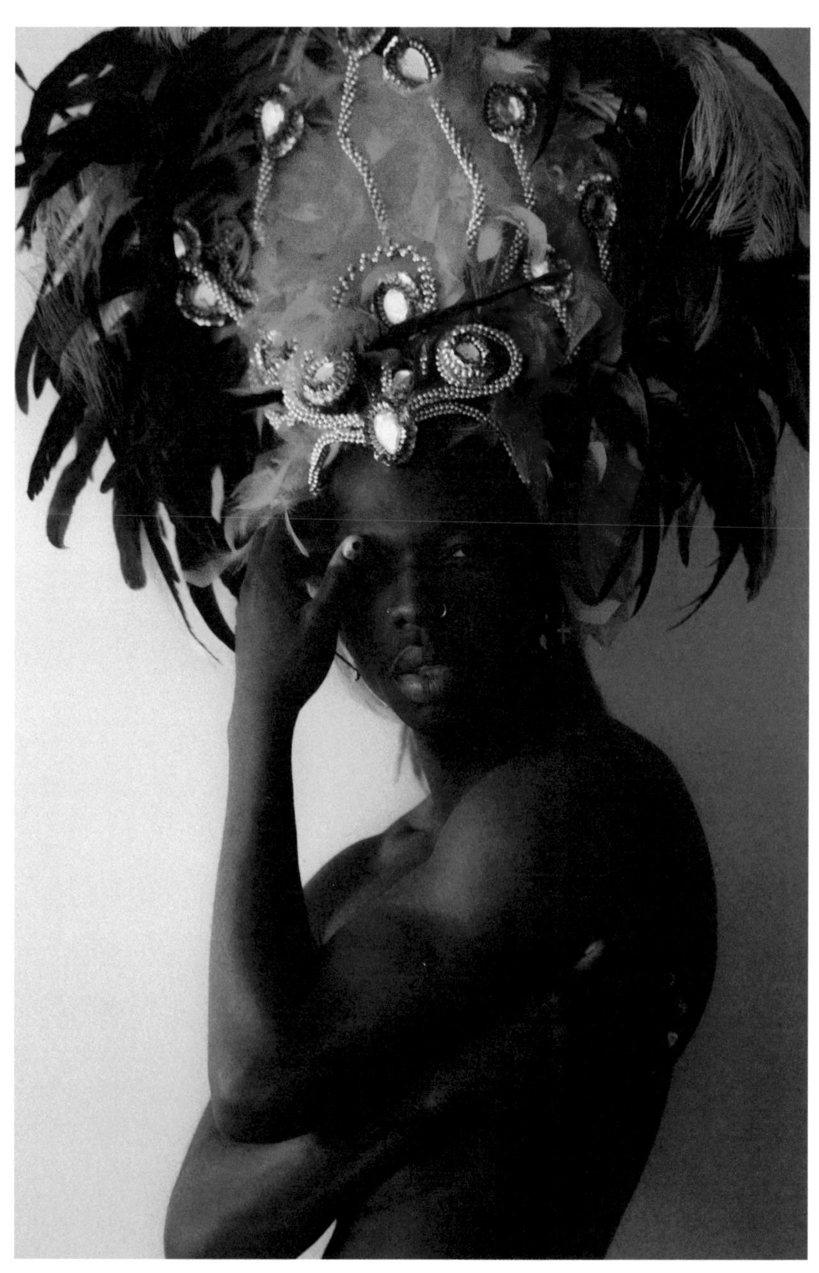

photos Mucio Ricardo *model* Jean Woolmay Denson Pierre – Haiti

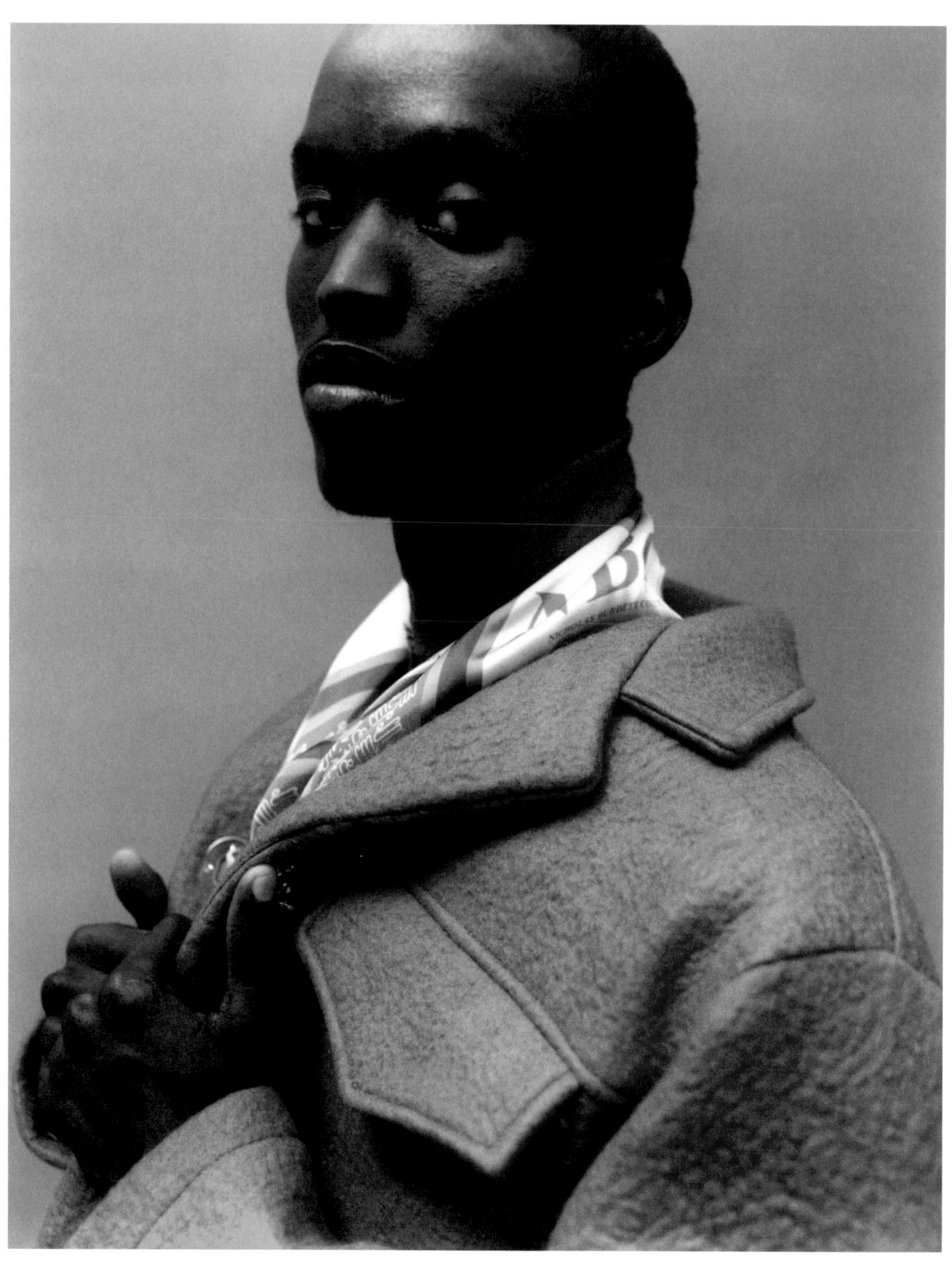

photo Luck Hoube *design* Lukhanyo Mdingi – South Africa
photo Maxim Vakhovskij *design* Fanoraine Dohr – Ukraine

photo Gleeson Paulino *design* Von Trapp – Brazil
photo Naguel Rivero *design* Marco Ribeiro – Brazil

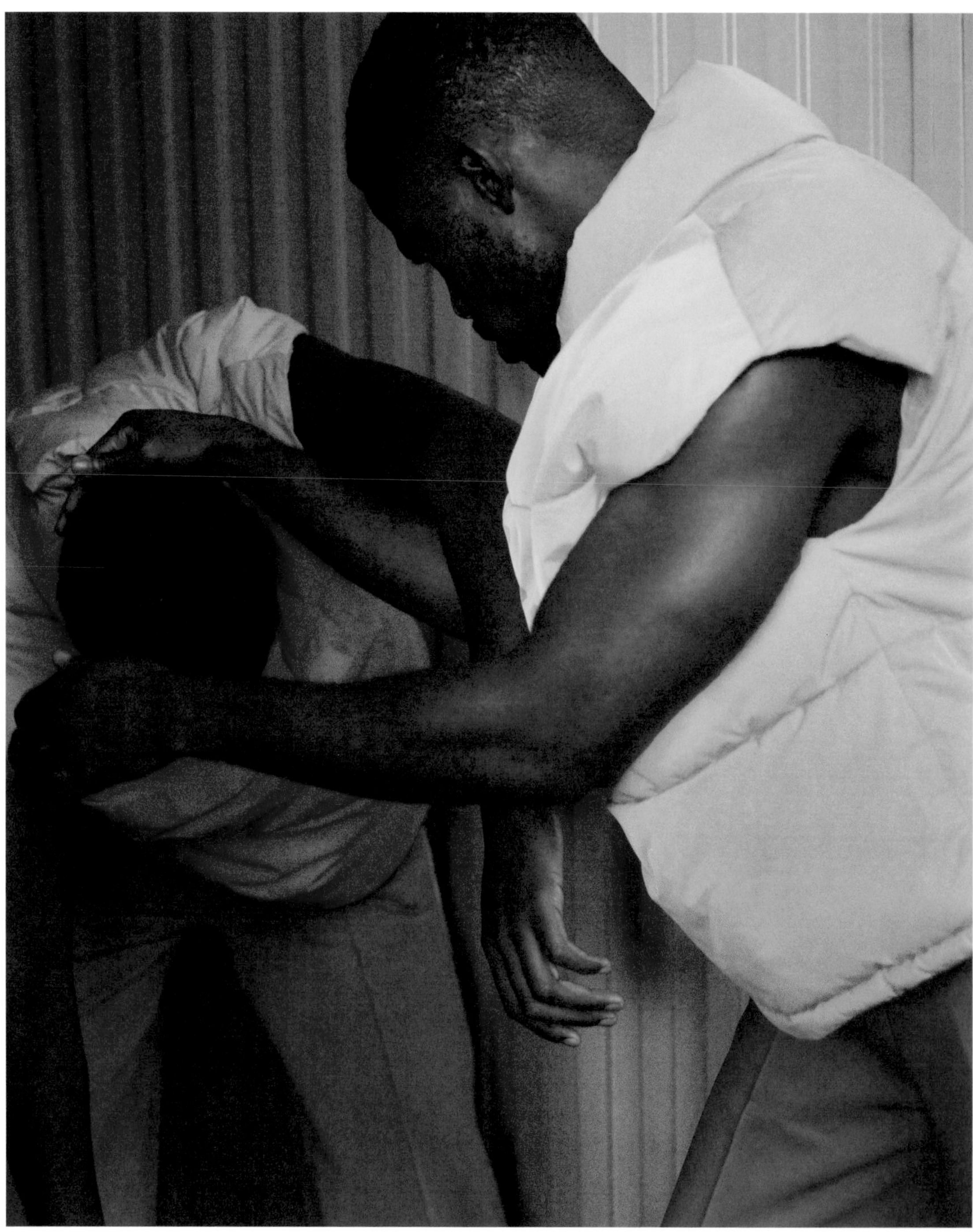

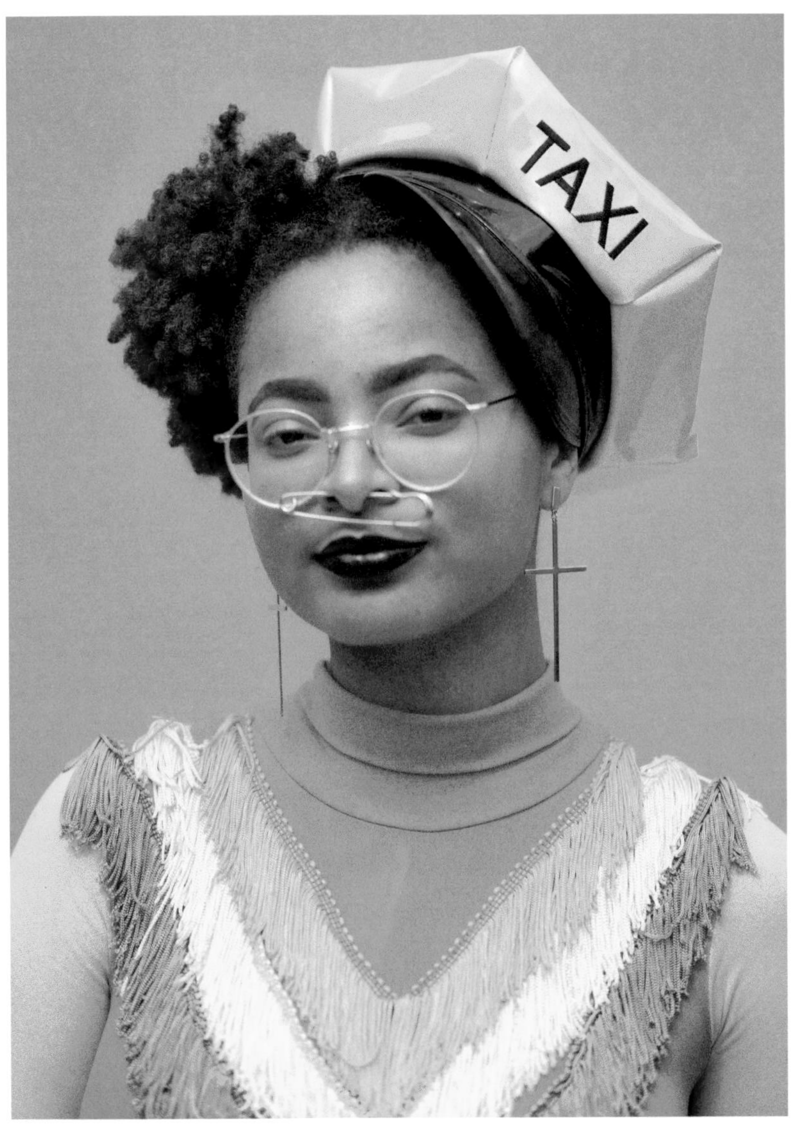

photo Francesco Visone *art direction & styling* Lauro Samblás – Tenerife
photo Leeroy Jason – South Africa

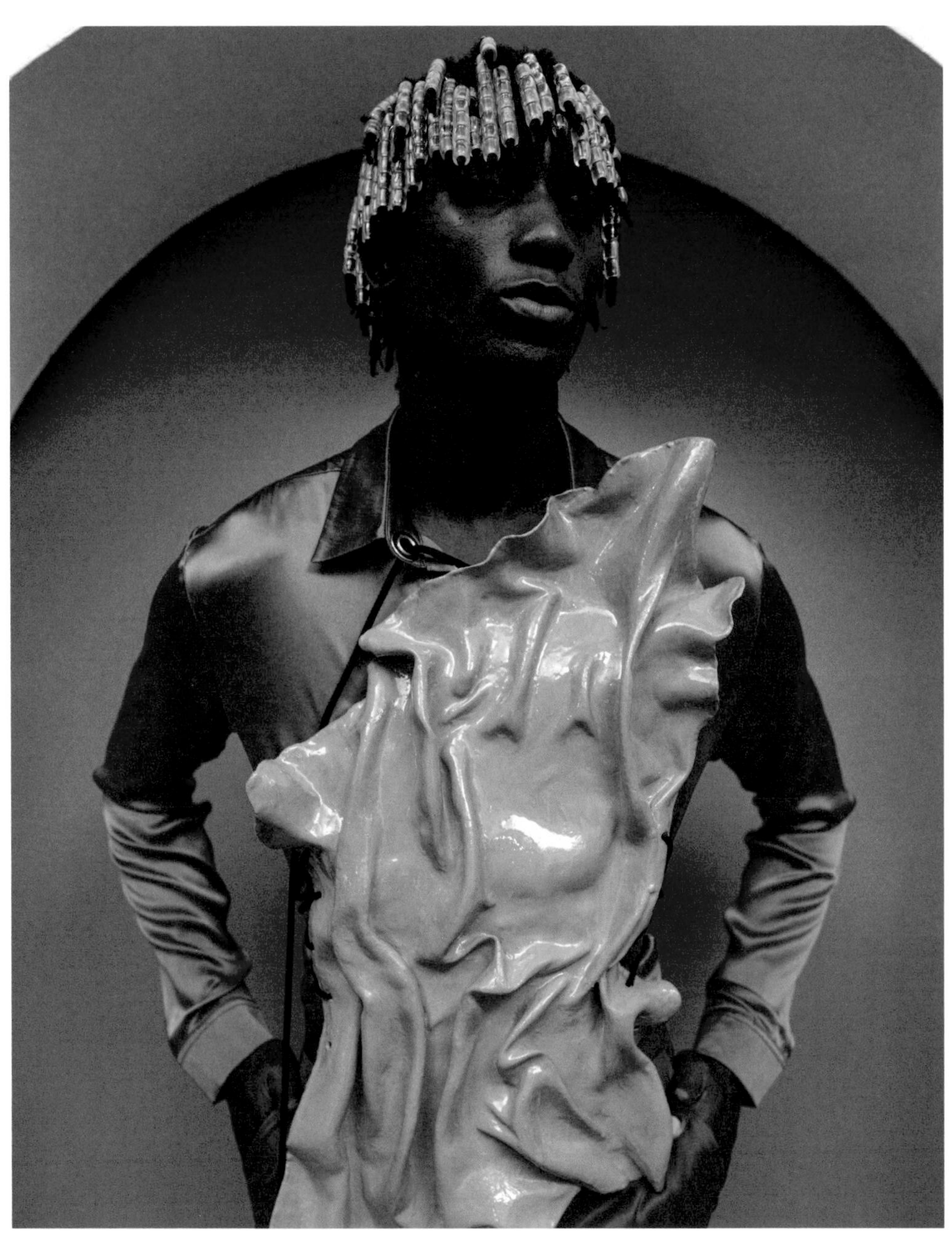

photo Eric Lafforgue – image taken in Papua New Guinea
photo Ricardo Simal *design* Rich Mnisi – South Africa

photo Namsa Leuba – Switzerland / Guinea
photo Gleeson Paulino *design* Von Trapp – Brazil

photos Gleeson Paulino – Brazil

PROUD & DOUBLE

◇◇◇◇◇◇◇◇◇◇◇◇◇◇◇

art by Omar Victor Diop
– Senegal –

One of the most remarkable talents to come out of Dakar is the great Omar Victor Diop. His vivid body of work is invariably interested in diverse cultural currents and his references are masterful and intelligent, taking the subject matter to extremes, layering them with icons from other universes to bring a subtle surreal aspect to the reading of his images. He is a self-taught heir to the great African portraitists and is inspired by the flatness of the colourful tradition of reverse painting on glass. Whether he is referring to the birth of photography, the origins of cinema, or the history of portraiture, he always uses the existing format and turns it around in creative caprioles, leaping from one obsession to another to land on his acrobatic feet, deserving of his accolades. His most fundamental work is the deeply personal series called *Project Diaspora* where he pictures his handsome self in historical clothes, accessories and poses that resemble famous artworks from the 15th to the 19th centuries, depicting heroic figures from the diaspora, exploring the forgotten historical encounters between Africa and the rest of the globe, including traders and diplomats that defied expectations and were educated, stylish and self-confident, outsiders observed by whites as the significant other. This historic context is disturbed with details from the world of football and illustrates how one can be venerated and at the same time isolated simply for being from the south. To break with that strained feeling of isolation, he now photographs himself as a group image, showing solidarity within himself, adding another mantle to the history of self-portraiture. *L.E.*

Portrait of Aquasi Boachi / Bergakademie, Freiberg – Germany

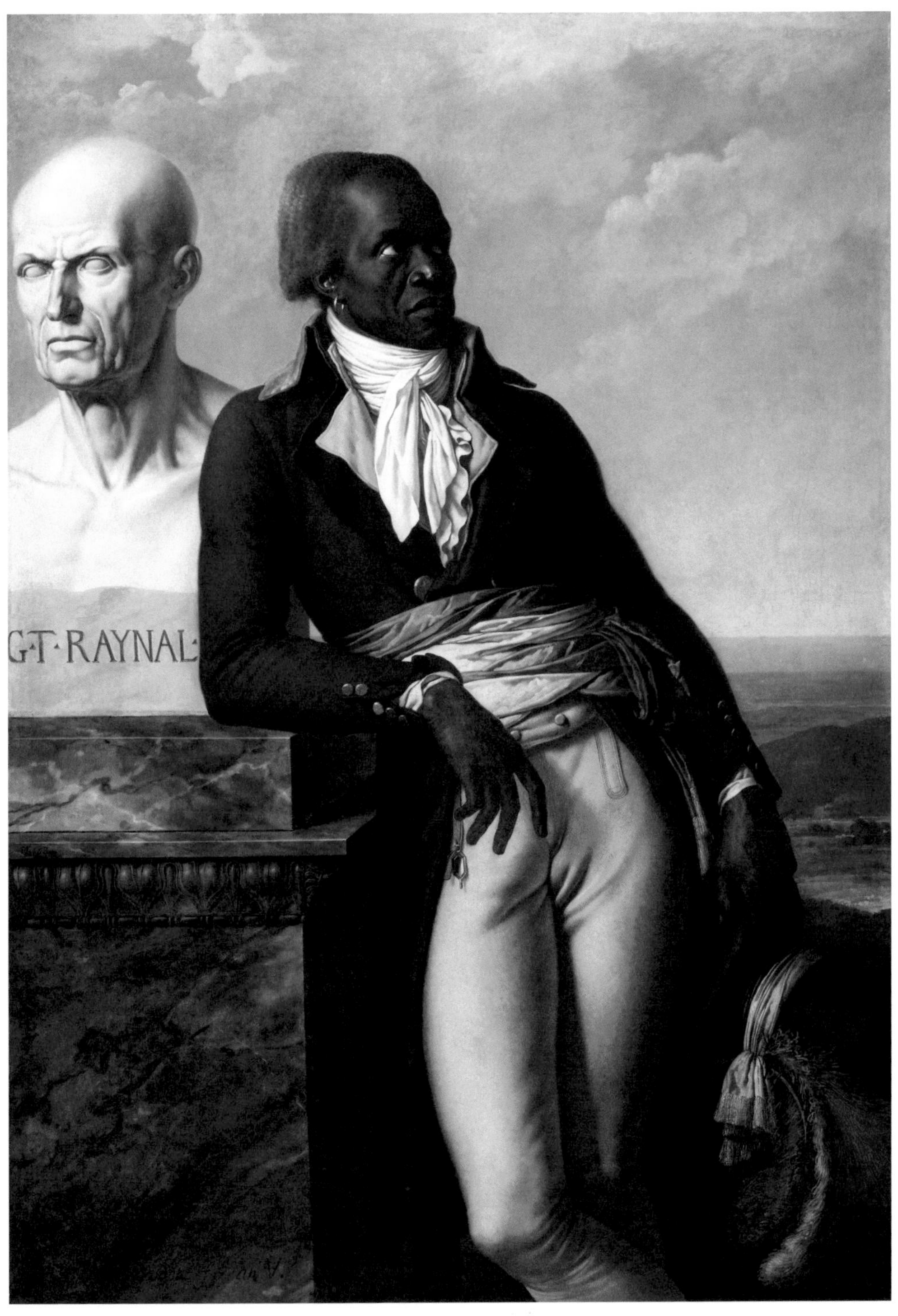

Portrait of Jean-Baptiste Belley / Anne-Louis Girodet
De Roussy-Trioson Château de Versailles – France

PROUD & SOUVENIR

Encouraged by recent reversals of rules and more advanced ways of perception, decolonialisation processes are designing new directions in photography and styling, taking the keys of colonial imagery and reversing them to include the current reflections on the matter. The highly symbolic millstone collar, enwrapping the indolent sitter, shows how clothes would tell tales of ascendancy. The mirror images of the past design a new present state of the southern arts, where symbols of power are replaced by symbols of poverty, where coifs of rulers become cynical turbans and where pristine white collars humorously contrast colourful patterns. At first glance these amazing photographs are just a memory recording beautiful imagery of the past. But! While the poses are regal, the regards royal and the atmosphere filled with pride, the pictures express a deep distress that cannot be hidden and becomes palpable through the symbolic artefacts of harvests and everyday objects. A myriad of pictures will still need to be conceived as part of a healing process, where beauty will be condensed with care. Appeasing the souvenirs of hardship. *L.E.*

photo Koen Hauser *design* Vlisco – the Netherlands

art Tamary Kudita – Zimbabwe

art Omar Victor Diop – Senegal

art Tamary Kudita – Zimbabwe

art Tamary Kudita – Zimbabwe

photo Erdi Doğan *design* Hatice Gökçe – Turkey

art Tamary Kudita – Zimbabwe

photo Arka Patra – India

photo Jamal Nxedlana – South Africa

photo Namsa Leuba – Switzerland / Guinea

photo Trevor Stuurman – South Africa

rt Tamary Kudita – Zimbabwe

art Omar Victor Diop – Senegal

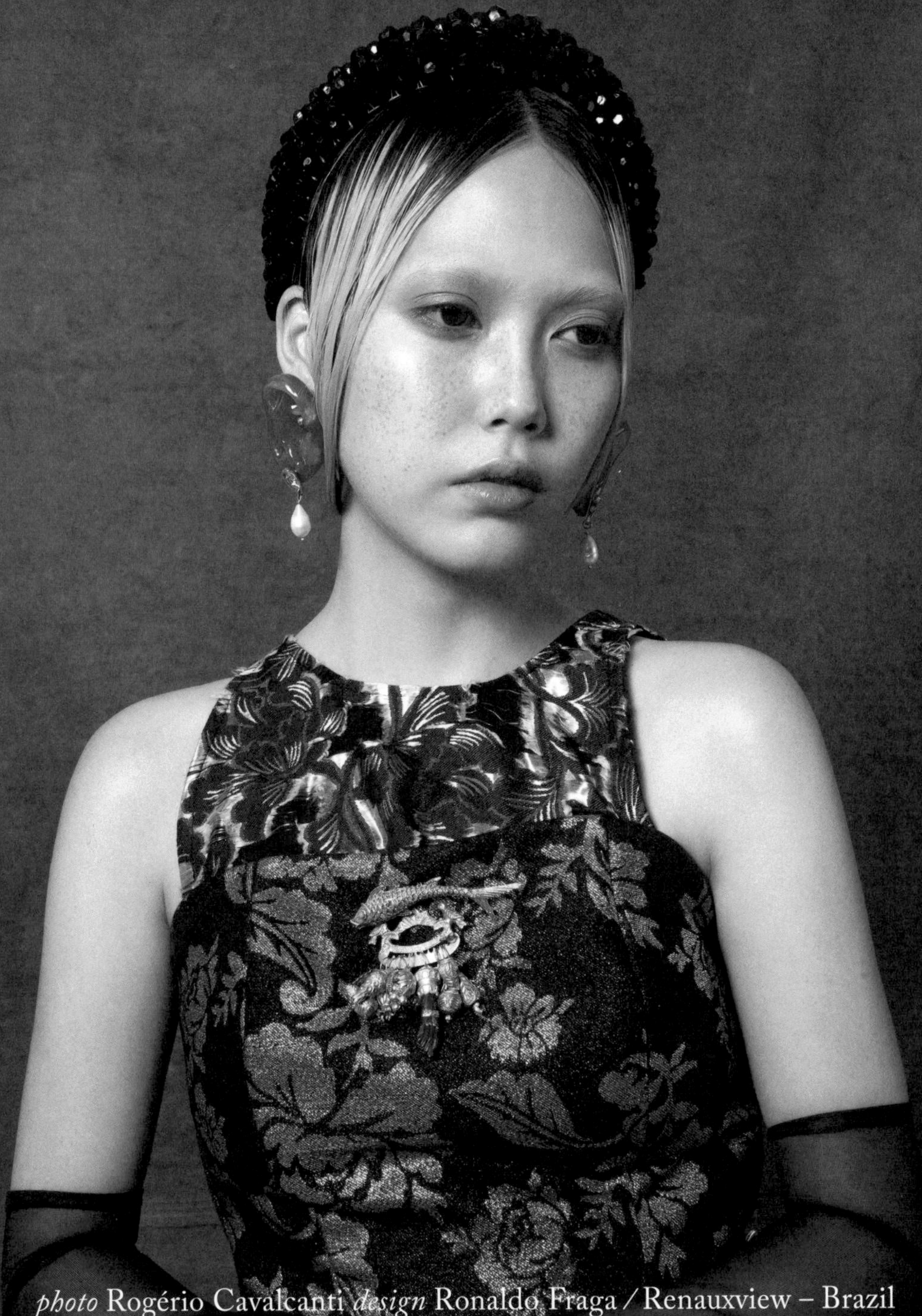

photo Rogério Cavalcanti *design* Ronaldo Fraga / Renauxview – Brazil

photo Tarun Vishwa *design* Sabyasachi – India

photo Erdi Doğan *design* Hatice Gökçe – Turkey

photo Tatenda Chidora *design* Thebe Magugu – South Africa

art Omar Victor Diop – Senegal

PHOTO CREDITS

◇◇◇◇◇◇◇◇◇◇◇◇

FOREWORD

page 02 *photo* Daniel Costa

PROUD & SOUTH

page 05 *photo* Rogério Cavalcanti *for* Bloom Earth Matters / *art direction* Le Petit Bureau / *assistant art direction* Antonia Cavalheiro / *photo assistant* Lucas Bianque / *image treatment* Factory Retouch

page 07 *photo* Rogério Cavalcanti / *design* Monica Carvalho *for* Bloom Lucius / *art direction* Le Petit Bureau / *styling* Lucius Vilar, Virginia Lamarco / *beauty* Raul Melo / *photo assistant* Jorge Escudeiro / *image treatment* Factory Retouch / *model* Raquel Radiske

page 08 *photo* Kyle Weeks / *design* Lukhanyo Mdingi / *model* Isaac

PROUD & GROUNDED

page 12 *photo* Eric Lafforgue / Suri boy with a painted body

page 13 *photo* Gleeson Paulino / GQ Brazil / *styling* George Krakowiak / *beauty* Liege Wisniewski / *model* Marcelo Lima / *image retouch* Helder Bragatel

page 13 *photo* Trevor Stuurman

page 13 *photo* Erdi Doğan / *design* Hatice Gökçe / *styling* Nur Eda İşbilir / *hair* Yıldırım Bozüyük / *makeup* Andrea Sheehan

page 13 *photo* John-Paul Pietrus / *design* Kenneth Ize / *styling* KK Obi

page 14 *photo* Eric Lafforgue / Suri woman with impressive bracelets

page 15 *photo* Kenji Nakamura / *design* Samuray Martins *for* Projeto Akra

page 15 *photo* Eric Lafforgue / woman wearing a leather dress

page 15 *photo* Eric Lafforgue / Woman With Traditional Leather Skirts

page 15 *photo* Gabrielle Kannemeyer / *styling* Berivan Dalgali / *model* Anyon Ansola / *makeup* Neveen Scello / *styling* assistant Yonela Makoba

page 16 *photo* Art Wolf / Karo male body painting, Lower Omo River

page 17 *photo* Leonor von Salisch / *design* Buki Akomolafe

page 17 *design* Marimekko

page 17 *photo* Heather Moore / *design* Skinny laMinx / *featured fabric* Flower Fields / *model* Ben Moyo

page 17 *photo & styling* Adele Dejak / *turban* Johanna Bramble / *dress* Diarrablu / *makeup* Sinitta Akello / *model* Shanelle Nyasiase

page 18 *photo* Eric Lafforgue / Mwila Mother With Her Albino Baby

page 19 *photo* Trevor Stuurman

page 19 *photo* Gleeson Paulino / Elle / *styling* Marcell Maia / *beauty* Renata Brazil / *creative direction* Luciano Schmitz / *executive production* Gregório Souza / *model* Cris Lopes / *image retouch* Thiago Auge

page 19 *photo* Bruno Gomes / *design* Meninos Rei

page 19 *photo* Ed Suter / *design* Tsidi Ramofolo / *model* Salim Ladjo

page 20 *art* Leonce Raphael Agbodjelou / Jack Bell Gallery

page 21 *photo* Naveli Choyal / *design* Tigra Tigra

page 21 *photo* Leslie Payró / *design* Carla Fernández / *poncho woven on loom* María Santiz / *hand-carved bracelets* Juan Alonso / natural fiber straw hat

page 21 *photo* Mous Lambarat

page 21 *photo* Pedro Santos / *design* Laura Laurens / *styling* Liliana Sanguino / *model* Jaima Yagarí *from* Emberá Chamí Trans Indigenous Community

page 22 *photo* Eric Lafforgue

page 23 *photo* Chris Saunders / *design* Sheila-Madge / *styling* Kristi Flok / *illustrations* Andel Olivier / *assistants* Blünke Janse Van Rensburg & L'mri Erasmus / *beauty* Liezl Leach / *model* Phetogo / *garden engineer* James Barry

page 23 *photo* Pretika Menon / *design* Shirin Salwan *for* 'the magazine' / *fashion assistant* Karishma Shah / *beauty & hair* Kin Vanity / *model* Akshara Balakrishnaa / *agency* Faze Management / *image title* 'East Wind'

page 23 *photo* Ivory Campbell / *design* Joy Julius / *models* David Alajiki, Adekemi Tej

page 23 *photo* Justin Polkey *for* Vogue India / *design* Victor and Rolf / *styling* Daniel Franklin / *beauty* Mitesh Rajani Publication / *model* Anugraha Natarajan

page 24 *photo* Tom McShane / Adventure in Focus

page 25 *photo* Pedro Loreto / *design* Uxuá / *styling* Bianca Nabuco / *hair* Fox Goulard

page 25 *photo* Bikramjit Bose / *design* Eka Design Studio / *styling* Nikhil Dudani

page 25 *photo* Bikramjit Bose / *design* Eka Design Studio / *styling* Nikhil Dudani

page 25 *photo* Menty Jamir / *design* Eka Design Studio / *creative direction* Rina Singh

page 26 *art* Leonce Raphael Agbodjelou / Jack Bell Gallery

page 27 *photo* Rogério Cavalcanti / *design* João Pimenta / *art direction* Jo Souza, Taiana Putti / *photo assistance* Lucas Silva, Isa Takikawa / *executive production* Fernanda Cintra, Karina Pierri / *scenography* Ana Fontana, Leticia Torres, Gabriella Zorzan, Lucas de Britto, Elka Apolinário, Gabriela Queiroz, Camila Gonçalves / *image treatment* Premedia Crop / *sponsor* Senac SP, Brechó Minha Vó Tinha

page 27 *photo* photographer unknown / Festival honouring elephants in Jaipur

page 27 *art* Leonce Raphael Agbodjelou / Jack Bell Gallery

page 27 *photo* Rogério Cavalcanti / *design* João Pimenta / *art direction* Jo Souza, Taiana Putti / *photo assistance* Lucas Silva, Isa Takikawa / *executive production* Fernanda Cintra, Karina Pierri / *scenography* Ana Fontana, Leticia Torres, Gabriella Zorzan, Lucas de Britto, Elka Apolinário, Gabriela Queiro, Camila Gonçalves / *image treatment* Premedia Crop / *sponsor* Senac_SP, Brechó Minha Vó Tinha

PROUD & DEVOUT

page 30 *photo & art direction* Marianne Marplondon / *model* Helen

page 31 *photo* Gleeson Paulino / *design* Nataal x Thom Browne x Farfetch / *art direction* Gleeson Paulino / *beauty* Branca Moura / *models* Yasmin Porto, Augusto Comuana / *set design* Yuri Godoy / *executive production* Yasmin Porto / *set design assistant* Ottavia Delfanti / *photo assistant* Theo Casadei / *production assistant* Carolina Monteiro / *image retouch* Nicolas Leite

page 32 *photo* Stephen Tayo / *models* Chris, Chuka

page 33 *photo & art direction* Marianne Marplondon / *model* Helen

page 34 *photo* Augusto Pena / *design* Ronalgo Fraga / *makeup* Marcos Costa / Carne Seca Agency Fotosintese

page 35 *photo* Mous Lamrabat

page 36 *photo* Mous Lamrabat

page 37 *art* Leonce Raphael Agbodjelou / Jack Bell Gallery

page 38 *photo* Mous Lamrabat

page 39 *photo* Gleeson Paulino / *image retouch* Nicolas Leite

page 40 *photo* Rogério Cavalcanti / *design* Ronaldo Fraga *for* Renauxview / *bijoux* Gansho / *styling* Bianca Nabuco / *beauty* Raul Melo / *photo assistant* Lucas Santos / *styling assistant* Alice Nigro / *image treatment* Factory Retouch

page 41 *photo* Ruy Teixeira *for* Bloom Lucius

page 42 *photo* Phyllis Galembo / Bambisana and Zoleli, Twasa Initiates, South Africa 2015

page 43 *photo* Ruy Teixeira *for* Bloom Lucius

PROUD & HUMOUR

pages 46 to 55 *all photos* Mous Lamrabat / Morocco

PROUD & LABOUR

page 58 *photo* Kristin Lee Moolman / *design* Thebe Magugu / *styling* Ib Kamara / *production* Jodie Ennik, Lampost Production / *photo assistant* Tatenda Chidora / *beauty* Orlioh / *jewelry* Githan Coopoo / *models* Annah Seroalo, Ashley Karah, Brian Sathekge

page 59 *photo* Jackie Nickerson

page 60 *photo* Menty Jamir / *design* Eka Design Studio / *creative direction* Rina Singh

page 61 *photo* Aart Verrips / *design* Thebe Magugu

page 62 *photo & art direction* Francesco Visone / *model* Mamadou Sarr

page 63 *photo* Jackie Nickerson

page 64 *photo* Lakin Ogunbanwo / Pure Water

page 65 *photo* Travys Owen / *design* Lukhanyo Mdingi / *model* Gandhi

page 66 *photo & styling* Ismail Zaidy / *model* Othmane Zaidy

page 67 *photo* Menty Jamir / *design* Eka Design Studio / *creative direction* Rina Singh

page 68 *photo* Jaime Rubiano / *design* Esteban Cortazar x TAEQ Collaboration / *creative direction* Jaime Rubiano / *styling & art direction* Stephania Yepes / *beauty* Daniela Uribe Perez, Simon Atehortua, Manuela Uribe, Isabel Montoya Vega

page 69 *photo* J'dee Allin / *design* Hamaji by Louise Sommerlatte / *models* Randy Gowan, Akidor Doye

pages 70/71 *photo* Omar Victor Diop

PROUD & SOURCE

page 74 *photo* Marie Taillefer / *design* Heartwear / *art direction* Le Petit Bureau

page 75 *photo* Trevor Stuurman

page 76 *photo* Cynthia Anderson / *design* Nur Zahra

page 77 *photo* Gabrielle Kannemeyer / *design* Daily Paper / *art direction & styling* Berivan Dalgali / *models* Victim, Litha Magawu / *grooming* Caroline Greeff

page 78 *photo* Marie Taillefer / *design* Heartwear / *art direction* Le Petit Bureau

page 79 *photo* Wilbert Das / *design* Uxuá

page 80 *photo* Marie Taillefer / *design* Heartwear / *art direction* Le Petit Bureau

page 81 *photo* Marie Taillefer / *design* Heartwear / *art direction* Le Petit Bureau

page 82 *photo* Justin Polkey / *design* Anavila

page 83 *photo* Bharath Ramamrutham / *design* Sabyasachi Mukherjee *for* CITTA Rajkumari, uniforms for the Ratnavati Girls School

PROUD & HOUSE

pages 90 to 95 *design* Péro / *photo* Dolly Devi / *makeup* Aien / *hair* Sonam Singh Solanki / *production* Akshay Ma

PROUD & TOUCH

page 98 *photo* Mous Lambarat

page 99 *photo* Trevor Stuurman

page 100 *photo* Vaishnav Praveen / *design* Ka-Sha / *model* Ridhiema Shahani Mehmi

page 101 *photo* Pedro Loreto / *art direction* Flora Velloso / *model* João Vitor

page 102 *photo* Ramiro Chaves, Dorian Ulises López / *design* Carla Fernández / *collection* Las flores y los espíritus / *styling* Erin Lewis, Diego Lacayo / *beauty* Maripili Senderos / *model* Fernanda Blaz

page 103 *photo* Sandra Blow / *design* Carla Fernández / *model* Bárbara Vergara / *makeup* Gustavo Bortolotti / *hair* Mariana Palacios

page 104 *photo* Tom Barreto / *design* Ana Clara Watanabe

page 105 *photo* Tom Barreto / *design* Ana Clara Watanabe

page 106 *photo* Alan Sosa Latournerie / *design* Thais Pérez Jaén / *stylist* Andrés Escarpulli / *model* Champ Jr

page 107 *photo* Pedro Santos / *design* Laura Laurens / *styling* Liliana Sanguino / *model* Roux Panchí *from* Emberá Chamí Trans Idigenous Community

page 108 *photo* Raphael Lucena / *design* Farm

page 109 *photo* Hick Duarte / *design* Fernanda Yamamoto / Vogue / *artist* Emily Nunes / *fashion editor* Pedro Sales / *beauty* Silvio Giorgio / *photo assistance* Edson Luciano, Naelson de Castro / *image treatment* Bragatel / *executive production* David Jensen, Wborn Productions

page 110 *photo* Gleeson Paulino / *styling* João Pimenta / *image retouch* Helder Bragatel page 111 *photo* Luke Houba / *design* Lukhanyo Mdingi / *styling assistant* Keenan Martin / *makeup* Inga Hewett / *model* Pivot Aurel, 20 model MNGNT Iternational

page 112 *photo* Rafael Arroyo / *design* Thais Pérez Jaén / *styling* Tino Portillo / *art* Ana Olhovich / *model* Lara Niamh

page 113 *photo* Pedro Loreto / *design* Uxuá / *styling* Bianca Nabuco / *hair* Fox Goulard

PROUD & YOUNG

page 116 *design* Sandrine Alouf

page 117 *photo* Jacobus Snyman / *design* Chu Suwannapha *for* Chulaap collection 'A West African Dream' / *makeup* Inga Hewett / *models* Anyon Asol, Jay Seigneur / *hat* Crystal Birch

page 118 *photo* Lakin Ogunbanwo / Forbidden Fruit

page 119 *design* Flavia del Pra

page 120 *design* CSAO / *Beaded Yoruba chair* Nigeria

page 121 *photo* Jackie Nickerson

page 122 *design* Sandrine Alouf

page 123 *photo* Jacobus Snyman / *design* Chu Suwannapha *for* Chulaap / *collection* Afor Joker / *model* Anyon Asola / *makeup* Inga Hewett / *hat* Simon and Mary

PROUD & ARDOUR

page 126 *photo* Ramiro Chaves *for* Carla Fernández

page 127 *photo* Ramiro Chaves *for* Carla Fernández

page 128 *photo* Ramiro Chaves *for* Carla Fernández

page 129 Ana Hop *for* Carla Fernández

page 130 Ana Hop *for* Carla Fernández

page 131 *photo* Ramiro Chaves *for* Carla Fernández

PROUD & LOUD

pag 140 *design* Maxhosa / *photo* Trevor Stuurman

page 141 *design* Maxhosa / *photo* Andile Buka

page 142 *design* Maxhosa / *photo* Gareth Cattermole / Getty Images

page 143 *design* Maxhosa / *photo* Trevor Stuurman

page 144 *design* Maxhosa / *photo* Arthur Dlamini

page 145 *design* Maxhosa / *photo* Andile Buka

PROUD & SOUK

page 148 *photo* Trevor Stuurman

page 149 *photo* Mous Lambarat

page 150 *photo* Carol Wehrs / *design* Farm

page 151 *photo* Rogério Cavalcanti / *art direction* Le Petit Bureau / *styling* Lucius Vilar, Virginia Lamarco / *photo assistant* Jorge Escudeiro / *image treatment* Factory Retouch / *beauty* Raul Melo / *model* Lucas Rufino

page 152 *photo* Travys Owen / *design* Orange Culture / *styling & art direction* Gabrielle Kannemeyer / *model* Kevwe

page 153 *photo* Stephen Tayo / *models* Ferdinand, Rasaq

page 154 *photo* Stephen Tayo / *model* Rukayat

page 155 *photo* Matilde Cunha / *design* Savio Drew *for* Casa Obi / *design* Cuscuz, Casa Obi, Fora de Jogo / *art direction* Savio Drew, Ana Mendes / *production* Ana Mendes / *asistance* João Januario, Diogo Matos / *model* J.P Bernabeu Avomo

page 156 *photo* Louis Philippe de Gagoue / *design* Ngadi Smart for Vlisco&co / *styling* Louis Philippe de Gagoue / *creative direction* Gabriela Sánchez, Sánchez de la Barquera / *prints* Ngadi Smart

page 157 *photo* Javier Falcon / *design* Meche Correa

page 158 *photo* Saskia Wegner / *design* Valoyi / *art* Harmonie Mbunga / *model* Tatenda Wekwatenzi / *bag* The KEDI

page 159 *photo* Bruna Sussekind / *design* Betina De Luca + Waiwai / *art direction* Raphael Tepedino / *stylist* Antonio Frajado / *beauty* Laura Peres / *model* Ana Patrocinio

page 160 *photo* Mous Lambarat

page 161 *photo* Pedro Loreto / *design* Ori Rio / *art director* Raphael Tepedino / *styling* Antonio Frajado / *beauty* Romulo Flores / *photo assistant* Daniel Sulima / *models* Peter Silva, Luan Schulz

PROUD & BOUQUET

page 164 *art* Atong Atem

page 165 *photo* Raphael Lucena / *design* Farm

page 166 *photo* Rogério Cavalcanti *for* Bloom Lucius / *creative direction* Le Petit Bureau / *fashion editor* Drica Cruz / *flower styling* Lucius Vilar / *fashion production* André Phergon / *beauty* Rafael Capello / *photo assistant* Jorge Escudeiro / *model* Jennie / *image treatment* Factory Retouch

page 167 *photo & art direction* Francesco Visone / *styling & headpiece* Francesco Visone / *model* Mo Sarr / *assistance* Verónica Vidal, Jonny Casamenti

page 168 *photo* Trevor Stuurman

page 169 *photo* Aart Verrips / *design* Thebe Magugu

pages 170 / 171 *photo* Mous Lambarat

page 172 *photo* B S Kameshwari / *design* Deeksha B / Handmade 3D fabric flowers on hand flat knitted / *model* Deeksha

page 173 *photo* Gleeson Paulino / *image retouch* Nicolas Leite

page 174 *photo* Saskia Wegner / *design* Shana Morland, Blünke Trotse Tert / *styling* Catharina Van Wyk / *makeup* Amy Tourell / *model* Newton Avies

page 175 *photo* Jamal Nxedlana

page 176 *design* Saloni

page 177 *photo* Arka Patra / *design* Bobo Calcutta / *jewelry* Eina Ahluwalia / *makeup* Rahul Nandy / *hair* Abinash Bhowmick / *models* Diya Palit, Ushoshi Sengupta / Missionaries of Bloom

page 178 *photo* Hick Duarte / *art* Uyra Sodoma / Vogue / *styling* Pedro Sales / *makeup* Uyra Sodoma, Silvio Giorgio

page 179 *photo* Fred Causse

page 180 *photo* Rogério Cavalcanti

page 181 *photo* Rogério Cavalcanti / *design* Diva / *styling* Andreia Ribeiro, Rodolfo Rubem / *beauty* Ricardo dos Anjos / *model* Samira

page 182 *design* FRANCES VH Mohair / *photo* Manesha Smit

page 183 *photo* Gabrielle Kannemeyer / *design* Daily Paper / *art direction & styling* Berivan Dalgali / *grooming* Hamïd Vijay / *first assistant* Arenze Chukwu / *model* Seth Bedzo / *lighting assistant* Jet Ofori

PROUD & ROUTE

pages 192 to 197 *art & craft* Namsa Leuba

PROUD & FIBROUS

page 200 *photo* Mous Lambarat

page 201 *photo* Eric Lafforgue / *Zangbeto guardian of the night spirit riding motorcycle in the royal*

page 201 *photo* Santiago Baravalle / *design* Anikena

page 201 *photo* Ruy Teixeira / *design* Osklen *for* Bloom Lucius / *art direction* Le Petit Bureau

page 202 *photo* Jackie Nickerson

page 203 *photo* Mous Lambarat

page 203 *art* Phyllis Galembo / *courtesy* Axis Gallery NY/NJ / Panther masquerade, Burkina Faso 2009

page 204 *art* Phyllis Galembo / *courtesy* Axis Gallery NY/NJ / Nigeria, 2004

page 204 *photo* Jamal Nxedlana

page 205 *photo* Jackie Nickerson

page 206 *photo* Eric Lafforgue

page 206 *art* Namsa Leuba

page 206 *photo* Bruna Sussekind / *design* Helena Pontes / *creative director* Helena Pontes / *styling* Lucas Magnof / *makeup* Piu Gontijo / hair Mabatha / *model* Bruna Di / *production* Yas Zyngier

page 207 *photo & art direction* Cai Ramalho

page 208 *photo* Gleeson Paulino / Elle Brazil / *creative direction* Luciano Schmitz / *styling* Marcell Maia / *beauty* Helder Rodrigues / *beauty assitant* Carlos Rosa / *art direction* Anderson Rodriguez / *ad assistant* Corinne Werner / *executive production* Isabela de Paula / *photo assistance* Theo Casadei, Gianfranco Vacani / *model* Bernardo Trez Pradella / *image retouch* Studio Marcio Moraes

page 209 *photo* Marvin / *design* Helena Pontes / *creative direction* Helena Pontes / *art direction* Nidia Aranha / *styling* Natalia Conti / *beauty* Piu Gontijo / *model* Nayara Oliveira

page 209 *photo* Kenji Nakamura / *design* Samuray Martins *for* Projeto Akra

page 209 *photo* Rogério Cavalcanti *for* Bloom Faith / *creative direction* Le Petit Bureau / *styling* Lucius Vilar / *photo assistant* Jorge Escudeiro / *beauty* Raul Melo / *image treatment* Iung Studio

page 210 *photo* Tinko Czetwertynski / *design* Paula Raia

page 210 *photo* Rogério Cavalcanti *for* Bloom Faith / *art direction* Le Petit Bureau / *styling* Lucius Vilar / *photo assistant* Jorge Escudeiro / *beauty* Raul Melo / *image treatment* Iung Studio

page 211 *photo* Fabrice Schneider / *design* Sarah Viguer / Hors Pistes project

PROUD & RIGOUR

page 214 *photo* Richard Ramirez Jr. / *design* Bagtazo / *styling* Caitlin Boelke / *model* Michael Rowles

page 215 *art* Edson Chagas / Courtesy of Stevenson Amsterdam / Cape Town / Johannesburg and A Palazzo, Italy / Salvador D. Kimbangu, Tipo Passe, 2014

page 216 *photo* Fleur Bult *for* Vogue Man Ukraine / *styling* Alex van der Steen / *beauty* Vanessa Chan / *model* Quintin *at* Models Rock Agency

page 217 *art* Edson Chagas / Courtesy of Stevenson Amsterdam/ Cape Town/ Johannesburg and A Palazzo, Italy / Untitled, Irmãos Carneiro Factory, Cazenga, Luanda, Angola, 2017

page 218 *design* Asakalugre *for* The Baba Tree / *photo* Azure Abotizure

page 219 *photo* Pedro Loreto / *art direction* Flora Velloso / *model* João Vitor

page 220 *photo* Daniel Obasi / *design* Orange Culture / *makeup* Sutchay / *model* Eze Meju

page 221 *photo* Gabrielle Kannemeyer / *design* Daily Paper / *styling* Berivan Dalgali / *model* Anyon Ansola / *makeup* Caroline Greeff, Tarryn Kelly

page 222 *photo* Mous Lambarat

page 223 *photo* Mous Lambarat

page 224 *design* Tiaan Nagel / *photo* Travys Owen / *beauty* Lesley Whitby / *model* Noelle Graobe

page 225 *photo* Diego Mateos / *design* Caralarga

PROUD & CLOUD

page 228 *photo* Trevor Stuurman

page 229 *photo* Niculai Constantinescu / *design* Buki Akomolafe

pag 230 *photo* Niculai Constantinescu / *design* Buki Akomolafe

page 231 *photo* Ruy Teixeira / *design* Thais Signorini Costa

page 232 *photo* Mous Lambarat / *design* Daily Paper

page 233 *photo* Jackie Nickerson

page 234 *design* Tiaan Nagel / *photo* Travys Owen / *beauty* Lesley Whitby / *model* Noelle Graobe

page 235 *photo* The Masons / Trunk Archive

page 236 *photo* Kristin Lee Moolman

page 237 *photo* Kristin Lee Moolman

page 238 *photo* The Masons / Trunk Archive

page 239 *photo* Ricardo Simal / *design* Rich Mnisi

page 240 *photo* Trevor Stuurman

page 241 *photo* Niculai Constantinescu / *design* Buki Akomolafe

page 242 *photo* Trevor Stuurman

page 243 *photo* Gleeson Paulino / Elle / *design* Colcci / *styling* Marcell Maia / *beauty* Dindi Hojah / *image retouch* Nicolas Leite

page 244 *photo* Gleeson Paulino / Elle / *styling* George Krakowiak / *beauty* Renata Brazil / *retouch* Nicolas Leite

page 245 *photo* Zander Opperman / *design* Rich Mnisi

PROUD JOURNAL

page 252 *photo* Manuel Álvarez Bravo / 'Margarita de Bonampak' 1949, © Archivo Manuel Alvarez Bravo, SC

page 253 *photo* Rudi Geyser / *design* Lukhanyo Mdingi

page 254 *photo* Gabriela Cajado / *design* Cajá / *model* Bruna Miranda

page 255 *photo* Graciela Iturbide / 'Vendedora de Zacate Oaxaca' (Sponge Vendor) 1974

page 256 *photo* Graciela Iturbide / 'Serafina', Juchitán, Oaxaca 1985

page 257 *photo* Graciela Iturbide / 'Cuatro pescaditos' (Four Fishes), Juchitán, Oaxaca, 1986

page 258 *photo* Eric Lafforgue / 'Miss Nashure' / Kibbish Village, Omo Valley

page 259 *photo* Jackie Nickerson

page 260 *design* Pége

page 261 *photo* Graciela Iturbide / 'La Ascensión' Chalma, State of Mexico, 1984

page 262 *photo* Graciela Iturbide / 'Madonna'/ Brooklyn Museum, Gift of Marcuse Pfeifer

page 263 *photo* Vaishnav Praveen / *design* Kaleekal

page 264 *photo* Tina Modotti / 'Woman with Flag' / The Museum of Modern Art, New York / Scala, Florence / Mexico page 265 *photo* Ashish Shah / *design* Raw Mango / *creative direction* Sanjay Garg / Cloud People - Chikankari

page 266 *photo* Original print owned by Jaipur City Palace

page 267 *photo* Sawai Ram Singh II, Maharaja of Jaipur 1860 / Portrait of a Courtesan from the Museum of Art & Photography Bangalore

page 268 *photo* Travys Owen / *design* Lukhanyo Mdingi / *model* Daniel / *collection* Macrame

page 269 *photo* Leah Gordon / 'Mulâtre from the Caste Portraits' / Port-au-Prince

page 270 *photo* Eric Lafforgue / Omo Valley

page 271 *photo* Joseph Moïse Agbojelou / *courtesy* Revue Noire Paris

PROUD & FLOUNCE

page 274 *photo* Kristin Lee Moolman

page 275 *photo* Kristin Lee Moolman

page 276 *photo* Erdi Doğan / *design* Hatice Gökçe / *styling* Nur Eda İşbilir / *hair* Yıldırım Bozüyük / *makeup* Andrea Sheehan

page 277 *photo* Cecilia Duarte / Elle / *art direction* Luciano Schimtz / *stylist* Lucas Boccalao / *beauty* Amanda Schon / *image treatment* Thiago Auge

page 278 *photo* Jamal Nxedlana

page 279 *photo* Cecilia Duarte / Elle / *art direction* Luciano Schimtz / *stylist* Lucas Boccalao / *beauty* Amanda Schon / *image treatment* Thiago Auge

page 280 *photo* Hick Duarte / *artist* Dionéia Ferreira *for* Vogue / *styling* Pedro Sales / *makeup* Silvio Giorgio

page 281 *art* Tamary Kudita / African Victorian II

page 282/283 *art* Tamary Kudita / 'The Gathering'

page 284/285 *art* Tamary Kudita / 'That evening sun goes down'

page 286 *photo* Mous Lambarat

pag 287 *photo* The Masons / Trunk Archive

page 288 *photo* Celine van Heel

page 289 *photo* Trevor Stuurman

page 290 *photo* Kristin Lee Moolman

page 291 *photo* Kristin Lee Moolman

pag 292 *photo* Kristin Lee Moolman

pag 293 *photo* Kristin Lee Moolman

PROUD & AURORS

page 296 *photo* Mariana Maltoni / *design* Casa Geração Vidigal School *for* Bloom Faith / *creative direction* Le Petit Bureau / *photo assistant* João Julio Mello / *image treatment* Doctor Raw

page 297 *photo* Mariana Maltoni / *design* Casa Geração Vidigal School for Bloom Faith / *creative direction* Le Petit Bureau / *photo assistant* João Julio Mello / *image treatment* Doctor Raw

page 298 *photo* Mariana Maltoni / *design* Casa Geração Vidigal School *for* Bloom Faith / *creative direction* Le Petit Bureau / *photo assistant* João Julio Mello / *image treatment* Doctor Raw

page 299 *photo* Demian Jacob *for* Bloom Faith / *creative direction* Bianca Nabuco / *production* Manuela Padilla / *beauty* Mariana Sixel / *beauty assistant* Luiza Goulart / *model* Aline Pommer

page 300 *photo* Rogério Cavalcanti / *scenography* Manuela Ferreira Alves, Karen Luza / *acknowledgements* Senac SP / *styling* Evandro Gueiros, Vitor Oliveira Nunes / *fashion production* Carolina Cavalheiro, Marília Mattos / *photo assistant* Jorge Escudeiro / *makeup* Alessandro Tierni / *model* Rodrigo Somalia / *image treatment* Factory Retouch / *thanks to* Jô Souza, Marcio Akiyoshi

page 301 *photo* Rogério Cavalcanti / *scenography* Manuela Ferreira Alves, Karen Luza / *acknowledgements* Senac SP / *styling* Evandro Gueiros, Vitor Oliveira Nunes / *fashion production* Carolina Cavalheiro, Marília Mattos / *photo* assistant Jorge Escudeiro / *makeup* Alessandro Tierni / *model* Rodrigo Somalia / *image treatment* Factory Retouch / *thanks to* Jô Souza, Marcio Akiyoshi

PROUD & TOUGH

pages 304 / 315 *photo* Neville Trickett / Carrot Pickers series

PROUD & HONOR

pages 318 / 323 *photo* Jackie Nickerson

PROUD & GENEROUS

page 326 *photo* Valentina Minette Escardó / *design* Gaia

page 327 *design* FVHxLM Mohair Knitwear Collection / *photo* Jacobus Snyman

page 328 *photo* Bruno Ilusorio / *design* Gaia

page 329 *photo* Bruno Ilusorio / *design* Gaia

page 330 *photo* Ryan Wijayaratne / *design* Amesh

page 331 *photo* Ryan Wijayaratne / *design* Amesh

page 332 *photo* Bruna Castanheira / *design* Anselmi / *art director* Pablo Quoos / *stylist* Carolos Esser

page 333 *photo* Bruna Castanheira / *art director* Pablo Quoos / *styling* Arthur Ribeiro / *beauty* Jake Falci / *photo assistant* Bia Garbieri / *beauty assistant* Jana Marques

page 334 *photo* Travys Owen / *design* Orange Culture / *styling & art direction* Gabrielle Kannemeyer / *model* Kevwe

page 335 *photo* Tenzin Lhagyal / *styling* Pandey Akanksha / *beauty* Bishhnupada Sinha / *model* Neeraj Saini

PROUD & COUPE

page 338 *photo* Eric Lafforgue

page 339 *photo* Duke Quarshie / *styling* Mathew / *model* Mathew / *makeup* Elizabeth Boateng

page 340 *photo* Eric Lafforgue

page 341 *photo* Hassan Hajjaj / Karima Rider 2010/1431 (Gregorian/Hijri)

pag 342 *photo* Eric Lafforgue

pag 343 *photo* Kevin Mackintosh / *design* Daryl McGregor / Windmill Woman

page 344 *photo* Eric Lafforgue / Hamer Man With A Chelsea Football Shirt

page 345 *photo* Haneem Christian / *design* Daily Paper / *styling* Yonela Makoba / Cast Nete Twins

PROUD & FAMOUS

page 348 *art* Leonce Raphael Agbodjelou / Jack Bell Gallery

page 349 *art* Leonce Raphael Agbodjelou / Jack Bell Gallery

page 350 *photo & art direction* Marianne Marplondon / *model* Helen

page 351 *art* Hassan Hajjaj /.'In The Basket' 2019/1440 (Gregorian/Hijri) Courtesy of Groupe Acrobatique de Tanger and the Artist

page 352 *art* Cecilia Paredes / 'El Susurro' 2021

page 353 *photo* Rogério Cavalcanti / *design* João Pimenta / *art direction* Jo Souza, Taiana Putti / *photo assistant* Lucas Silva, Isa Takikawa / *executive production* Fernanda Cintra, Karina Pierri / *scenography* Ana Fontana, Leticia Torres, Gabriella Zorzan, Lucas de Britto, Elka Apolinário, Gabriela Queiroz, Camila Gonçalves / *image treatment* Premedia Crop / *sponsor* Senac_SP, Brechó Minha Vó Tinha

page 354 *art* Omar Victor Diop

page 355 *art* Hassan Hajjaj / 'Zezo' 2011/1432 (Gregorian/ Hijri) / Courtesy of Zezo Tamsamani and the Artist

page 356 *photo* João Bertholini / *design* Isaac Silva *for* Havaianas

page 357 *art* Omar Victor Diop

page 358 *art* Thandiwe Muriu

page 359 *art* Thandiwe Muriu

PROUD & COLOUR

page 372 *photo* Tinko Czetwertynski

page 373 *photo* Luca Oliva / *design* Misci

page 374 *photo* Koto Bolofo / *paper design* Daryl McGregor *for* Arjowiggins / *makeup* Houda Remita / *model* Marie Ndao / CRUSHED

page 375 *photo* Mous Lambarat

pag 376 *photo* Jaime Rubiano / *design* Esteban Cortazar x TAEQ Collaboration / *creative direction* Jaime Rubiano / *styling & art direction* Stephania Yepes / *beauty* Daniela Uribe Perez, Manuela Uribe, Isabel Montoya Vega, Simon Atehortua

pag 377 *photo* Gabrielle Kannemeyer / *design* Daily Paper / *art direction & styling* Berivan Dalgali / *makeup artist* Giselle Ali / *photo assistant* Arenze Chukwu / *model* Ottawa Kwami / *lighting assistant* Jet Ofori

pag 378 *photo* Mucio Ricardo / *model* Jean Woolmay Denson Pierre

pag 379 *photo* Mucio Ricardo / *model* Jean Woolmay Denson Pierre

page 380 *photo* Luck Hoube / *design* Lukhanyo Mdingi

page 381 *photo* Maxim Vakhovskij / *design* Fanoraine Dohr

page 382 *photo* Gleeson Paulino / *styling* Von Trapp / *model* Loïc Koutana / *image retouch* Nicolas Leite

page 383 *photo* Naguel Rivero / *design* Marco Ribeiro / *styling* Imruh Asha

page 384 *photo* Francesco Visone / *art direction & styling* Lauro Samblás / *art assistant* Andrea Balloch / *models* John Diego, Charlie Oyo

page 385 *photo* Leeroy Jason

page 386 *photo* Eric Lafforgue / Woman From Autonomous Region Of Bougainville In Traditional Clothes

page 387 *photo* Ricardo Simal / *design* Rich Mnisi

page 388 *photo* Namsa Leuba

page 389 *photo* Gleeson Paulino / *design* Von Trapp / *model* Loïc Koutana / *image retouch* Nicolas Leite

page 390 *photo* Gleeson Paulino / *styling* Marcell Maia / *beauty* Mika Safro / *production* Raphael Lobato, Mirrorage / *graphic design* Estudio Margem / *fashion production* Carolina Albuquerque / *photo assistant* Theo Casadei / *beauty assistant* Nathalia Almeida / *styling assistant* Pepa / *model* Loïc Koutana / *image retouch* Nicolas Leite / MJournal *Partners* João Pimenta, Leandro Castro, Ana Clara Watanabe, Igi Ayedun Lucas Carinhoso, Zopelar

page 391 *photo* Gleeson Paulino / *styling* Marcell Maia / *beauty* Mika Safro / *production* Raphael Lobato, Mirrorage / *graphic design* Estudio Margem / *fashion production* Carolina Albuquerque / *photo assistant* Theo Casadei / *beauty assistant* Nathalia Almeida / *styling assistant* Pepa / *model* Loïc Koutana / *image retouch* Nicolas Leite / MJournal Partners João Pimenta, Leandro Castro, Ana Clara Watanabe, Igi Ayedun Lucas Carinhoso, Zopelar

PROUD & DOUBLE

page 394 *art* Omar Victor Diop

page 395 Portrait of Aquasi Boachi in the Bergakademie in Freiberg, Saxony, between 1847 and 1848 / Bergakademie, Freiberg

page 396 *art* Omar Victor Diop

page 397 Portrait of Jean-Baptiste Belley / Anne-Louis Girodet De Roussy-Trioson / photo © RMN-Grand Palais (Château de Versailles) / Gérard Blot

PROUD & SOUVENIR

page 400 *photo* Koen Hauser / *design* Vlisco / *art direction & styling* Maarten Spruyt / *hair* Margot van Essen

page 401 *art* Tamary Kudita / Gladys

page 402 *art* Omar Victor Diop

page 403 *art* Tamary Kudita / African Victorian

page 404 *art* Tamary Kudita / Roots, IV

page 405 *photo* Erdi Doğan / *design* Hatice Gökçe / *styling* Nur Eda İşbilir / *hair* Yıldırım Bozüyük / *makeup* Andrea Sheehan

page 406 *art* Tamary Kudita / Lady With Corn II

page 407 *photo* Arka Patra / Dionysus / *styling* Shreyashi Debnath / *beauty* Dhiman Ghosh / *model* Amartya Ray

page 408 *photo* Jamal Nxedlana

page 409 *photo* Namsa Leuba

page 410 *photo* Trevor Stuurman

page 411 *art* Tamary Kudita / Body as an archive

page 412 *art* Omar Victor Diop

page 413 *photo* Rogério Cavalcanti / *design* Ronaldo Fraga *for* Renauxview / *bijoux* Gansho / *styling* Bianca Nabuco / *beauty* Raul Melo / *photo assistant* Lucas Santos / *styling assistant* Alice Nigro / *image treatment* Factory Retouch

page 414 *photo* Tarun Vishwa / *design* Sabyasachi / *models* Anuj Choudhry, Archana Akil Kumar

page 415 *photo* Erdi Doğan / *design* Hatice Gökçe / *styling* Nur Eda İşbilir / *hair* Yıldırım Bozüyük / *makeup* Andrea Sheehan

page 416 *photo* Tatenda Chidora / *design* Thebe Magugu / *styling* Chloe Andrea Welgemoed / *model* Phumla Mtolo / *production* Lampost

page 417 *art* Omar Victor Diop

PROUD & TEAM

◇◇◇◇◇◇◇◇◇◇◇◇

concept & art direction
Lidewij Edelkoort

editor-in-chief
Lili Tedde

book design
Mariola López Mariño

editing
Lidewij Edelkoort
Philip Fimmano

research
Lydia Caldana, Marcella Echavarria, Lidewij Edelkoort, Le Petit Bureau, Ambika Magotra, Rodrigo Muller, Bianca Nabuco, Alice Nigro, Nicolas Rico, Lili Tedde, Lucius Vilar

texts
Lidewij Edelkoort, Carla Fernández, Modupe Oloruntoba, Kavita Parmar, Keith Recker

executive production
Alice Nigro

proofreading
Michelle Dominique Anderson

printing
robstolk®

isbn
9 789462 264441

publishers
EDELKOORT EDITIONS
a division of Trend Union, Paris
edelkoort.com

Lecturis, Eindhoven
lecturis.nl

supported by

Firmenich

FOCUS
TÊXTIL

RENAUXVIEW